Early praise for How

Without doubt, human capab⎯⎯⎯⎯⎯⎯⎯⎯⎯⎯
+ HR) initiatives create increasing value for all organization stakeholders. This book does a thoughtful and thorough job exploring how to upgrade talent by building a stronger HR function. The practical ideas make this a useful 'how to' guide.
- **Dave Ulrich**, Rensis Likert Professor, Ross School of Business, Partner, The RBL Group

This book is a 'must read' for any aspiring CPO or someone who is new into the role. It brilliantly guides the reader not only through the modernised purpose of the CPO role (particularly important in the changing world of work) but also provides super practical information and insights on the key operational elements. I found I was able to dip in and out of it to different sections as well as read page to page which for me is the essence of a great book. It will take pride of place on my bookshelf.
- **Linzi Blakeley**, Global Head – Client Coverage, Human Resources CCIB, Standard Chartered Bank

Not only is the book a concrete, comprehensive and clear handbook for a modern people leader, it is also written by customer and business-oriented people with impressive international experience. It includes many practical views on how to improve our CPO function and the infrastructure supporting it.
- **Sampsa Laine**, CEO, Manna Group

Not only a comprehensive introduction to the role and importance of the Chief People Officer for business leaders wanting to take their organisation to the next level, but a very useful handbook for HR professionals wanting to take the next step in their career and for Chief People Officers themselves.
- **Beth Austin**, Head of HR, Sponsors for Educational Opportunity

If you're a seasoned, first time or aspiring CPO, this book is for **YOU**! Packed with practical solutions, insights and real life case studies to show you how to put humanity back into HR. Sit back, relax and prepare to be guided on the impact a CPO role can truly have! Move over, robots / ChatGPT. This book is bringing humanity back to the workplace! It's like a cup of coffee for your soul...or your HR department.
- **Rob Knight**, Director, HRBP, Immutable

As the strategic enabler of a truly sustainable organisation, one that is powered by humanity, the enabling role of the CPO has never been more important...this highly relevant and pragmatic book addresses the critical context of today's world of work and deals with all of the modern-day CPO priorities in an incredibly consumable way.
- **Ger Mitchell**, Chief People Officer Permanent TSB

The authors own advice conveys the immense potential and responsibility of the role: "As CPO, never forget your outsized impact on the human race for one single minute. It's a truly wonderful gift with which to be presented – grasp it with both hands." How to be a Chief People Officer is a well-researched and well-structured handbook which provides us with the tools to meet that potential and responsibility, covering all aspects of the role of the CPO and the function they lead. The book is an invaluable and comprehensive resource for CPOs, HR professionals and people leaders.
- **Stephen Groarke**, European CFO & Executive Director, Elavon Financial Services, Former CRO & Executive Director, Permanent TSB

An awesome read! Highly practical and well-structured and an essential handbook for any new/aspiring CPO, or even HR Professional who wants to succeed, but also for anyone new to Executive Coaching who doesn't have previous experience of HR.
- **Jill Maidment**, Director, Natural Talent

For all HR Professionals looking to take the next strategic step in their career, a guide like this is so timely and valuable, giving not only an overview of the key aspects of the HR Leadership role but also a practical guide to the various tools to move towards strategic people centric decision making and planning. I also loved the idea of the book being in the CEO toolkit to help cement the people agenda as we move from traditional Human Resources Management to Human Experience Management.
- **Joanna Murphy**, President EMEA, Rizing HCM

Anne Kiely is an amazing HR professional and has written (with Jennifer Geary, a seasoned C-suite member and business author) a must-read, not only for CPOs, but anyone in the People space. This book touches on balancing leadership with both the business and people in mind and is infused with intelligence from two experienced professionals. Well written with great guidance.
- **Tami Floden**, Global TA professional

HOW TO BE A CHIEF PEOPLE OFFICER

Enabling people in the evolving world of work

ANNE KIELY

JENNIFER GEARY

Cover design: Tehsin Gul

Editor: David Woods-Hale

Copyright © 2023 Anne Kiely and Jennifer Geary. All rights reserved.

Published by Kindle Direct Publishing

For more information about the authors and further materials, visit www.coo-author.com

ISBN: 978-1-9997683-4-8 (print)

ISBN: 978-1-9997683-5-5 (e-book)

For Dad, Mom, Emer, Elaine, Jonathan, Joshua, Lucy and Christopher. A x

For Conor, Jack, Anna and Dad. J x

About the authors

Anne Kiely is a HR Director with 20 years of experience in the finance, technology and consultancy sectors, across a number of diverse organisations. Prior to that she worked for 10 years in banking. Anne is also proud to be a non-executive director of the Special Olympics Ireland. She has a master's degree in social and organisational psychology, and recently completed the Professional Certificate in Governance. She lives in Dublin with her husband, three children and Brodie the cockapoo.

Jennifer Geary is a senior executive with more than 25 years of experience in finance, technology, risk and legal, across diverse industries from finance to not-for-profit. Jennifer is also an author, speaker and advisor to emerging businesses and serves as a mentor on the Enterprise Ireland Scale programme. She has attained qualification as a chartered accountant, PRINCE 2 practitioner, CISA and CISSP and most recently completed a course in Sustainable Finance and ESG Investing at NYU Stern. She lives in London with her husband, two children and two cats.

Table of Contents

Introduction

Why this book is needed

This book is the third in the *'How to be a...'* series and represents the first time that we have tried a co-authoring approach, blending the framework created in the first two books with deep expertise from an industry practitioner. After Operations and Risk – and given the seismic changes we have seen in the HR industry and in the social construct – People seemed like a very logical next area to tackle.

There is a wealth of reading available on the topics of leadership, people management and culture for aspiring or new-to-role Chief People Officers. We list some of these at the end of the book. However, as with the first two books, we saw a gap in the market for a practitioner's handbook; an accessible read that looked at the entirety of the people life cycle, and the technical expertise that was needed to provide an excellent experience for people as they journey through an organisation.

From HR Director to Chief People Officer

The position of CPO is a substantial step up from a HR Director role. It requires being a 'T-shaped' leader – understanding the breadth of responsibilities that your Executive team, or C-suite colleagues face, while having deep expertise in your own specialism. Few people will come to their first CPO role 'fully formed'. Ordinarily, they will have depth in certain areas, but this is not what will allow them to succeed in their new, elevated role. To be successful, a new CPO needs to hand over some of that depth and hands-on experience to others in their team, while embracing some new and unfamiliar areas. They will now own a great degree of responsibility for culture, values, perhaps sustainability. They will have a new set of stakeholders on the Board and will face scrutiny like never before around their financial management, appointments and reward strategy. To be successful, they need to equip themselves and their teams, and be armed with a framework for how to think about their position, what to focus on and how to execute quickly.

Moreover, being a CPO is not simply a matter of executing a bunch of people-related workstreams in isolation. CPOs who focus on their own agendas slavishly, without sensitivity to the wider context, will gain few allies around the executive table. Managers and leaders face an overwhelming amount of expectation from their people in terms of how they will be managed. Shovelling HR task after task at them will not help. As we outline in more detail later in the book, one of the most important priorities for the CPO is to *unburden* managers, being selective about what needs to be done, maximising automation of people-related activities, giving them precious time back. Time to think; time to be human.

As the authors of this book, we have more than 50 years of experience between us working in international, multi-cultural environments. We have witnessed growth, success, crisis, closure. We have seen the best and worst in people behaviour. We have had to bootstrap –to figure things out in roles – and we have been frustrated by the lack of access to clear, readable, 'how-to' guidance when navigating new and complex roles. We have distilled all this experience into this book, in the hope of helping others on that same journey.

As a new CPO, you will be stretched as never before. We hope this book makes that journey a little easier and allows you to maintain the joy and passion that brought you here in the first place.

"Now is the time." Martin Luther King

Now is the time for the CPO and the People function.

Who this book is for

This book will be of use to you if you are already on your HR journey, whether an aspiring manager, HR Director or someone new to their CPO role. It should supplement any missing areas of expertise, helping you approach the role in a more rounded, balanced manner – not simply favouring the areas you know well, but looking objectively across your brief, and surveying calmly where to apply your time and attention.

This book will also be useful to CEOs who may be working out what they need from a CPO and what kind of people leader that they want, at the particular stage of their organisation's life cycle.

Finally, for newly appointed Board members, or members of a Nominations / Appointments or Remuneration Committee, this should illuminate and explain the likely challenges their CPO is facing and help the non-executive in navigating the oversight role they need to play.

We hope you find this book beneficial and would love to hear your feedback. You can reach us via LinkedIn, or you can email Anne at anne.kiely@thehrpartnership.ie or Jennifer at jennifer@coo-author.com.

Chapter 1

The role of the Chief People Officer

Introduction

"As CPO, you are now part of running the business. Sitting on the executive committee, working with the remuneration committee, reporting to the board, and building relationships with the chair and CEO are all significant steps up from the responsibilities of the HR director."

Heidrick & Struggles[1]

For a long time, the People function has fought to exert the appropriate level of influence on an organisation. It is only very recently that most CEOs are seeing the People function for what it truly is: a core element – sometimes *the* core element – of the success of their organisation.

Forty years ago, personnel management was 'done' by Personnel, a team of people pushing paper around, often behind a locked door. Personnel represented a cost line on the P&L of the organisation, was operational, and was not seen as adding much value.

Forty years and several name functional changes later (i.e. Human Resource Management, Human Capital Management, People or Talent Management, Human Capability Management), the function now has a seat at the C-suite table, is one of the core elements of strategic business planning, is regularly visible on the actual and virtual office floor, is viewed as creating value and is a key driver of differentiation and success for the organisation.

As an aspiring, or new-to-role CPO, you have a unique opportunity to harness and develop the human *capital* and human *capability* of your organisation to help it achieve its goals. You play a pivotal role in shaping the culture, in aligning the full organisation behind the strategy and in executing change at critical points in the organisation's life cycle. You are responsible for every stage in an employee's journey, from attracting new people, to helping them reach their potential, through to managing their exit from the organisation. You will preside over a team – small or large – of HR experts, all of whom must execute complex functions, from performance management to pensions, repeatedly and accurately.

Perhaps most honourably of all, you get to support people on their journey of self-actualisation, helping them to achieve their life and career goals, while they deliver value for your organisation.

Why be a CPO?

Like all C-suite positions, CPO roles are hugely satisfying. They often represent the pinnacle of the role-holders' career aspirations, and the CPO position is no different in that regard. However, CPO is not an easy role. Of all the C-suite roles, we would argue that it carries the highest emotional toll. You are in role because of your love of people and your natural empathy. You will get to see the best and – at times sadly – the worst of people. You will be privy to highly personal and sensitive information. You will witness elation, success, disappointment and devastation. You must be available and empathetic, physically and emotionally, while also being able to make rational, data-based decisions about what is right for the organisation. You will have a critical say in people's livelihoods. You will get to support people in achieving their dreams and will have to witness others experiencing gut-wrenching failures and frustrations too. It really is a roller-coaster ride.

So why be a CPO? You get to see across the whole organisation, and witness where the personal meets the organisational. You will have access to more sensitive data than most other roles and be privy to the intricate detail of hirings, firings, scaling-up programmes and redundancy plans. You get the opportunity to be and do a lot of things:

- An extrovert, getting energy from the workforce, and an introvert, focusing on your inner self to work out a challenge;
- Work in a field that is a science, making data-led decisions, as well as an art, following gut instinct to make people-led solutions;
- A collaborative leader, facilitating agreement around the table, and an authoritative leader, charting a course and encouraging followership;
- An ally, supporting other senior C-suite executives when they need it, while at other times holding them to account;
- A person who needs to judge the right time to take action, when to maintain the status quo, make incremental change, or lead transformational change, making big bets on how people have outsized impact.

The position of CPO is a solemn responsibility, and it's all-encompassing. Depending on what's needed, you lead from the front when the organisation loses its way, you guide from the back to steer everyone forward in the one direction, and you cheer from the side lines every single opportunity you get.

For the right person, it is exhilarating.

The career path to CPO

A successful CPO will usually be an experienced practitioner with relevant HR qualifications. They will also need to stay on top of current business and people-related trends to ensure they meet today's people and organisational needs while preparing for tomorrow's challenges.

The obvious route to CPO is development through the People function, with qualifications in Human Resources (HR). Relevant qualifications for a CPO may include: an undergraduate diploma or degree in HR; a postgraduate degree in HR, organisational psychology or organisational behaviour; and / or specialist qualifications in, for example, data analytics, learning and development, diversity, equity and inclusion (DEI), career framework design, organisational psychology, remuneration and talent acquisition.

We will see throughout sections 2 and 3 what those specialisms are. However, it's likely that a CPO will have had at least some generalist experience in HR operations or HR business partnering at some point in their career.

That being said, senior experienced professionals from other functions are moving increasingly into CPO roles directly from other organisational areas, where they have the necessary characteristics to be successful in the role and encircle themselves with that specialist knowledge required to execute the People strategy. The role of the CPO must move away from being a functional specialist within their own silo to being a business leader, who thinks like a CEO:

> *"There is a rising belief in the value of a CHRO who brings business strengths gained outside HR,"* observes *EnBW CHRO Colette Rück-ert-Hennen. "Experience like this cements the kind of business-impact mindset that chimes with the board,"* she says. *"It gives a CHRO the confidence to drive business-centred decisions, such as how overhead costs can be saved or what form of organisational development makes sense. For the same reason previous P&L experience is also exceptionally useful."* [2]

The characteristics of a good CPO

As CPO, you are leading a function that is responsible for the world's greatest and most complex assets, humans. You are tasked with making sure they are safe, well and thriving during the time they spend in your organisation. And yet you're also leading a cost centre, and will need to beg, borrow and steal (!) in any given year to deliver on your responsibilities. The CPO comes from a tough breed – broad shoulders, thick skin, always-on brain, eyes scanning the horizon, and a heart for every single one of their charges. Nothing is more intimidating, challenging and rewarding. You'd forgive the CPO for being head-down busy, stern with the burden of responsibility, and... yet they will be in the front row, cheering for every single celebration that takes place.

Let's face it – the CPO needs to ensure many of those celebrations actually happen. And we don't forget to bring fun back to the workplace. We are inherently social beings – even introverts enjoy being with other humans.

Some of the attributes of a strong CPO that we have observed include the following:

- **High integrity:** the CPO must have a strong moral compass and the highest values and beliefs to ensure good decisions are made within the organisation and in the best interest of those working there.
- **Empathetic:** while you need to be analytical and rational in how you get things done, you must show understanding, compassion and humanity in how you do it. Despite often having to make the most difficult decisions involving people, CPOs will do it in a way that respects the dignity of those involved. Humanity is key.
- **Courageous:** the CPO is one of the bravest people at any table. You must be ready and able to speak truth to those in power (the Board, the CEO) when there's something they don't want to hear. You must be brave when your subject matter is the wellbeing of people.
- **Diplomatic:** the CPO is entrusted with the most personal and sensitive information about everyone within the organisation. You must be discreet and respectful in your use of this knowledge.
- **Humble:** this is a hard-working, often thankless position. Ambition, assertiveness and leadership is at the core of the position, however a CPO that seeks the limelight or is self-oriented will likely not be effective.
- **Calm and consistent:** you must be one of, if not the, most approachable person in the organisation. The CPO is the epitome of trust, dependability and credibility. You will regularly need to deal with an issue in the moment in a way that those involved feel safe.
- **Patient:** the CPO often needs to play a slow, long-term game, with plenty of setbacks along the way. You have to be fixed on the long-term and able to bounce back from disappointment. If you are driven by early, tangible results, this may not be the position for you.

- **Resilient**: you need broad shoulders and thick skin to be a successful CPO. It's not a position for someone who is highly sensitive. You will often be on the receiving end of a person who is having a challenging time and seeks to assign blame. It's not personal, and the successful CPO will understand that.

Putting together the above knowledge, experience and attributes, Gartner's framework for a world-class CPO captures how they come together in delivering under five core pillars:[3]

Drive business results				
Board and CEO's leader of human capital & culture	Win in a dynamic talent landscape	Leader of enterprise strategic change	Leading through evolving stakeholder scenarios	Trusted advisor and coach
Plan and support CEO and C-level succession	Ensure top talent and capabilities for critical roles	Create organization agility and resilience capability	Anticipate and respond to external trends	Advise and coach the CEO
Build effective compensation supported by shareholders	Embed DE&I into talent and culture strategy	Assess and catalyze actions to drive competitiveness	Align and link organizational metrics to stakeholder expectations	Maximize senior team effectiveness
Drive culture and purpose	Deliver a compelling employee value proposition	Integration of organizational levers to sustain change	Focus on workforce as a primary stakeholder	Coach and develop key enterprise talent
Business acumen		Business strategy development		
Functional business leader				
Create a future-focused, technology oriented, operationally capable, and financially disciplined team to run the HR function.				

Figure 1.1: A framework for a world class CPO, Gartner for HR Leaders.
Introducing the Model of a World-Class CHRO

If you are stepping up into your first CPO role, the changes in how you operate are enormous. Your first CPO position is a time in your career – more than ever before – to ensure that you have the right support structures around you. An assistant or (for more comprehensive support) a Chief of Staff, will provide bandwidth in your day, to allow you to keep focused on your vision. Technical experts in your team will support you in doing the complex work and in managing the day-to-day – which you now need to let go of. An executive coach, who knows and understands you – and all your personality foibles – can be a useful sounding board and reflect back to you when you are falling into any personal traps or bad habits.

Taking care of your home life and getting support if you have additional caring responsibilities, will reduce the guilt and the worry we all feel at times, and allow you to keep focused. Finally, a network of peers and professionals you can ask and lean on will reduce the feelings of isolation that sometimes come from now being at the top and having 'nobody to turn to' when stuck with a problem.

Key relationships for the CPO

Your success as CPO will also depend on your ability to forge strong relationships with your peers and colleagues. For the first time, as a member of the Executive committee, you will be expected to take an interest in the whole workings and full success of the organisation. Not just the People function; not just your silo. You are as invested in the success of your peers as yourself. This is a fundamental mindset shift. You also have a whole new set of stakeholders with whom to engage.

Some of the key dynamics with the other senior disciplines that you will encounter – perhaps for the first time – are outlined below. Also, don't neglect that you often play a key role in shaping the interpersonal dynamics at Executive Committee (ExCo) level; so, while you are getting to know the stakeholders, finding your place and providing challenge, you're also trying to get everyone else to operate constructively together – a delicate balancing act…

- **Board, Remuneration and Nomination committees.** The talent strategy is recognised as a core and consistent item on the Board agenda, and the CPO is accountable to the Board for devising and executing on the People strategy in furtherance of organisational goals. The CPO will also report on the 'health' of the organisation, and on the Objectives and Key Results (OKRs) that you have jointly agreed are most important. Issues such as succession planning, unfilled / vacant roles, attrition, grievances and whistleblowing will usually be reported by the CPO. Further, as Boards and investors now look at culture and employee engagement as drivers of value, you play a more strategic role than ever, and can drive the market capitalisation of the organisation directly, through the success of your People strategy. As the organisation matures, you may have formal committees in place around senior appointments, the creation of long-term incentive plans (LTIPs) and other significant People programmes. You'll be expected to understand investor / shareholder priorities for the organisation and ensure the reward structure reflects that. Bear in mind as well that you will play a role in the setting of executive compensation, which adds a nuance to your relationship with the rest of the executive team. According to Paul DeNicola, a principal in PwC's Governance Insights Center: *"Talent management is more critical than ever – and so is director oversight."* [4]

- **Chief Executive Officer (CEO)**. Usually your direct reporting line, although you can report into other roles such as the COO or CFO. As well as advising on all aspects of the people agenda, you can often build a relationship of deep trust with the CEO, and be their confidante and trusted partner, like no other person on the Executive team. If you are new to the organisation, this relationship will require a deep investment of time and trust by you both. Sometimes you may have to reflect back to the CEO when something they are saying or doing is not resonating well with the organisation, and great tact and diplomacy are needed here. Finally, you may be called upon to assist the Board in looking at CEO performance and succession – a uniquely sensitive role to play with your line manager.

- **Chief Operating Officer (COO).** Hopefully, the COO is someone with whom you will work hand-in-glove to execute the strategy of the organisation. The COO has one of the broadest briefs in the organisation and often has a large proportion of the headcount, so you may spend a lot of time with them on their people plans. They may also work with you on the execution of key transformation programmes and corporate development activity.

- **Chief Commercial Officer / Chief Revenue Officer (CCO).** The person responsible for the top-line revenue / sales performance of the organisation. This person may field a large sales team and have to work with you jointly to devise large-scale commission programmes. This person is expected to drive the organisation hard, and you may at times have to play a role in ensuring wellbeing is considered and that they strike a balance between short-term performance and long-term resilience.

- **Chief Financial Officer (CFO).** The CFO will usually set the people budget for the year ahead – hopefully working in collaboration with you – or it may be handed to you as a *fait accompli*! They have to ensure the organisation grows in a balanced way, and they have to ensure both periodic performance and the long-term viability of the organisation, maximising return for shareholders (in a commercial organisation) and careful management of spend. Understanding the financial 'rails' you are on and where there is (and is not) scope for flex, will pave the way for a productive relationship. In-keeping with your role having broad executive responsibility, you should ensure that you understand the financial fundamentals of the organisation. You don't need to be a chartered accountant, but you should understand how the organisation makes money, the basics of the P&L and where the people-related elements fit in. Don't be naïve about your HR budgetary requests – contextualise them and ground them in a knowledge of what the organisation can sustain. If it would boost your confidence to take a 'Finance for non-Finance professionals' course, now would be a great time to do so.

- **Chief Legal Officer (CLO) / General Counsel (GC).** The General Counsel (GC) is often a great support for the CPO, especially in times of difficulty, such as grievance procedures, capability discussions, terminations and / or redundancies. While the CPO will be expected to have a strong grasp of employment legislation, they will lean on the GC for specialist support at certain times and in areas such as Employee Relations. In turn, the CPO can advise the GC on the optimal balance of in-house vs. third party support for their own legal team, balancing cost and expertise.

- **Chief Marketing Officer (CMO).** You will work with the CMO to ensure that the brand, values and ethos of the organisation are reflected internally, to employees, as well as externally, to the market. Without that consistency, the organisation will lack authenticity and there will be a dissonance at its heart. When a new employee joins, they transition from having the outside view to being an insider. If that recruitment, hiring and onboarding journey is a disappointment relative to what they were led to believe, trust is lost and is very hard to regain. The same applies when it comes to Diversity, Equity and Inclusion (DEI), promotion and pay. How employees are exited also has a bearing on whether they remain an advocate for the organisation. On the lighter side, you get to collaborate on elements such as office look and feel, merchandise / swag (hoodies!), Corporate Social Responsibility (CSR) days out, sponsorships and plenty of other enjoyable things that bring the spark to your organisation. A rewarding relationship when it's working well.

- **Chief Technology Officer (CTO)**. The CTO often has some of the most neurodiverse employees in their team – from those who love the buzz of collaboration to those who cherish the opportunity to working in their own way, in a more peaceful setting. It's also a place where great developers can get promoted into team leaders, which will suit some people really well, and others not at all. The career development path in Technology requires particular support from the People team and building a trusted relationship between the CPO and CTO really helps. In addition, you may find yourself collaborating with the CTO to deliver the people systems required to support your team, so this really is a two-way relationship.

- **Chief Risk Officer (CRO).** The CRO heads up the 'second line of defence' in the organisation. We will discuss this further in chapter 19, but what this essentially means is that they hold the rest of the organisation – including you – to account, to ensure there's a robust system of controls in place to manage risk. They should be a supportive, constructive but critical friend to you in this, helping you ensure that you manage the employee lifecycle appropriately and guard against errors, data loss and legal challenges. They also manage a team and will need all the same supports as any other part of the organisation in looking after their talent.

Building successful relationships with this cohort from the outset is key. According to Rachel Farley, a Partner at Heidrick

& Struggles: *"To succeed you must have the Board's ear, the Executive Committee's ear and your ear to the ground."* [5] Plus, you want to have an impact early. It's important to structure your first 100 days; use a framework like the one outlined in Niamh O'Keeffe's book *Your First 100 Days: How to make maximum impact in your new role.* [6] Once you have set those goals, you need to adopt a regular habit of reviewing them and holding yourself accountable.

Summary

Starting out in your new position as CPO is exciting and nerve-wracking in equal measure. You are in a position to take the organisation on a new journey under your leadership. Having a clear view on where to start, building trust and allocating your time appropriately are all key. It's also an opportunity to bring a fresh, unique view, decide what you want to continue, and what to change.

We've covered the role of CPO, routes to get there, personality characteristics that are helpful, and not helpful, to the CPO and the nature of some of the relationships with the rest of the C-suite. Next, we examine how to structure your work and the fundamental pillars of how the CPO will have impact; through shaping culture, aligning strategy and executing change in the organisation.

SECTION ONE – THE FOUNDATIONS

Chapter 2

Culture and engagement

Introduction

"If you look at companies that have struggled, more times than not, it's not about the quality of their strategy, it's much more about around execution or culture. We've seen some massive failures in corporate America around culture." [7]

F. William McNabb III, Former Chairman and CEO of Vanguard

We've been talking about organisational culture for almost 50 years, since Edgar Schein, founder of the discipline of organisational behaviour, introduced us to it.

There is an abundance of definitions of organisational culture, and they all centre around employees in the organisation having a set of shared ways of thinking, acting and being. When the organisation's espoused mission, vision, purpose, values and goals are mirrored in how people actually think, act and operate in reality, the organisation has a strong culture. When an employee aligns with that strong culture, they are fully engaged. So culture is 'how we really do things around here', and high engagement depends on whether or not employees have bought into that culture. Psychological safety is a core element of culture as it allows people to speak up and learn from their mistakes. Without it there is no healthy culture and, therefore, no high engagement.

The role of the CPO in shaping culture

The CPO is a steward and keeper of employee culture, safety, wellbeing and engagement.[8]

The CPO does not own it – it's the role of the Board and the entire Executive team to:

- Create a mission, vision, purpose and set of values that will underpin everything the workforce does to achieve business success;
- Align with the culture of the organisation, in order to achieve the mission, vision, purpose and values successfully;
- Build an environment where employees feel safe to ask questions, raise concerns and make mistakes; each executive will be held to account on this being the case within their own function, and the Board will regularly examine that to be the case in reality;
- Espouse and role model the culture consistently; the workforce should be under no illusion about what good looks like, as they will see it in how their Board and executives behave from the top; and
- Safeguard the culture by actively dealing with situations where it is not being displayed throughout the organisation – what we tolerate is what we are deemed to accept.

It is however the role of the CPO to put in place the processes, systems, training and measurement to capture how well the organisation is doing on the agreed shared culture. The CPO should create a framework to capture the organisation's culture, as well as a process to measure it regularly, share the results and ensure improvements are made when gaps start to appear.

Creating a culture framework

There is no shortage of tools to measure culture in the organisation; these include surveys, key performance indicators, anecdotes, analytics and insights. One simple assessment involves looking at two dimensions, similar to the Goffee and Jones model:[9]

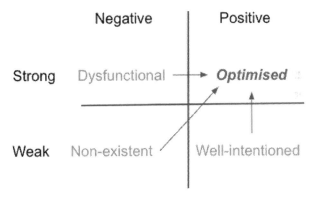

Figure 2.1: A framework for measuring culture

Culture can be:

- **Strong:** high degree of behavioural similarity and repeated behaviours exhibited by employees, even across locations. Everyone knows how they need to act.
- **Weak:** high degree of behavioural differences and ad hoc behaviours exhibited by employees. There are few behavioural norms to fall back on.
- **Positive:** positive disposition towards mission, vision, purpose and values. Good sentiments expressed between and towards employees.
- **Negative:** cynicism, lack of trust and defensiveness permeate the organisation.

Depending on where the organisation sits, there are four approaches that you as CPO can take to move the culture in the direction it needs to go for success:

- **Dysfunctional:** intervene to address a toxic culture;
- **Non-existent:** build the right culture for the organisation;
- **Well-intentioned:** reinforce and consolidate the positive behaviours; and
- **Optimised**: work within it to ensure ongoing and future business success.

Where a culture is not strong, or there are gaps in – or emerging in – your culture, good employees leave. In measuring emerging gaps in the organisation's culture, Melissa Daimler assesses three elements:[10]

- **Behaviours:** we've said already how leaders must role model values. To measure behaviour gaps, you need to invest time in identifying the behaviours and skills that express each organisational value. Once expected behaviours are clarified, employees can focus on emulating them rather than trying to identify them.
- **Systems:** there are five systems that can either reinforce or dilute culture: hiring, strategy and goal setting, assessing, developing and rewarding. These should feed into and off each other when a strong culture exists – where they don't, gaps emerge, and culture is weakened. We will cover each of these areas in this book.
- **Practices:** these include everything from company events, feedback culture, how meetings are run and how decisions are made. Practices should evolve with the organisation, that is when it grows, re-organises or faces new threats. Where practices continue to meet mission, vision, purpose and values as they change, a strong culture will remain. Practices are also the small, everyday things

that subtly but powerfully reinforce culture; a kind word, holding the door open, sacrificing your agenda to help someone else. Do not underestimate these.

Traditionally we look at culture as an internal matter. Dave Ulrich however proposes that, as one of HR's unique contributions to business success, we need to consider the future of culture from the 'outside-in', or from the customer's perspective:

"The 'right' culture can be defined as the identity of the firm in the mind of its best customers that then shapes employee behaviours and HR practices... the right culture focuses on customer identity to help organizations stay connected to customer changes rather than being focused on internal values."[11]

In order to future-proof the success of the organisation, it certainly makes sense to consider taking the customer perspective when considering the mission, vision, purpose and values of the organisation, and testing how the 'outside-in' view of culture measures up.

Psychological safety and the link to culture

Psychological safety was defined originally in 1999 by Amy Edmondson as,

"The belief that one will not be punished or humiliated for speaking up with ideas, questions, concerns or mistakes, and that the team is safe for interpersonal risk taking."[12]

Edmondson adds that when an employee feels psychologically safe, they,

"feel able to ask for help, admit mistakes, raise concerns, suggest ideas and challenge ways of working / business operating model and the ideas of others on the team, including the idea of those in authority."[13]

Psychological safety is a crucial component of culture as it allows people to learn from their mistakes and near misses, reducing the chances of future errors.[14] High-performing teams need psychological safety so individuals feel invested in, empowered and impactful. The leader needs to allow people to be curious, to listen to each other intentionally, ask and answer questions openly, to not blame or point the finger when mistakes are made and to elevate and appreciate difference.

While it's incumbent on the full team to build this safety, it needs the right leader to drive and guide it. Psychological safety should be measured via employee surveys, whistleblowing activity and grievance tickets raised with the HR team and tracked intentionally to make sure psychological safety evidenced throughout the organisation. An organisation that does not have psychological safety will never reach its full potential. Not tracking psychological safety intentionally nor maintaining it actively across the entire organisation may render everything else people-related ineffective.

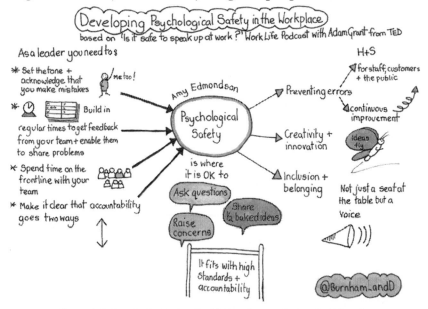

Figure 2.2: Psychological safety[15] Sketch note by Rachel Burnham

Engagement and how to measure it

It's time to talk engagement. At its most uncomplicated, culture is 'how we do everything around here', and engagement is 'whether I'm bought into that or not'. This includes candidates, employees, managers, the Board, contingent workers, suppliers, customers – everyone who interacts with the organisation making it a success.

High engagement is defined by Paul Zak in his book *The Neuroscience of Trust*, as,

> *"…having a strong connection with one's work and colleagues, feeling like a real contributor, and enjoying ample chances to learn [which] consistently leads to positive outcomes for both individuals and organisations. The rewards include higher productivity, better-quality products and increased profitability."* [16]

High engagement impacts the bottom line and is a lofty, but necessary, goal of the People strategy. But how do you pin it down? It's difficult as engagement is something you feel in your heart. When you send out employee surveys, people answer most of the questions with their head. For example: "Do you have the tools to do your job?". Engagement questions such as the following are answered more with your heart:

- "Are you proud to work at this organisation?"
- "Will you be working here in two years?"
- "Would you recommend the organisation to your friends?"

For practical purposes though, let's try to pin it down to something less ethereal and more tangible. A look through the main business psychology articles presents the following as key areas on which to focus to achieve high engagement:

- Have a clearly articulated company vision and purpose;
- Ensure employees feel valued and recognised;

- Empower employees and give them a voice;
- Build trust in leadership and management; and
- Communicate honestly, transparently and often.

HR training provider AIHR offers five potential strategies for measuring engagement:[17]

1. **Point in time surveys:** the traditional annual employee survey, in which questions cover all elements of the employee experience, quantitative and qualitative results are collated and actions are taken to address areas of concern or to elevate areas of strength.
2. **Interval employee surveys and focus groups:** specific surveys and focus groups set up to discuss and find solutions to specific challenges.
3. **Pulse surveys and check-ins:** ongoing, small surveys with immediate follow up actions to improve scores.
4. **Employee lifecycle measures of moments that matter:** gathering feedback around a particular employee experience to assess and improve it continuously.
5. **Continuous dialogue and analytics:** increasingly popular, these are continuous conversation platforms that collect qualitative data on themes on an ongoing basis and use technology scale to capture the information.

There are a multitude of engagement surveys on offer, depending on the budget, time and resources available, as well as depending on what you want to focus. Equally there are plenty of consultancy organisations to help you deliver these surveys to the highest quality. Whatever tool you use to gather the data, you absolutely must action the data when it's collated. One of the most heart-breaking questions to see answered poorly is: "Do you believe the organisation will act on this feedback?"

Build trust in the engagement survey process by having a consistent and visible follow-on action planning process to address the survey outcomes. Your data analytics team – whether within the People team or an organisation-wide analytics team – should be committed to investigating the data as soon as the survey closes, or the subsequent focus group content is submitted. They should analyse and provide the story of the data in tables, trends, infographics and proposed areas for action.

Make sure employees, managers and leaders are given the time and space to co-create improvements and solutions to the survey outputs. Take the time to look at this rich data forensically yourself with the analytics team, taking a company-wide perspective. Consider deeply what the data is telling you and, crucially, what you have in your gift as CPO to do with the information. What policies, processes and behaviours can you leverage to address issues and grasp opportunities? What would the customers of the organisation say about the survey results? Are the strengths of the organisation reflected in the Employee Value Proposition?

After the business leaders make their commitment to their actions, and when you have decided where you can make changes, do it all over again by measuring what effect all the changes have on your employees – crucially measuring if what we are doing is increasing employee engagement.

Questions for a new CPO

- Does the feedback culture align with the company values?
- Do managers create psychological safety for their teams intentionally and consistently?
- Would everyone in your organisation say they can speak up without fear of retaliation?
- Do you measure engagement?
- What direction is the engagement score trending towards?

- How vibrant is the action planning post-engagement survey?
- How well is your organisation learning and iterating on the back of survey data?

Summary

Mission, vision, purpose and values provide the direction of travel for everyone in the organisation. Culture is the shared thinking, actions and behaviours across the workforce that underpins everyone moving in the right direction, leading to organisational success. However, according to authors Greg Satell and Cathy Windschitl, hiring for skills and capabilities is not sufficient for organisational success: *"There is a fundamental difference between hiring people to do what you want and hiring people who already want what you want."*[18]

That is where culture, psychological safety and engagement come into the equation. Identify the culture carriers in the organisation – those who have deep institutional knowledge and embody the company values – and elevate them. They are the best role models for company culture and provide employees with clear expectations of what it takes to be successful. When everything aligns, a strong culture leads to highly engaged employees, resulting in business success.

With a firm handle of organisational culture, the next foundational item the CPO needs to consider is strategy.

Chapter 3

People and strategy

Introduction

As a new or aspiring CPO, you need to know, understand, digest and buy into the business strategy of the organisation, so you can craft a People strategy that aligns to it. Every element of your HR framework – your organisational design, job framework, hiring, performance management criteria, remuneration and benefits structure, learning and development, succession planning – should all be in furtherance of the organisation's goals. Strategic people management, and engaging the Board, ExCo and workforce in your People vision is the over-arching role of the CPO.

The business strategy can and should also be informed to a degree by the People function. In looking at the key strengths and capabilities of the organisation, the elements that create a 'strategic moat' around its offering and make it hard for others to break in and emulate, the CPO should be putting forward what they view as the core capabilities and know-how that are valuable and should be optimised in furtherance of the strategy.

Also, the CPO should provide a clear-eyed assessment where capability gaps and blind spots are creating areas of weakness and risk for the organisation, while putting forward strategies to counter them. Executive search firm Heidrich & Struggles says about CPOs:

> *"We create an edge through people, in an ever-changing environment, in a way that is impactful and low cost."* [19]

It also follows that, as strategy is bespoke to an organisation at a particular point in time and is constantly evolving, the People strategy will evolve as well. While certain aspects of the role, such as striving for value for money and operational excellence, will always hold true, there will be flex in other areas, and you will be respected by your executive peers for regularly checking in on the alignment of your people measures to the overall goals. Conversely, if they see a CPO as operating in an ivory tower, pushing ahead on a dozen initiatives for the sake of it, oblivious to what's going on in the rest of the organisation, they will be frustrated, roll their eyes, comply with the 'essential' parts of the HR strategy but not engage with you on a serious level.

Linking strategy and the People function

Take a look at one commonly used strategic framework – the McKinsey 7S model; every aspect of it touches on the People function in some capacity.

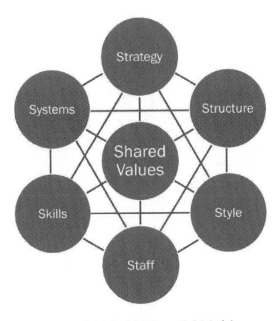

Figure 3.1 The McKinsey 7-S Model

Strategy

Let's look at how certain business strategies impact on the People function, and how different approaches are required at different stages of the organisational life cycle.

- **Growth phase:** this phase of the organisation's development is characterised by a land grab in a new or innovative area. There's often a war for talent, at times paying over the odds for the skills needed in the time available (either in terms of permanent or outsourced workforce). By necessity, there is sometimes a shortened recruitment cycle, which may yield a few failed hires along the way. Capability is nascent and lots of things are being figured out on the fly. The small generalist People team is working hard to try and create a great employee experience, but often short of the suite of tools they need. It's a hard-working, challenging, energising time.

The CPO gets to try to build and differentiate on culture, office experience and perks. There's lots of fluidity in how the organisation works and lots of bootstrapping. This time in the organisation involves rapid decision-making, often without all of the information available.

- **Scaling phase:** the organisation has found some product / market fit and some investment and is hiring at scale, developing fast. The People team should be watching for over-stretch, stress, over-promotion and burnout. It's also often a time of launching in new territories, with all the attendant infrastructure needed, and working to maintain the culture as you do so. Mass induction programmes need to be built, while keeping close to new people and preserving the values and ethos of the founders. A common challenge for the founding team at this stage is being able to devolve certain tasks; In *7 Entrepreneurial Leadership Workouts,*[20] authors Jones and Tynan state that one of the key muscles that leaders need to work at this time is the *"letting go of autonomy"*. This is one area where many founders fail – giving up some of the early control they had. It's also often a time, at executive level, when you need to bring in some additional skills and integrate some new personalities, with all the associated risk.

- **Stability:** this is a slightly less manic period of consolidation. This should be the time when the CPO gets to build some of the systems and processes that may have been neglected during the hyper-growth stage. It's a time of maturing the model, building in elements such as more formal succession planning, learning and development (L&D), and internal talent mobility. The formalisation of people policies and processes can cause push-back from those who loved the easy, fluid way of doing things, but it's often required, for example, when an organisation goes through an investment round and where investors and regulators simply expect more due process and consistency.

- **Efficiency and optimisation**: we're seeing a wave of this in the tech sector at the moment. With valuations a fraction of what they used to be, and revenues faltering, some organisations have realised that they have over-hired, over-promoted and over-compensated. Layoffs and cost cuts can follow. This is deeply challenging for organisations that have been on the journey where, previously, the only way was up. It's when culture and values are tested like never before – it's easy to stick to your values when things are going well. What people remember is what you do, and how you do it, in tough times.

- **Crisis:** not all organisations go through this, but every now and again, an established institution goes through some kind of crisis. It can be a business continuity event (physical disaster, political upheaval, technology hack), or a public relations issue, where the organisation's products, values or ways of working are put under the spotlight and held to account in the eyes of the public like never before. This is one of the most challenging situations for the whole Executive team and the CPO. The role of the CPO must be to gather people together, to reassure, to listen (*really* listen), sometimes to bring in independent experts to play back to the organisation what has gone wrong and to plot a way forward. The CPO must help and counsel the organisation and its people to 'take its medicine', be humble, examine what went wrong, not sweep things under the carpet, support its people and eventually re-build (see re-invigoration below). Displaying strength of character authentically, counselling your Executive team and supporting your people (including / especially the whistle-blowers, culture carriers and the people who care most about the organisation) are key at this difficult time.

- **Defensive:** this is when an organisation finds itself in some kind of race to the bottom; perhaps on price or features. It's often characterised by commoditisation of products or services, outsourcing or offshoring to reduce cost. It's not a strategy to be envied, but it does exist and requires its own HR response. It's a challenging time, characterised by a lack of investment and innovation. There can be loss of talent and a retention drive to try and retain key staff. It can become a death spiral, leading to…
- **Retrenchment / wind down:** the wind down of the organisation. The organisation may be seeking to divest lines of business or other valuable assets. From a People standpoint, this involves phasing the letting go of staff and managing the redundancy programme, while keeping enough critical people around, often tied in with retention packages, to manage the last of customer services, finance and other essential functions through to orderly closure. It involves keeping just enough of the People team around to finalise payrolls, support skeleton staff and wind down.
- **Re-invigoration:** Some organisations that go through flat or difficult times find a way to be re-born, to find new markets, or to re-capture what was great about the offering in the first place. In his book *Net Positive,* [21] former Unilever CEO Paul Polman discusses the transformation that took place at Unilever and the need to *"capture the soul of the organisation"*, finding its true purpose, and then aligning all of the organisation, including all aspects of it People framework, around that purpose. We discuss this more in chapter 21.

HR has a critical function to play when an organisation undergoes a corporate development activity, such as a merger, acquisition, joint venture or divestment. We'll talk more about the role of HR in Corporate Development in the next chapter.

Continuing through the McKinsey 7-S model:

Structure

The organisational design needs to mirror what operating model the strategy needs. Typically, leaders look to devolve decision-making for speed and empowerment when they need to move quickly. They usually centralise control and decision-making either in the very early days, when things are quite immature, or when they need to take control of, for example, costs and effort. The depth, spans and layers of the organisation have a direct impact on the velocity at which it can move, and a mismatch between structure and strategy will frustrate efforts. We look at organisation design in more detail in the next chapter on Execution.

Style

The organisation's brand should permeate all aspects of the People function too; from the look and feel of the office space, to the hiring process – modern and agile vs. traditional. Many of us will have gone through a recruitment process with a supposedly agile organisation, only for it to be slow, impersonal, linear and rigid. HR is usually the first and final function that an employee experiences – make sure that the employee experience lives up to expectations. Chapter 5 focuses on what needs to go into the Employee Value Proposition (EVP) to entice new hires to the organisation and to keep the existing workforce engaged in the employer brand.

Staff

The attributes of the people you hire and promote should reflect the organisation's purpose, culture, brand and values. The values and behaviours that are rewarded should be aligned completely with what is espoused, as we saw in the last chapter on Culture and Engagement. Is the product or service you are offering highly commoditised, or is it specialised and bespoke? What does that imply for the skillsets of the front-facing staff that you need? Look at composition, skills and tenure and make sure they are all serving the organisation.

Skills

As well as the people you hire in, your L&D strategy should build directly on the needs of the organisation. Consider the bar you set for people you bring in, linked to pay – are you hiring in the top percentile or is market average good enough? This is not a trivial question – sometimes market average may be just fine for what you need, and your role is to ensure the organisation hires the right people at the right price point for what it needs. What competencies does the organisation need, and how can those be further developed in-house? What leadership development training is required to reinforce and implement the strategy, so the organisation can thrive in its sector? What formal training do you want to complement the on-the-job learning that staff are getting? We discuss talent development in more detail in chapter 10.

Systems

How much is the organisation prepared to invest in systems that make life easy for its people; both in relation to HR and more generally? How much self-service is allowed? Stripe[22] devoted significant resource to building its own quality assurance software, Sorbet, to empower and free up their own coders to work better, signalling the value it places on time and efficiency of its expensive developers. Chapter 17 on information systems for people management discusses this in more depth.

Shared values

As outlined in the previous chapter, the CPO plays a significant role in shaping culture, the set of values that underpins everything. Culture is not for the CPO to devise in isolation, but you play a pivotal role in ensuring that what's written on the wall is what is 'lived' every day. Actions that undermine the shared values will be picked up on quickly.

As per the sister handbook to this one, *How to be a Chief Risk Officer,*[23] another 'S' should be added for stakeholders. As for the Chief Risk Officer, stakeholder mapping is a critical exercise for the CPO to embark on. Key stakeholders include:

- Customers / external clients;
- Employees;
- the Board;
- Suppliers;
- Regulators;
- Investors;
- Shareholders;
- Media;
- Government; and
- The public.

Developing a strong understanding of internal stakeholders will be intuitively straightforward for the CPO. However, the relationships with external stakeholders such as investors, shareholders and media are increasingly important to cultivate, with the increasing focus on human capital being seen as a strategic investment (rather than a cost) and on Environment Social and Governance (ESG) matters.

Putting strategy into action for the People function

The best strategy in the world is no good unless it's put into action. Your role as CPO is not just to formulate a People strategy with the Executive team – it's to execute it across the organisation. You do this by taking the business strategy, aligning the key elements of the People framework with it, turning it into an actionable plan, and putting measures in place to track progress and outcomes. This also requires a clear-eyed assessment of the current state of the People function, so that the path from here to there can be clearly and realistically charged.

Gartner[24] recommends four steps to turning a business strategy into a HR one. They are;

1. "Identify a shortlist of metrics to describe the function's target state.
2. Document and monitor key assumptions.
3. Identify the key initiatives and milestones required to move to the end state.
4. Craft a concise statement that encapsulates the essence of the strategy."

Gartner stresses – and we agree – that a small number of metrics (it suggests four to seven) is optimal; any more than that and it loses focus. Then, once these metrics are achieved, you celebrate the achievement, review for effectiveness, capture the learnings and start all over again. A list of OKRs for the People function is provided at the end of the book – be selective!

Summary

We started with the role of the CPO in shaping culture. We've now aligned the strategy of the business with the People strategy. Now we need to take a look at the differing role of the CPO in executing that strategy holistically, effectively and resiliently.

Chapter 4

Execution

Introduction

"...the aim of workforce planning is not to create a workforce plan; the aim of workforce planning is to create the right workforce. Without delivery a plan is just an idea... Success is taking that workforce plan ... and executing it effectively to deliver the workforce that the organization needs." [25]

Adam Gibson

The people plan will be made up of 'business as usual' elements to meet current specific business or functional goals. However, as CPO you also need to deliver the above-mentioned *"workforce that the organisation needs"*, that is the *right* workforce for the long term. This requires taking a helicopter view of the organisation and executing a people plan that is flexible, resilient and continues to meet the ever-evolving needs of the organisation.

Your People strategy will need to incorporate alternative scenarios to ensure its success in an increasingly volatile, uncertain, complex and ambiguous (VUCA) world. Sticking to a people plan rigidly will not be a recipe for success for you, your People team, your business leaders nor your external stakeholders.

In this chapter, we will discuss several distinct areas of focus for the CPO, all of which play an important role in executing an impactful People strategy successfully and continuously. Some are associated with *what* you need to deliver – for example securing your HR budget and having great organisational design – and some are associated with *how* you deliver this – including thoughtful change management and respectful relationships with unionised workforces.

Executing the People strategy successfully is *the* most important aspect of your role as CPO. It requires to you get above and stay above day-to-day transactional HR so you can orchestrate the talent in the organisation in harmony to reach its greatest potential, thereby impacting current and future business success directly.

Organisational effectiveness

You will need to create a blueprint for how value will be created for the customer using the human resources that are in, or need to be in, the organisation. We saw at the end of the previous chapter that the People strategy emanates from the business strategy. Your People strategy will have an overarching vision, aligned to that business strategy, and will be broken into a number of operational people plans, each captured in a series of Objectives and Key Results (OKRs). You are therefore tasked not only with a plan for meeting today's goals, but also one that secures business success tomorrow.

Three of the most strategic tools at your disposal to consistently check the organisation is delivering value are:

- **Organisation design** – a framework used to identify the gap between how the organisation is currently designed and how it needs to be designed in order to continue performing;
- **Organisational development** – tools and processes used to sustain that required level of continued organisational performance; and
- **Change management** – the discipline used to continuously close the gap between current and required organisational performance.

Let's take a look at each in turn.

Organisation design

Described by the Chartered Institute of Personnel and Development (CIPD) as *"the review of what an organisation wants and needs, an analysis of the gap between its current state and where it wants to be in the future, and the design of organisational practices that will bridge that gap"*,[26] designing or redesigning the structure of the organisation will be a function of a number of elements, including its size, strategy, where it is in its life cycle, the external environment and technology.

Organisation design takes account of all elements of the organisation. An organisational design review will usually be undertaken when there is a change in business strategy, when the current design is no longer fit for purpose, or when there are significant changes in the external environment. The process will generally inspect the current and required future state of the following parts of the organisation:[27]

1. Chain of command – how authority flows through the organisation;

2. Span of control – the number of subordinates a superior can effectively manage;
3. Centralisation – where decision-making power is concentrated;
4. Specialisation – the degree to which tasks are broken down into individual jobs;
5. Formalisation – the rules and procedures which govern how an individual job is done; and
6. Departmentalisation – how jobs are group together to coordinate tasks.

Great organisational design also considers the values, communication channels, aspirations, culture and leadership styles within the company. The People plans focus on the programmes, systems and processes associated with the employee journey, whereas organisation design is focused on the bigger picture, *"ensuring that the mechanics of your organization are optimised so that your business can perform as well as possible."*[28]

Organisation design is complex. There are a number of open-source guides to help you check that your structure is fit-for-purpose for now and the future, however where financially possible, seek specialist support to create one that truly identifies a future-state structure that will deliver success. The fundamental steps to review your design are:

1. Understand the strategic context, in order to understand strategic priorities. This step includes creating design principles to be followed throughout the process, which will help in the latter stages, particularly when selecting the final model.
2. Identify priority opportunities for change to develop an initial vision of the future state. This includes assessing the capabilities needed for the organisation or function being assessed. Specific metrics, for example spans of

control, number of layers, customer service or quality can be used to unearth where the redesign opportunities lie.

3. Design conceptual options based on what needs to change based on opportunities identified. Inputs into this step include current organisation structure, as well as the design priorities and agreed metrics from step 2. Drivers of design options can include the following examples:
   a. Growth (organic and inorganic) – re-aligning the organisation with the biggest growth opportunities;
   b. Customer centricity – designing the organisation to optimise excellence in customer experience;
   c. People and culture – driving clarity and accountability;
   d. Leveraged and scalable – breaking down silos and increasing efficiencies;
   e. Geographic need – adapting to meet the needs of new jurisdictions;
   f. Capability – addressing capability gaps in marketing, finance, sales ops etc.; and
   g. Governance – clarifying decision rights, strengthening management processes.

4. Build the future state organisation, by developing the detailed components of the chosen organisational model and measuring the strength of each option based on the agreed design principles from step 1 and the organisation design priorities from step 2. Include a measure of the overall impact on the current structure for each option.

5. Implement, by developing a roadmap and timeline of change, including headcount implications. In confirming the agreed option, work with business lead(s) and finance to agree and effect the future state headcount.

The outcome from carrying out an organisation design or redesign is the identification of a future optimal design and a plan to achieve it (using change management discipline) and how to maintain it (using organisational development tools).

Workforce planning, an element of organisation design, is defined by the CIPD as, *"a core business process which aligns changing organisation needs with a people strategy"*.[29] This is a follow-on step from step 5 above, where new headcount requirements are filtered through the finance headcount planning process.

Later in the book you will see a number of references to organisations needing to become more agile, to move more quickly to react to the external environment for continued business success. Consideration should be given to creating an agile, flexible organisation design should also, and Kevan Hall's book *Making the Matrix Work*[30] is an excellent and practical guide in this regard.

McKinsey focuses on answering four questions to create an agile company blueprint:[31]

1. Where should profit-and-loss ownership lie?
2. How does one create incentives for teams that do not own a P&L?
3. What is the framework for coordinating among teams?
4. How does culture need to adapt to make this work?

Organisation development

Organisation development (OD) is described by the CIPD as *"a planned and systematic approach to enabling sustained organisational performance through the involvement of its people"*.[32]

As with organisation design, organisation development is a complex activity. There are a number of open-source guides to help you identify and use the tools needed to check and maintain organisation performance at the required level. However where financially possible, seek specialist OD support to periodically examine how well the company is performing and what tweaks and adjustments can be made to keep the engines running to the highest level. Using principles from behavioural science to consider how to design and deliver change to how we work (i.e. relationships, behaviours, culture), organisation development is fast becoming a key tool used by organisations to ensure continued future success in a fast-paced world of business. This process can also be referred to as achieving the organisation's target operating model. While the business strategy and goals define *what* the organisation will deliver to achieve business success, the company's target operating model defines *how* it will achieve it.

Organisation development is comprised of the organisation's people, processes, systems and structure / governance and the CIPD advises that *"companies should take a proactive approach to examining their current processes, systems and organisational structures to assess if they align with their goals and future needs".* [33]

OD specialists use tools such as SWOT analyses, Lean/Six Sigma and Total Quality Management (TQM) to diagnose what interventions may best fit gaps between current and future states, and these may include human processes, techno-structural and strategic interventions.

How do organisation design and organisation development work together? Both are critical in taking a holistic approach to business transformation.

Peter Turgoose and Mark LaScola, Founders of organisation design firm On The Mark, explain: *"The first step is deciding what is the purpose and the function of the business: that is the Organization Design part. The next step is deciding how to maintain the purpose and function: that is the OD part."* [34]

Next, we focus on how to implement change, including how to close the gap on the current and required organisation design.

Change management

Change management is the activity that will take you from current state to desired future state. There are two scenarios for the CPO to consider when thinking about how and when change management discipline should be exercised by the people function: in support of the organisation's overall change management strategy, and to drive people-related change through the organisation.

The CPO should have oversight of and influence over the organisation's change management programme of work, given all change invariably involves people to a greater or lesser degree. For medium to large companies, there will often be a Programme Management Office (PMO) housed within the Operations function under the remit of the COO. They will be charged with oversight and delivery of all change management projects across the company. In smaller companies, there may be decentralised project teams within individual functions, delivering smaller bespoke projects within those businesses. However change management is set up in your organisation, your perspective and influence will be needed to ensure it is done successfully. If the change capability of your organisation is not well-developed or if you sense change fatigue, consider asking the following ten questions to assess how well the workforce is dealing with the company's change agenda:[35]

1. What is the workforce's attitude towards change? What is their experience of it?
2. What is the change capability within the organisation – both in project teams and among the workforce?
3. What are the most recent changes in the organisation? How have they landed?

4. Does management accept change management as something that needs to be taken into consideration or is project success just assumed?
5. How much change has the organisation been through in recent years?
6. Who leads the change in the organisation? Is it viewed as led by management, or is it federated and staff-initiated?
7. What is the governance around the change portfolio and around incepting new projects?
8. Do projects generally get implemented on time and on budget? If not, what lessons have been learned?
9. What must-do projects have been implemented this year? Were they appropriately resourced?
10. Is there a clear line of sight between the strategy and the change portfolio?

Seek to create a culture that involves the greater workforce in as much of the change as possible – that is your gift as CPO. You can – and should – be the voice of the employee in protecting them from change fatigue, and giving people control in that change is one of the best tools to do just that. Flipping change management from top-down change to open-source change involves:

- Employees co-creating change decisions.
- Employees owning implementation planning.
- Employees talking openly about change in order to sustain it.

All change projects are not created equal. Traditionally the change function will measure the number and impact of all the change programmes of work. However, Gartner reports that there is differing impact on the disruption factor of change on employees[36] which should be an additional data point when considering 'air traffic control' and deciding what projects to land when and with whom.

The second lens through which to consider change management is in overseeing the change required to deliver on the People agenda, i.e. implementing changes to move towards your chosen organisational design. You may consider establishing a project team within your People team, or at a minimum, ensuring there are people on the team with project management capability to execute the organisational changes. The types of change that you will want to deliver may include anything from the purchase and implementation new company-wide people technology to do compensation planning to delivering new policy and processes on how, where and when we work into the future. Dave Ulrich provides a practical six-step process and 10-question assessment for constantly checking that the HR function remains consistently effective in delivering it programmes and creating value:[37]

Steps to a More Effective HR Function

Figure 4.1: Improving HR Value Creation

HR Function Dimension	Diagnostic questions	How well do we do this? 1 low, 5 high	How important is it? 1 low, 5 high
1: HR Reputation	Have a reputation for creating value for all stakeholders?		
2: HR Customers	Serve all stakeholders inside (employees) and outside (customers)?		
3: HR Purpose	Share an HR mission about who we are, what we do, and why we exist?		
4: HR Design	Clearly allocate roles and work together to make knowledge productive?		
5: Human Capability	Build human capability (talent, leadership, organization) in businesses?		
6: HR Analytics	Access relevant and rigorous information to make better decisions?		
7: HR Digital Technology	Invest in and use technology / digital tools to do work and connect people?		
8: HR Practices	Innovate, align, and integrate HR initiatives?		
9: HR Professionals	Define and upgrade HR professional competencies to be effective?		
10: HR Relationships	Form positive working relationships within HR and with others?		

Figure 4.2: Measuring the core dimensions of HR

Business-as-usual HR will maintain performance. As CPO, you need to focus on identifying and maintaining organisational effectiveness to deliver value from the People organisation consistently. Organisational design, organisational development and change management are your tools in that regard.

Corporate development

HR has a critical function to play when an organisation undergoes a significant corporate development activity, such as a merger, acquisition, joint venture or divestment. It's crucial for you as CPO to have early sight of these changes, which is where close relationships with your CFO and their top team will be of benefit. When these arise, consider putting a temporary project team together from your People team, potentially including representation from your HR Business Partners (HRBPs), total reward, internal talent, legal / industrial relations and Diversity Equity and Inclusion teams, led by a project manager, to complete this work in a singular focused way.

Never forget the importance of aligning or realigning culture and values post the completion of the deal – there are too many stories to tell in which the work stopped on the day the deal closed leading to discontent, legal issues and attrition only to start on that same date. Put a team in place to continually care for and (re)integrate those in the workforce who join or remain in post, following these large-scale transformational change events.

Organisation effectiveness, including design, development and change management, is a top HR priority for CPOs, and change fatigue and work friction are driving attrition.[38] It's likely that a significant amount of your time and energy will – and should – be spent on organisational effectiveness: that is, making sure the size and shape of the workforce is aligned to the business purpose (i.e. organisational design); ensuring there will be sustained people performance to deliver business goals (i.e. organisational development); and that where a gap that appears in either the workforce or what it's delivering, it will be closed (i.e. change management).

As Deloitte reports, you – as the CPO – are the best placed person at the C-suite table to enable this organisational performance:

> *"Business leaders must also constantly reinvent their organizational formula to drive sustained performance now and into the future. Discarding old thinking is key to enabling an adaptive organization, accessing new capabilities, and creating high performing teams and a winning culture."* [39]

The HR budget

Another responsibility for the CPO in delivering the people plan successfully is to do it within an agreed budget. We'll see later in the book the importance of positioning the People function as an investment in talent, not an input cost. As CPO, you must be financially astute, creating a sustainable people budget that meets the current and future organisational needs, and being prepared to defend and stand over it.

Your CFO will be your biggest collaborator, and likely challenger, in this matter. According to Gyöngyvér Martin, a consultant at HR Lead, close collaboration between the CFO and CPO leads to stronger performance improvement.[40] In chapter 15 on remuneration, we look at how to finance one of the biggest elements of organisational spend: that of payroll. For now, and taking the strategic perspective, in financing the People function you should be able to understand not only the full budget figure, but how this overall figure breaks down line-by-line. You will also need to stand over how you plan to finance the People team in support of the organisation-wide HR budget.

The following graph from Gartner provides a useful starting position against which to check your current allocation of HR spend by category, as well as your current allocation of People team spend against each of those categories. Note the biggest investment in the overall people spend is talent acquisition (20%), talent development (14%) and total reward (13%), however your own graph should be reflective of the design, maturity, sector and other nuances of your organisation:

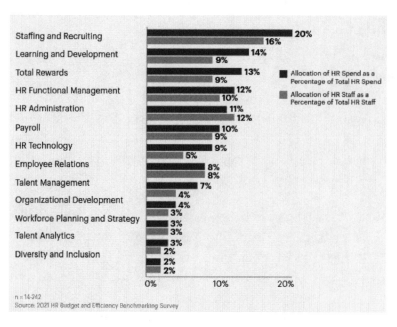

Figure 4.1: Allocation of HR spend and People team spend[41]

Working within a unionised workforce

You may, over the course of your career, operate within a workforce that is represented by a union. While union activity is not as prevalent in the UK and Ireland as in other jurisdictions across Europe, representation is increasing. Representation is also increasing in the US. There are collective consultation requirements for mass redundancies and Transfer of Protected Undertaking (TUPE) situations, as well as a legal framework which protects union activity and provides immunity from certain litigation subject to matters such as secret ballots and proper notice.

The other area of activity for union representation is in the disciplinary process, as employees going through this process are often legally allowed to have union support in the room with them.

At its most basic, "*'employee relations' describes the relationship between employers and employees*".[42] Borne out of the Industrial Relations period of the 1960s, when the balance of power between employer and employee was very much in favour of the employer, and employees joined external trade unions for better representation, trade unions collectively harnessed the power of individual employees to ensure workers' rights were being met.

Fast forward 50 years, the employer-employee contract has evolved into a more balanced bilateral agreement, with stronger legislation backing employee rights, and a workforce made up of individuals who are increasingly inclined to stand up for their own rights. Notwithstanding improvements in the balance of power between employer and employee, collective representation of employees within a union looks set to remain in the workplace for some time to come.

As a CPO, you will need to be aware of the employee relations (ER) landscape for your industry and within your geographical jurisdiction and work within the required parameters to ensure your organisations' legal obligations under ER legislation are respected. In parallel, however, all organisations can and should seek to harness the collective voice of their employees internally anyway to create a positive, transparent relationship between leaders and individual contributors – whether formalised into a union or not.

Workplace conflict is not going away. In fact, with the increasing pressure on people's lives in general, it will remain a prevalent part of working life – and one that the People team will need to proactively manage in some capacity. A positive relationship with either formally or informally organised groups of workers should be an imperative to keep your finger on the pulse of the organisation. At a minimum, it is an opportunity to understand the culture of the organisation, what motivates people to stay, and what drives them to leave.

There are a number of ways to influence good relationships with union representatives outside of the relationship itself. The company should upskill managers who work in a unionised environment proactively, to understand what is required of them, and more importantly, what activities are outside of their remit. A manager should never treat an employee represented by a union any differently than an employee that is not in a union, in the same way they should never discriminate anyone from a particular group. Not only should this upskilling focus on the legality of unions and employee rights, it should also include behavioural aspects such as communication, negotiation, influencing and compromise. There will be an expectation that, when leaders have been upskilled and supported in how to manage a team who are members of a union, they will not make unilateral decisions that disrupt the relationship unnecessarily.

Two-way public fora, as well as tools like 'employee councils' and regular 'listening events', are additional channels that can provide consistent opportunities to share company information, changes of strategic direction, financial concerns and other important updates. These can help create that trusted environment where employees feel they have a strong voice that is listened to, considered and where appropriate, actioned on by leadership.

Stay vigilant – listen, learn, pivot and keep executing

Business planning generally occurs at a set cadence during the year. However, people planning should be a consistent focus for you and the People team at all times. You should have a licence from your CEO, CFO and other key stakeholders to re-plan when needed and not have to return 'cap in hand' for every headcount adjustment.

You're working with human beings who, with all their wonderful gifts and foibles, are susceptible to change. Take an insights-driven approach, lead with data, use your business acumen to listen, learn, pivot and repeat. Quarterly business reviews (QBRs) are set meetings with key senior stakeholders to discuss how well or otherwise execution of the People strategy is going, and are very useful for regular check ins. These meetings should not comprise staid, mundane reporting of tables of people data and pretty graphs – the story of the current state of the people investment should be sent in advance for pre-read (and it should be a story, not just a data dashboard with a bit of commentary), with the meeting time used for a vibrant, honest, 'papers down, heads up' discussion about what needs to stay, what needs to change, and what needs to go.

From time to time, you will need to make a call on what goes into the people plans, and crucially what does not (or indeed what comes out of them). The people strategy has several dependencies and key stakeholders. You will need to work fastidiously to figure out what you want them to do in furtherance of the business goals, as well as to understand what they want from you.

A useful barometer is to look from the outside in – only do things that positively impact the customer. Use something like this useful the Gartner checklist to plan and replan for ongoing success:[43]

Project Name:

Project Owner:

Instructions: The following table provides a list of questions for checking and ensuring the successful execution of each of the five steps for updating HR strategy. After executing each step, HR leaders should refer to the questions listed in the second column. The answer to each question should be "yes" before HR leaders move to the execution of the next step.

Key Steps	Key Questions to Answer	Yes
Step #1 **Prepare for HR Strategy Planning**	Have you identified the key stakeholders who need to be involved in the HR strategy planning process?	☐
	Have you aligned your corporate strategy planning process with your HR strategy planning process?	☐
Step #2 **Understand Business Strategy and Its Talent Implications**	Have you had significant interactions with relevant business leaders about the strategic direction of the organization?	☐
	Do you understand the business's short- and long-term strategy?	☐
	Do you understand the emerging trends that may impact future business strategy?	☐
	Have you identified the talent implications that are critical to achieving each business strategic objective?	☐
Step #3 **Connect HR Strategy to Business Strategy**	Do you understand the current state of HR capabilities?	☐
	Do you know the strengths and weaknesses of your current HR efforts?	☐
	Have you conducted a gap analysis to identify the most critical HR activities where current capability is lacking?	☐
	Does your HR strategic plan have a set of integrated actions across the HR subfunctions?	☐
	Do you have a list of clearly defined metrics associated with each of your HR strategic objectives?	☐
Step #4 **Communicate HR Strategy**	Have you identified all the stakeholders who need to be aware of the HR strategic plan?	☐
	Have you developed an HR strategic communication plan that targets employees, other functions and management?	☐
	Have you developed a storyline to effectively convey your strategy to the identified stakeholders?	☐
Step #5 **Adapt and Monitor HR Strategy**	Have you identified triggers for revisiting your HR strategy?	☐
	Do you have a decision framework for adapting your HR strategy when business conditions change?	☐

Figure 4.2: HR checklist for successful execution of People planning

Case study

Pulling it all together – an interview with CPO Paul Cutler

In an interview for this book Paul Cutler, an experienced CPO currently leading the People strategy at international healthcare consultancy Lucid Group, brought everything we have discussed so far to life with his own career journey: what led him into HR (not his initial career choice), what he experienced in the people space and what keeps him there.

Initially starting out as a digital marketer, Paul realised early in his career that he was motivated more by the unpredictable, complex, unique elements of the workplace than with formulaic processes, numbers or technology. He became fascinated with the question of why some people were satisfied with their careers while others were frustrated, and he found himself considering that if some of those colleagues changed roles by "moving three chairs over, they could be really happy"; and so began the life of a highly successful CPO. Several years later, having worked in sectors as diverse as consumer goods, healthcare, the third sector and fintech; and in companies from small scale ups to those employing many thousands globally, Paul has celebrated the highs, suffered the lows, and experienced a lot in between. Suffice to say, he has seen it all.

Paul's initial foray into HR began, like many of us, in one of the centres of excellence: learning and development. From there, he moved into a generalist role, onto HR Director, and ultimately to CPO. In between all that, he founded his own successful consulting company and upskilled as an executive coach. Here's what he wanted us to know.

The role of the CPO: *there is nothing more important in work right now than the People function – as the world becomes more complex and the needs of our people more nuanced, it is what will be the ultimate differentiator between companies that succeed and fail. And yet C-suite colleagues may never have experienced exceptional People leadership before. Because of this, in some instances, they may look down on you and treat your job as if it's still the 'personnel administration' of yesteryear, merely enforcing policies and managing processes such as the annual salary review.*

Navigating and influencing these C-suite relationships successfully is one of the biggest differences between being an HR People Partner for the C-suite and being a CPO colleague of – and peer to – the C-suite, but this brings an equally large challenge. These C-suite relationships are crucial to success and call for a completely new set of skills to build them. At one extreme you may find yourself partnering with the inspiring, morally-driven leader who believes in the importance of people, and whom you can get behind and rally; and at the other, you may work alongside the task-orientated, self-driven, controlling leader who is far more difficult to partner with.

'Managing' your C-suite colleagues as you would a sophisticated key stakeholder is imperative to determining whether they will be a blocker or an enabler of your People agenda, and how best to positively influence them. The World of Work Project's Trust Equation, which says that an individual's trustworthiness is equal to their credibility, reliability and intimacy divided by their level of self-interest, is a useful tool to use to assess where your peers sit on this spectrum.[44] The key to building your coalition, so you are not constantly fighting an uphill battle, is to find your genuine allies and ensure you have their support for your strategy and plans.

Culture and values: *in my experience I have encountered two extremes of HR leader – your 'favourite auntie' who is always there with a hug and a smile but might duck the tough messages and shy away from difficult decisions; and the night club bouncer on a power trip who is obsessed with process and following the rules.*

The CPO of the future is the person who can marry the empathy of the former, understanding deeply the individual and organisational needs on a very human level, and connect that to the latter's bias for action and transformation, together with a commerciality that has sadly been lacking in the People function historically.

The CPO role requires us to both uphold the needs and responsibilities of the business while having a moral accountability to do what is right for the people within that business. In a healthy organisation these are normally in lockstep so this is not an issue. However you will, at times, be put in positions where you will need to soul search and interrogate your own values, to work out what kind of person you are and what kind of organisation you are leading and to which you belong.

When your values and those of the organisation do not match up, you may be in the position of having to challenge leadership and the establishment. Keep your morals, your values and your core intact in those most difficult moments. You may need to rely on that gut instinct during the times when the organisation is being short-sighted, balancing the need to make decisions that are right for both the company and the individuals within it. Managerial courage in the CPO role is often required to be at a level above everyone else — it's a core competency, not a nice-to-have.

Business strategy, People strategy and transformation: *there will always be an element of change in your job. In my experience, whatever organisation you go into as a CPO, you are always transforming the function and the organisation's capabilities. This is because the People function has been underinvested for decades, until recently, and we have a huge amount of ground to cover in order to catch up with some other functions. You'll likely have to conduct a major transformation wherever you go, starting with wherever that greatest need is; it is often in the operational basics of having the right systems, processes, policies and tools in place in order to administer the day to day needs of the business, and establish your credibility before aiming for bigger things.*

People operations is one of those spaces where paradoxically one of the greatest things to aspire to is to deliver great service silently and invisibly behind the scenes. In these departments people face problems when they become visible for the wrong reasons, and that is a massive credibility drain for the function. So, start with getting brilliant basics in place. From there, determine the HR centres of excellence in which you need to invest, as these will depend on the particular business you are in.

Another driver for the constant need for people transformation is technology, which has never before expanded so rapidly and extensively. There is amazing technology in the people space and, as a CPO, you need to be deeply networked and integrated with the evolving marketplace, because everything you learned even two years ago will become obsolete quickly, thanks to innovation in areas such as talent management, compensation and benefits, wellbeing, benchmarking and analysis.

One of the most difficult challenges facing the CPO right now is transforming the People function within a cost-constrained environment, alongside the continual commercial imperative to grow the business. In this context you will always be fighting to reframe the argument that investing in people is ultimately a source of profit and not just a cost. Levels of engagement, retention and the skills and capabilities of your people also matter to a company's valuation, and these all require sustained investments of time and money. You will need to find a way to repurpose the people imperative in commercial language consistently.

SECTION TWO – PEOPLE EXPERIENCE: TALENT MANAGEMENT AND THE EMPLOYEE JOURNEY

Chapter 5

Talent management

Introduction

"Talent management is an HR process designed to gain and retain qualified talent. The goal of talent management is to keep workers engaged and motivated so that they perform optimally."[45]

Ringo

Talent Management is the management of people through the entire employee journey; from identifying fresh talent to maximising the potential of current employees, to offboarding when the journey is complete. McKinsey attests that talent management is *"a distinct competitive advantage, matching talent to where the most value is at stake".*[46]

This section is all about executing the talent management strategy through the lens of the employee, often called the People experience (PX), employee experience (EX) or employee journey. This chapter on talent management will focus first on five fundamental basics which underpin that entire journey, namely:

- a fit-for-purpose career framework;
- a bespoke employee value proposition;
- a strong feedback culture;
- a dynamic culture of recognition; and
- a resilient employee:manager relationship.

After considering these important foundational building blocks of the employee experience, the following five chapters will focus on breaking down the employee journey into five phases:

- **Talent acquisition:** recruiting new employees into the organisation (chapter 6)
- **Talent assessment:** assessing employee performance in their current position and assessing employees for their next and future positions (chapters 7 and 8)
- **Talent mobility:** moving talent around the organisation to new levels and into new positions (chapter 9)
- **Talent development:** growing and developing employees into the workforce of the future (chapter 10)
- **Talent offboarding:** exiting employees from the organisation (chapter 11)

While it is helpful to categorise the employee journey into these five phases, the journey is by its nature dynamic, complex and different for every one of us. Building a talent-first organisation places the employee as a key partner in the organisation, in a position that truly puts them in the driving seat to achieve business success.

What are we solving for?

There are a number of ways to consider how to manage talent, and the framework used in this book is just one way to visualise it:

TALENT MANAGEMENT				
Talent acquisition	**Talent assessment**	**Talent mobility**	**Talent development**	**Talent offboarding**
Recruiting new employees into the organisation	*Assessing employees in current and for next positions*	*Moving current talent around the organisation*	*Developing employees into the workforce of the future*	*Exiting employees from the organisation*
Talent acquisition strategy	Performance management	Promotion	Talent development strategy	Voluntary leavers
Source and attract	Talent planning	Internal talent marketplace	Learning and development curriculum	Regretted leavers
Recruit and select	Succession planning		Leadership and management training	Re-hiring
Induct and onboard			Building organisational capability	Retirement
Career framework				
Employee value proposition				
Feedback culture				
Recognition culture				
Employee:manager relationship				

Figure 5.1: The talent management framework

At the heart of successful talent management is placing the employee in a position where they truly are able to bring all their skills, knowledge, aptitude and energy every day to tackle challenges, innovate and create, and facilitate the organisation reaching its potential. Traditional methods of managing people will no longer work in our VUCA world: organisational structures built around hierarchies will stymie potential; measuring performance based on fixed roles and goals achievement will frustrate employees; not providing ongoing stretch growth opportunities will cause boredom; and not planning ahead for the next skills and competencies needed for business success (or survival) is a risk no company should be taking.

Talent management must be vibrant, real-time, continuous and have real momentum from the employee perspective. The People function will need to meet that challenge head on.

What does success look like?

Career framework

A career framework, also called a competency framework or job architecture among other names, is defined by the CIPD as *"a structure that sets out and defines each individual competency … required by individuals working in an organisation or part of that organisation"*.[47]

It forms the backbone of almost everything within talent management. It informs internal and external job ads for internal mobility and external recruiting; it sets expectations for how to assess current performance; it informs future moves via the promotion, talent planning and succession planning programmes; and it helps the talent development team articulate what goes into their learning and development programmes and why.

Without a career framework, all the actions around hiring, assessing, developing and recognising talent risk being done subjectively, inconsistently and at the behest of individual manager biases. A current, relevant, agile framework on the other hand will inform all the key talent management processes concurrently and consistently.

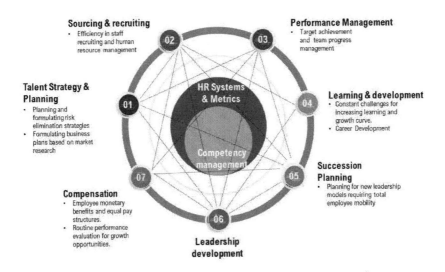

Sourcing & recruiting
- Efficiency in staff recruiting and human resource management

Performance Management
- Target achievement and team progress management

Talent Strategy & Planning
- Planning and formulating risk elimination strategies
- Formulating business plans based on market research

Learning & development
- Constant challenges for increasing learning and growth curve.
- Career Development

Succession Planning
- Planning for new leadership models requiring total employee mobility

Compensation
- Employee monetary benefits and equal pay structures.
- Routine performance evaluation for growth opportunities.

Leadership development

HR Systems & Metrics

Competency management

Figure 5.2: An integrated talent management framework[48]

There is a wealth of publicly accessible templates available for you to help create or review a career framework. Here are some of the core considerations when you are setting one up or reviewing an existing one for your organisation:

- Once you create a career framework, update it systematically and regularly, and use it widely. Your framework should be an input into practically every HR programme, resource and project you undertake, even outside the talent management framework. Invest time getting this important HR tool right – you won't regret it.
- Inputs into the career framework include: the current business strategy and goals, the current organisational design (workforce numbers, functional teams, hierarchies, layers, spans of control); current job family frameworks; current job descriptions; current workforce planning strategies and, if known, future positions needed in the organisation. When considering your workforce numbers, account for your entire workforce, not only permanent employees

but agency workers, contingency workers, temporary employees, gig workers, consultants and managed services. The career framework is about capturing the positions and skills needed for the work to be done – not about who will be doing it.

- In creating your framework, you should be answering the following:[49]
  - o What are the skills and people we need to compete now and in the future?
  - o Do we have the right job structures in place and are we flexible enough to adapt our workforce as needed?
  - o Where do the different jobs fit into our organisation? Where does the work get done and by whom?
  - o How do we provide our employees with career opportunities that are both vertical (i.e. promotion to the next level within the same job family) and horizontal (i.e. a lateral move into a new role in a different job family)?

- Depending on time and budget, you can leverage publicly available frameworks, which may be either generic and applicable to all industries or bespoke for certain sectors. For example, the Canadian Professional Sales Association[50] has created a robust sales competency framework which includes the following capabilities: Sales Planning, Building and Leading a Sales Team, Supporting the Sales Cycle and Sales Conduct, to name a few. if budget allows, you can buy in support from specialist consultants.

- Each competency outlines expectations for each level of ability, as well as differentiating expectations between a manager / leader versus an individual contributor. You will also see that some competencies are focused on technical skills, others around behaviours, and others are a mix of both. The Organization for Economic Cooperation and Development (OECD) has made its competency framework publicly available, and it frames its competencies around three clusters: Delivery-related, achieving results; Interpersonal, building relationships; and Strategic, planning for the future. Each cluster has a number of competencies within it, each with a description of expectations by level.[51]

- Most frameworks will include a different track for individual contributor (IC) and manager. An IC is someone who will build deep specialist knowledge during their career and will share that knowledge through projects and other temporary work structures such as coaching and mentoring. A manager is someone who will have specialist technical knowledge and will share that knowledge by leading a team of similar specialists permanently. This career path therefore requires the person to have people management skills in addition to technical skills.

- Don't stop at creating professional competency frameworks. With the continued pressure on finding and hiring great employees, create a framework around your internships, apprenticeships and graduate development programmes. Link these inextricably to the company goals and behaviours like the professional career frameworks, as well as to the related qualifications associated with each job family.

Once you create your framework, share it widely and transparently on your intranet site or through other internal communications channels. Differentiate between organisation-wide core competencies – behaviours expected by all (broken down by level) – and specialist technical skills required in specific functions.

Your managers should see the framework referenced throughout all facets of HR including promotions, talent planning, talent mobility moves and succession planning. And finally, it should be pervasive in your people team programmes, not only those working in the People Experience team who interact directly with employees, but throughout your DEI, remuneration and benefits, systems, analytics, compliance and other Centre of Excellence teams. All HR programmes should have the career framework as an input into their design.

Don't expect everyone to know how and when to use the career framework. Educating and upskilling employees and managers regularly on the correct use and understanding of the framework is also an important part of making it a success. Your learning and development (L&D) team will feature the career framework in the resources they create for HR programmes, and your programme management office (PMO), which runs the cyclical HR projects, should do the same.

Don't stop there though – one of the most powerful uses of a career framework is to help employees and candidates visualise their potential career journey in your organisation. Show employees, and their managers, how they can not only climb vertical ladders to success, but also benefit from broader growth opportunities to acquire additional skills. Allow them to be an explorer and access a number of different roles, controlling their own journey across the organisation. Some organisations create a persona or journey map of key careers to show what 'great' looks like at key moments along the way – where there are key challenges and how to show up and overcome them.

The power of creating career journeys rather than ladders will only be successful if you create a company that embraces agile working – let's focus on what that means exactly. Traditional career frameworks are staid, vertical job families that employees climbed up every couple of years, rung by rung, each of which was associated with a new title and an increase in salary.

The CIPD defines the career framework as *"a starting point that outlines broad expectations of skills and behaviours, but which needs to be applied flexibly".*[52] Deloitte describes how structured jobs are no longer the way that work gets done, rather flexibility and agility are needed for success in a boundaryless world:

> *"...a growing number of organizations are beginning to imagine work outside of the job – turning workforce management on its head by increasingly basing work and workforce decisions on skills – not formal job definitions, titles, or degrees."* [53]

A framework that seeks to reward skills will only be successful if we recruit and resource for those skills, reward those skills, and move people into new positions based on those skills. Similarly, talent development must seek to grow and develop those skills across the entire workforce, and the reward philosophy must focus on paying for those skills. A successful career framework will not work in isolation and needs to be considered in a much wider context when being written and revised.

Going forward, the focus of the People function will need to move away from focusing on specific roles and hierarchies doing specific jobs, to assigning people with specific competencies to complete a distinct piece of work. Elevating competencies above specific jobs means that employees will be more marketable for a variety of positions, rather than just the job they were hired to do – and employees will view this as a positive.

In parallel, work will be designed increasingly around specific pieces of work, to be completed by temporary teams within a fixed window. The People function will need to prepare the organisation for these new ways of getting work done. It's a high priority item for the next few years, according to the main HR research houses. In his recent article, business author David Green places *"building the skills-based organisation"* at number three in terms of HR priorities.[54] This work involves revamping how the organisation completes work and will be felt in the workforce tangibly, when employees move fluidly between pieces of work, defined by set outcomes, timeframes and budgets, and likely completed by a cross functional team.

In an interview specifically on this topic, Orla Stafford, Senior Manager in the Deloitte Human Capital Consulting team in Dublin, describes the importance of skills-based organisations to future organisational success:

> *"More and more organisations today are looking to redefine their HR and talent processes by putting skills at the centre and becoming a more skills-based organisation (SBO). Unlike the traditional organisation which emphasises job rules and hierarchy, an SBO prioritises skills, projects and outcomes over job titles.*
>
> *As work becomes far more variable, bundling all that people do into a job means that there are untapped skills and capabilities in our people leading to trapped value in our organisations. Skills rather than jobs are now being used to make decisions about work and the workforce - from who performs what work, to performance management to rewards to hiring. Work is now being adapted so that skills can be fluidly developed to keep pace with work as it evolves. This is leading to more agility, flexibility and greater realisation of every worker's true potential, and the confidence that the organisation has the right talent to meet their ever-evolving business needs and outperform their competition"*

We will see through the subsequent chapters on talent management how this trend towards creating an SBO can happen in reality.

Employee Value Proposition

The Employee Value Proposition (EVP) is part of the employer brand and is defined by Gartner as *"the set of attributes that the labour market and employees perceive as the value they gain through employment with the organization".*[55]

The EVP is another tool that should be bespoke to the organisation, used frequently in HR programmes and shared widely and transparently inside and outside the organisation. Internally, it should be communicated with the current workforce as part of an internal employee referral programme – this has the added benefit of reinforcing why they chose the organisation in the first place. It can also be tweaked for use with new employees coming on board as part of a merger or acquisition. However, one of the most impactful uses of it is with external hiring.

A truly differentiated EVP will have an outsized impact on external candidates who have not (yet) had the opportunity to experience how great your organisation is. Take a holistic approach to creating it, covering the following four distinct areas:[56]

1. Material offerings (remuneration, benefits, wellbeing).
2. Growth and development opportunities (talent planning, talent development).
3. Connection and community (recognition, values, engagement).
4. Meaning and purpose (Diversity, Equity and Inclusion (DEI), Corporate Social Responsibility (CSR), Environment Social and Governance (ESG), Sustainability.

All four elements are equally important, but some candidates will place higher value in some over others. Check your offering against the competition to see where you sit in each area; you may find you have a better offering but are just not selling it, or you may see where you need to boost it. Candidates usually think in terms of immediate gratification so make sure your talent acquisition (TA) team also highlights and intentionally sells the longer-term benefits that will materialise over time with the organisation.

Stand over your EVP proudly, and don't dilute it unduly with sign on bonuses, compromises or horse-trading salaries against a higher bidder. Make sure it's authentic and that what you sell in your EVP is what your successful candidates will experience when they start. That will be their first experience of your strong culture. In this hyper-connected world, it will not take long for candidates to lose trust in your company with the reputational damage that may be caused if an EVP is not authentic – keep it real, and always linked to your company purpose.

Finally, measure the impact of your EVP regularly with your new hires, including each of the four elements individually to highlight any specific area bringing the offering down. Ideally break the feedback down by DEI cohort if you can, to ensure the offering is equally appealing to a diverse cohort of candidates. Make sure you gain internal validation from your current workforce too – check with them that it's realistic, effective and inspiring. Ask them would they use it to recommend to a friend to come work for your organisation – a powerful measure of the engagement of your current workforce.

Feedback culture

Healthy organisations talk, and the conversations are vital to a strong heartbeat in a company. According to author and social entrepreneur Matt Tenney, in a feedback-rich culture:

> *"employees receive regular, helpful feedback from direct supervisors, and they are empowered and encouraged to provide meaningful feedback to co-workers and leadership."*[57]

The best organisations will have an energetic network of conversations: from executives up and down through the organisation, laterally across managers and leaders, 1:1 between manager and employee, and socially among everyone. Time and resources spent creating a pervasive ethos of sharing feedback regularly and recognising greatness publicly and consistently, will elevate the mood of the organisation and ensure everyone knows what great looks like, aspires towards achieving it, and is informed regularly about where they are on that journey to greatness.

That all sounds a little fluffy, however the opposite is true. Organisations that do not talk, that do not have a hum of conversation, are not healthy and will not reach their potential. We have already seen in chapter 2 how a strong positive culture creates a successful organisation. Owned by the Board and the Executive team, culture establishes what the expected ways of working and behaviours need to be in order for the organisation to achieve success, by creating the values and code of conduct that they want everyone to live by. We will see in the talent development chapter the importance of supporting, training and coaching your manager layer to grow and develop their teams to ensure individual and team potential is reached.

How is this healthy feedback conversation achieved? Certainly not by burying heads in the sand because it's too hard. Your parents might have taught you that 'if you cannot say something nice, don't say anything at all' (or that may just be an Irish thing!). But, in the context of creating a high-performance culture and achieving business success, this approach doesn't work. Sometimes something might have to be said that feels 'not nice', but it still needs to be said. It's important for the employee's success, the team's success, the company's success – or all three. What is vital is *how* it is said, *when* it is said, that it's said with the goal of making things better, and making sure the recipient of the message is prepared for it, open to it and able to respond to it.

Healthy transparent ongoing conversations between employee and manager, across peers, and inside and outside the organisation about what is working and what is not working are crucial.

Start by creating and communicating the feedback philosophy clearly for your organisation, which must be agreed in collaboration with the Executive team for commitment. This will ensure everyone knows what is expected when discussing feedback. This book's co-author, Jennifer, can recall the refreshing experience with a prior manager who said: *"Tell me bad news fast".*

Great leaders will seek to bring issues to the surface, and great organisations will provide the right environment in which employees will be comfortable sharing issues and challenges proactively. In doing so, consider the following questions:

- How mature is the organisation in terms of having performance and growth and other potentially challenging conversations?
- Do we need to be prescriptive and have clear rules to ensure these conversations happen, or can we trust our managers and employees will do it, and do it well, autonomously?
- How good are we as individuals in the organisation at giving feedback?
- Crucially, how open and available are we as individuals in the organisation to receiving the feedback?
- What is the role of feedback in the organisation – evaluating current performance, assessing competence for a role, checking in on wellbeing, coaching for future potential, or all the above?

Once you have agreed on what role feedback plays in your organisation, you need to weave it into all the HR programmes, and indeed the entire people experience journey. Remember, feedback is more than about performance and potential – it's all the crucial conversations through the employee journey.

We saw during the pandemic lockdown that wellbeing check-ins were as important, if not more so, than performance feedback. Some organisations continue asking for feedback on how well employees are doing post-pandemic and for a manager it's a quick, easy and often enlightening question to start every 1:1 meeting. Most organisations do return to work meetings to get feedback on how well equipped the employee feels to re-engage after an absence, as well as to give the manager the opportunity to update the employee on what has been going on. In many jurisdictions, it is required by law after an absence.

However, conversations around performance and potential are likely to be the ones that offer the greatest motivation, and indeed cause the most tension and disappointment. Some organisations like Screwfix and Google are moving to continuous, real-time feedback in recent years, in conjunction with real-time rewards to validate great achievements in the moment.[58]

The following are some of the most important feedback moments in the employee journey that are worth special consideration to get right in your organisation:

TALENT ASSESSMENT					
	What	Why	Who	When	How
End of Probation	Current performance assessment	To be made permanent or not. Often legally required	Manager provides to employee	Once at the end of probation or probation extension	Formal written assessment
Regular check in	Current performance discussion	Set ongoing expectations of performance level and for employee to ask for guidance, help etc.??	Manager provides to employee and vice versa	Weekly, monthly or ad hoc – whatever works for both	Written or verbal during usual 1:1 meeting
Annual Performance Discussion	Past year performance assessment	To provide rating and / or merit increase	Feedback provided by number of inputters; final feedback completed by manager	Annually at the end of the performance year	Formal written assessment
Talent Planning	Assessment of past and current performance and potential	Retention	Feedback provided by number of inputters	Annually at fixed point in HR cycle	Feedback often not shared directly with employee
Succession Planning	Assessment of potential future roles	Risk management	Feedback provided by number of inputters	Annually at fixed point in HR cycle	Feedback often not shared directly with employee

TALENT MOBILITY					
	What	Why	Who	When	How
360° feedback	Selection of employee data to assess past and current performance	Multi-voice inputs into an employee's performance, often for most senior levels	Manager, leader, team executive, peer feedback, plus other employee reports	Often used for year-end performance, for promotion or for internal hiring	Formal written assessment, often a formal and confidential survey
Promotion	Assessment for performance against next level	Assess employee's current ability or future potential for next level	Feedback provided by number of inputters; final feedback completed by manager	Ad hoc intervals during the employee's tenure	Formal written assessment
New internal role	Application for a for new role	Employee seeking growth opportunity	Employee requests feedback for application	Ad hoc intervals during the employee's tenure	Formal written application and interview
Anytime feedback	Ad hoc feedback in the moment	Recognise something done well or discuss something that could have been done better	Manager or project leader to employee and vice versa	Real time when the action is being completed	Verbally, potentially with follow up email

TALENT DEVELOPMENT				
	What	**Why**	**Who**	**When**	**How**
Growth plan	L&D discussion on filling current gaps and taking future opportunities	Current performance and future retention	Joint discussion with manager and employee	Annually at fixed point in HR cycle, revisited during regular 1:1s	Formal growth Plan
Coaching	Focus on future action by giving practical instruction	Improve future opportunities	Coach (usually manager) to employee	Set cadence of meetings	Discussion often captured post session
Mentoring	Guidance offered on long term career	Alternative perspective for employee	Mentor advises employee on options by sharing their skills and experience	Set cadence of meetings	Employee may capture guidance in own notes

Table 5.1: Feedback opportunities throughout the talent management framework

As with all elements of your organisation's culture, the feedback element needs to be felt tangibly and seen everywhere – from how the organisation celebrates when things are done well to how it deals with disappointment and missed targets.

Consider using a single model for giving and receiving feedback for consistency as well as encouraging a set language for how it is to be offered and received. Short, punchy – albeit mandatory – training, with reminders and hacks will set expectations on how to provide effective feedback, including role model exercises, cheat sheets, FAQs and employee / manager guides. That way everyone can expect a process steeped in dignity, with the betterment and growth of the employee and company at its heart. A set structure and a bias for a future action is core to all of them. A non-exhaustive sample of the more well-known and used models in the workplace include:

- **SBI model:** feedback is given by the specific Situation that arose, the Behaviour that was observed, and the Impact the behaviour had on the person, team, situation. One of the most frequently used in organisations.
- **McKinsey ABC model:** feedback is given by the specific Action event or behaviour to be changed, the impact of that Behaviour (how it made you feel) and a suggestion for what Could be done differently the next time.
- **STAR model:** feedback is given by the Situation that arose, the Task that was being carried out, the Action the recipient of the action took, and the Result or outcome of the action that the recipient took.
- **Pendleton model:** feedback is given by asking the recipient what went well, telling the recipient what went well, asking the recipient what did not go well or could be improved, and telling the recipient what did not go well or could be improved.
- **HUWUMU model:** *how* useful / good was something out of 10; *what* was useful, what would make it *more* useful.

In many ways, the model selected is immaterial. It is more important that everyone in the organisation knows what is expected in terms of giving and receiving feedback and is therefore aligned with it and expects it. According to recruitment firm Indeed, this will result in the key benefits of good feedback being achieved:[59]

- **Structure:** for giving actionable, helpful feedback.
- **Increase confidence:** to act on employees' good ideas.
- **Improve communication:** for increased clarity and effectiveness of meetings.

Adam Grant, an organisational psychologist at Wharton Business School, provides a great practical tool:

Adam Grant ✔ @AdamMGrant · Mar 10, 2021
When **people hesitate** to give **honest feedback** on an idea, draft, or performance, I ask for a 0-10 score.

No one ever says 10. Then I ask how I can get closer to a 10.

It motivates them to start coaching me—and motivates me to be coachable. I want to learn how to close the gap.

    💬 82   ⟲ 1,333   ♡ 6,633   ᵢⱼᵢ   ⬆

Figure 5.3: Tips for getting honest feedback

Doing feedback well is hard but there is plenty of help at hand. Whether you want to complete a full review or revamp of your feedback philosophy, or you want to keep it simple with managers regularly asking, *"What is the one goal you are working on where you would like some specific feedback?"*[60], or something in between, make sure you do something proactive and visible on feedback. It's too important to skip over it just because it might make people feel uncomfortable. An excellent feedback culture can be a solid differentiator in attracting and retaining people at your organisation. Not doing it well is a missed opportunity. Let's finish this section with some practical wisdom, a simple go-to reminder of everyone's responsibilities in an organisation with a great feedback culture:[61]

What leadership and HR can do	What team leaders and feedback givers can do	What recipients can do
Don't just trumpet benefits, explain trade-offs	Model learning, request coaching	Remember you are the most important person in your own learning
Separate appreciation, coaching and evaluation	As givers, manage your own mindset and identity	Watch, ask questions, solicit suggestions
Promote a culture of learners	Be aware of how individual differences collide in companies	Whatever people suggest, try it on, experiment

Figure 5.4: Roles and responsibilities for creating a great feedback culture

Recognition culture

We see the headlines everywhere: create a happy organisation, bring joy to the workplace, make sure humans flourish. According to Claire Hastwell, Senior Content Marketing Manager at Great Place to Work, a culture of recognition is *"all the ways an organization shows its appreciation for employees' contributions. It can take any forms and may or may not involve monetary compensation"*.[62]

Rooted in the field of positive psychology, there is little doubt that we as a human race thrive on being recognised for doing something great, and we see it appear more and more in relation to work in recent years. Where better indeed to create an environment that celebrates greatness than in the workplace, given we spend a lot of time there? How do we as CPOs build this muscle? Where does recognition even sit? Is it part of performance management, internal talent marketplace, succession, coaching and mentoring, inclusion and equity, internal comms or benefits? It's all of the above actually, and there is robust science behind it. Adam Grant again:[63]

 **Adam Grant** ✓
@AdamMGrant

Being appreciated doesn't just make you feel good. It helps you get stronger.

Evidence: receiving gratitude improves cardiovascular stress responses, boosting resilience and performance by turning threats into challenges.

Being thanked fortifies our bodies along with our bonds.

Figure 5.5: Positive impact of being appreciated

Like feedback, a consistent, transparent recognition culture should be in the company's DNA. At its most basic level it's saying thank you, as Melody Beattie attests: *"Gratitude... turns what we have into enough."*[64]

Recognition makes colleagues smile, and its scientifically proven that it's very hard to frown when someone is looking at you and smiling – try it. A UC Berkeley study even revealed that smiling makes people appear more competent, and it reduces stress.[65]

But recognition is more than saying thanks and beaming smiles at colleagues. An excellent recognition programme is increasingly important way to celebrate in a hybrid workplace as it's a channel to share what great looks like publicly. There is a multitude of tools, growing by the day, to run your programmes from and for efficiency and effectiveness. The recognition tool you select should talk to your HR information system (HRIS) and performance systems too – more on that in the people systems chapter later.

Your programme should offer everything from verbal gratitude and written thank you notes, to monetary and other tangible gifts as a starter. However it needs to be much more than that. Recognition can be giving an employee access to an influential mentor, or by being coached by a senior technical expert, or by shadowing an important sponsor or influencer in a person's career.

Whatever the offering, and as with many people-related initiatives in the workplace, it should be customisable and personal – build something that provides the giver and receiver with choices. It should be sincere, credible, readily and easily available, self-service driven and crucially, recognise effort as well as achievements.[66]

Deloitte[67] offers the following four-phase approach to designing, or redesigning, your recognition programme:

1. Develop a holistic recognition strategy: what do you want to achieve? How will it integrate with talent management? Can it be used as part of the EVP?

2. Consider your audience: will the offerings be unique to some parts, levels or segments of the organisation or will they be available for all?

3. Design the programme: alignment with business goals will strengthen the business case for investment. How will it be executed and governed? How visible will the programme be? What rewards offering will be given?

4. Measure the programme: agreed before launch, your metrics should measure the impact of the programme on a variety of employee data.

Don't underestimate the impact of a visible recognition programme – it's powerful stuff, and a potential differentiator for your organisation for candidates and employees alike when created thoughtfully. The most appreciated and valuable elements of the programme are free – credible and public recognition of a great piece of work or an outstanding behaviour by a peer or manager are the acknowledgements that resonate most with employees. Imagine how great it feels when it results in a senior leader or executive making a follow up call to ask the person to take part in a further piece of work on the back of the shoutout? Powerful stuff.

It's useful to wrap up this chapter by thinking about how feedback and recognition are core tools for supporting the creation of a healthy employee:manager relationship.

The employee:manager relationship

It is widely accepted that an employee does not usually leave an organisation, they leave a manager. While the reality is a little more complex than that, and often involves a multitude of push and pull factors, there is sufficient research showing that the employee-manager relationship is indeed one of the most important relationships in the organisation. We know the success of business and people strategies are wholly linked to how leaders show up to articulate plans, celebrate business achievements and role model values. Feedback and recognition are important manager tools to effect this success because they create trust. Neuroeconomist Paul Zak[68] outlines how to use them to maximum effect:

- Recognise excellence: publicly, regularly, and including wider employee inputs (i.e. not just selected or called out by the executive or leaders).
- Induce 'challenge stress': charge teams with difficult but achievable challenges and watch them rise to the occasion.
- Give people discretion in how they do their work: employees allowed to work autonomously feel empowered and will deliver.
- Enable job crafting: allow people to organise themselves around work, not job titles and fixed teams.
- Share information broadly: uncertainty causes stress which hampers trust. Communicate regularly and openly. Trust your people with the information.
- Intentionally build relationships: everyone needs to socialise, albeit to differing degrees. Showing empathy, caring and making strong social ties drives performance.
- Facilitate whole-person growth: high-trust organisations grow their employees personally and professionally. Retention and engagement ensue.

- Show vulnerability: Ask for help – this resonates with colleagues and team members. It helps leaders and manager build authenticity and credibility.

Review your company values and your HR processes and programmes to elevate trust throughout. Building a high-trust organisation does not compromise accountability and performance – they are not mutually exclusive. On the contrary, they work together beautifully. Gallup[69] highlights that this is:

"the most important relationship at every stage of the employee journey. Managers affect employees' work experience in how they engage them and develop their strengths. Managers are in a position to continually help the employee see their current value and future in the organisation."

Questions for a new CPO

- Do you have a career framework to inform all your people processes?
- Does your career framework encompass the organisation-wide competencies that will be needed for future business success?
- Does your career framework appear robustly in your hiring, promotion, internal mobility, feedback, performance and development frameworks?
- How captivating is your employee value proposition?
- How healthy are the conversations between employees and their managers?
- Does everyone in the organisation know how to give and receive feedback?
- Does feedback result in measurable positive behaviour change?
- Do you have a recognition programme?
- How well used is your recognition programme?

- Is data from your recognition programme linked to HR data and performance data?
- Do your employees stay because of their manager? Do they leave because of their manager?

Summary

The topics dealt with in this chapter are significant. They form the backbone of HR programmes and frameworks. A robust, agile, fit-for-purpose career framework will be used everywhere there are people in the organisation. A unique EVP that truly differentiates the organisation from everyone else is a game changer for candidates and existing employees alike, to tell and remind everyone why this organisation is a great place to work. The whole talent management framework is underpinned by healthy conversation (feedback) and appreciation (recognition) throughout. High engagement, visible through tenured employees who hold multiple roles throughout their career with the organisation, is proof the organisation is working well together. Create focused programmes of work around tools and initiatives as they build trust between the employee and manager, confidence in the leadership and the Executive team and a collective belief in the organisation. All excellent foundations on which to build your talent management framework.

Chapter 6

Talent acquisition

TALENT MANAGEMENT				
Talent acquisition	**Talent assessment**	**Talent mobility**	**Talent development**	**Talent offboarding**
Recruiting new employees into the organisation	*Assessing employees in current and for next positions*	*Moving current talent around the organisation*	*Developing employees into the workforce of the future*	*Exiting employees from the organisation*
Talent acquisition strategy	Performance management	Promotion	Talent development strategy	Voluntary leavers
Source and attract	Talent planning	Internal talent marketplace	Learning and development curriculum	Regretted leavers
Recruit and select	Succession planning		Leadership and management training	Re-hiring
Induct and onboard			Building organisational capability	Retirement
Career framework				
Employee value proposition				
Feedback culture				
Recognition culture				
Employee:manager relationship				

Figure 6.1: The position of talent acquisition in the talent management framework

Introduction

Workforce planning is the system that calculates if there are enough people with the right skills to achieve the business goals of the organisation. The associated annual process often starts in the third or fourth quarter of the year when senior leaders create the forthcoming year's goals, which will include headcount asks for particular skills to supplement the existing team. If funds exist, Finance will allocate an additional headcount number or additional headcount budget to the leader to spend on bridging the gap early in the calendar year. The senior leader allocates the headcount number or budget to where they think it will have the greatest impact, and the applicable hiring managers go to work with their talent acquisition partner to find the new skills in the market.

There are options on how and when to fill the skills gap throughout the process: permanent or temporary hires; scale hiring for a cohort of new employees; ad hoc bespoke hiring for a senior or hard-to-find skill; not hiring employees and using outsourcing, partnering and other people resources; how much artificial intelligence (AI) to use for efficiency and objectivity while staying compliant. There will be plenty of solutions on offer to get the right people in for the right cost with the right skills in the appropriate timeframe.

We've been hearing about global skills shortages for a long time, building up mild panic in senior executives, and placing a lot of pressure on talent acquisition processes. At this stage, it's safe to say that the world of work is evolving at a pace that no education system is ever going to keep up with. Constant work redesign and workers wanting more control over their careers than ever, when combined with the aforementioned evolution, accumulates in a perfect storm for talent.

The concept of hiring for broad organisational capabilities, via general job descriptions with expansive titles, into positions that are always going to need new skills and knowledge every couple of years, will all go towards helping to bring some degree of calm to the situation, without compromising on getting extraordinary talent into the workplace. Even when the organisation cannot or does not want to articulate a small number of broad organisational capabilities to solely hire for, they should still be prepared to hire for potential; that is, hire transferable skills where candidates can be upskilled to meet with talent shortage for other related skills. Add to all the above a greater use of a contingent workforce to widen the talent pool and pipeline, and then it feels like organisations might just be able to get in the right skills to bring organisational prosperity – turns out, organisations do have more control than they think in getting the required talent in.

The biggest challenge with accepting this new way to think about TA is in resetting the expectations of all the stakeholders involved that this new approach will in fact work – from the CFO who holds the purse strings, to hiring managers who want the best and quickly, to you as the CPO who knows that doing this work under less pressure will result in successful hiring campaigns for all involved.

What are we solving for?

Talent acquisition (TA) is a prominent element of the People strategy – there will always be a need to bring new people and skills into the organisation, by hiring managers who are excited to get the best people out there into their team. The TA process for every hiring manager should be consistently positive, efficient and successful. The TA partner should be skilled at getting commitment from the hiring manager to the process from the outset, provide additional support to those who are less experienced in the hiring process, expect and pre-empt hurdles with being adaptable and agile, and set and reset hiring manager expectations throughout the process to keep them on track for a great outcome.

The TA strategy and philosophy underpinning any given hiring project will remain largely unchanged – that is, the skills we hire for will remain tied to corporate goals and company values throughout. By taking responsibility for maintaining this link, the TA partner creates alignment with that team's vision and goals, ensuring they tie into the greater business objectives.

This, in turn, allows the TA partner to communicate those goals and the possible impact of that team to prospective candidates, increasing engagement with candidates – in particular passive candidates. What will change with every annual TA plan is the different hiring projects that any particular year brings. And remember, when there is a vibrant internal talent marketplace in place, which we will discuss more in chapter 8, the new hires you are seeking will ideally be fewer in number and earlier in their career, creating a bigger talent pool into which to dive.

In sourcing and attracting candidates to the company, the TA team will want to find people with the right skills from the outset. When you are sourcing broad organisational skills for expansive positions rather than specific skills for specific roles, which we saw earlier in the career framework section, the number of sectors and industries that can be sourced from is greater. The employee value proposition (see chapter 5) will entice candidates in, articulating clearly how your organisation is different from the others who are trying to woo them too.

Once a talent pipeline has been created for the vacant positions, the process of selecting the right candidates kicks off. How this is done, and with what resources, will differ depending on position type and number of vacant positions. If your organisation is in a hypergrowth phase – for example a tech scale-up – your hiring plan will be different from a mature industry, such as professional services, hiring its annual intake of employees straight from university.

A successful outcome will be an efficient process for all involved, hiring managers and candidates alike, that results in a choice of diverse candidates being brought to the final selection stage. While the entire selection process should have a razor-sharp focus for all involved, the importance of the moment the offer is made to the selected candidate should not be underestimated. Sealing the deal with candidates who have agency and will often have other offers may actually be the start of a different negotiation process, one in which control of the final outcome is increasingly with the candidate – the hiring manager and TA partner will need to stay alert until pen is put to paper, and the offer is signed.

Finally, signing the contract is only the beginning of a pre-day one process that engages your new hire continuously, maintaining excitement which reaches a crescendo on the first day in your organisation. Even then, induction (usually a week-long process) and onboarding (which can last for several weeks) cements the excitement into a solid foundation for the employee, the hiring manager and the TA partner upon which everyone anticipates this new employee doing great and loving it here. According to research published by HR system provider HiBob, 64% of employees are likely to leave a new position within their first year following a negative onboarding experience.[70] Make your onboarding experience an unforgettable one.

While these steps are reasonably well defined, the function responsible for completing them is open for discussion. There is a strong argument for the TA partner maintaining the relationship with the new hire through to the pre-day one period, into induction and perhaps even into of onboarding new hires. The TA partner is the person who personified the company brand from that initial connection – how wonderful it would be for that same person to continue the journey with the new hire through to welcoming them to the organisation, helping them through those awkward first days, until there is a warm handover to the hiring manager. Food for thought.

What does success look like?

Let's look at each part of the talent acquisition framework in turn.

Talent acquisition (TA) strategy

The Society for Human Resource Management (SHRM) describes the TA strategy as:

> *"developing, implementing and evaluating programs for sourcing, recruiting, hiring and orienting talent and getting the right people, processes, technology and partners together around the strategy."* [71]

The strategy will always be linked directly to business goals, in that any recruitment of new headcount will be focused on sourcing the skills required to meet those goals. The strategy will also be linked to the TA philosophy of the organisation. In thinking about the TA strategy and philosophy, the organisation may consider some of the following:

- **Build organisational capability:** rather than hiring for specific skills in specific roles, identify broad organisational skills that you know your organisation currently needs and will need next. More about this in chapter 9 on talent development. This will mean committing to hiring for potential above hiring for experience, which must be aligned on from the outset. It will mean assessing candidates for what they have done as well as what you can see they will be able to do. Hiring for potential also requires assessing candidates for being 'coachable' at selection stage.

- **Hire those that fit with the organisation values and culture:** if your organisation has a robust set of values and a strong culture that celebrates them, hiring employees who do not align with these values is not going to end in a successful relationship. Behaviours and how someone approaches work are difficult to teach, or unteach. However, while hiring for fit at a minimum, also look for those people who will enhance and develop the organisation's values and culture – this brings diversity of thought to how the organisation approaches business success.

- **Agree the diversity rubric:** align on a plan for how you will hire a diverse cohort of candidates. Some of the most common approaches include committing minimum diversity hiring targets against every member of the Executive team; creating a diverse slate where a certain percentage of underrepresented populations must be present at each stage of the recruitment and selection process and having a diverse interview panel, for example when half the hiring panel is made up of women. In planning a diversity strategy for a campaign, the TA partner will seek to understand the demographic in which they are operating, as it will vary by region and by position. They will gain an understanding of the under-represented populations in that region and / or for that function and use that information to commit to matching that demographic in the workforce.

- **Don't move the goal posts:** commit to hiring within the agreed level and remuneration strategy for new hires.

Aligning on a level for the role is important as the TA partner will clearly define criteria around it in terms of impact and contribution. In terms of remuneration, the hiring manager must commit to hiring within the agreed salary bands and, if relevant, long-term incentive plans at the point that matches the candidate's ability and expectations, while also considering the degree of difficulty hiring for the role. Any governance around sign-on bonuses should also be pre-agreed, as well as an efficient escalation process for requests for exceptions.

- **Stay legally compliant:** make sure your people, processes and systems adhere to the legal requirements of the jurisdiction into which they are hiring. There has been a signification increase in the amount of regulation relating talent acquisition in recent years. While each country will have their own specific requirements which you will need to stay on top of, it's likely that there will be GDPR, data privacy, data protection and freedom of information requirements with which to be complied. This growth in compliance will continue with the increasing impact AI, neurolinguistic programming (NLP), machine learning and other similar developments like ChatGPT have on HR processes in general, and on the automation of talent acquisition in particular. We discuss some of these developments in chapter 16.

- **Invest in supportive technology:** as with all aspects of HR, TA has huge potential for digital transformation. There are a multitude of tools and systems available to automate the steps in the TA process, leaving the human aspects of the role – that of establishing quality relationships with the best candidates – being the largest part of the role for your TA team. Technology can support action tracking, applicant tracking, background checks, candidate updates (only when we don't want a human touch of course), job analysis, job descriptions, job postings, legal compliance, orientation / onboarding and recruitment.[72]

How you set up your TA team to execute the strategy will depend on a multitude of factors, including the size and maturity of your company and your people team, where the organisation is in its lifecycle, the products or services it sells and the skills you need to get into it. You may also task your TA team to deliver the internal hiring process as well as doing external talent acquisition. The skills needed are similar and providing this additional type of programme of work for your TA partners may enthuse them, and even lead them to other HR roles on the team – for example, expanding the internal talent marketplace to include a career management offering where HR associates cultivate long-term careers with employees. More food for thought.

There are plenty of other options for getting TA work done if you prefer to keep your core in-house TA team small, and / or focus them on specific types of internal or external hiring. These include:

- **Recruitment agency:** usually used to support the hiring of a small number of difficult to hire roles or senior executive roles. They may also be used where a specialist type of hiring is needed that is not available on your TA team. Agencies can also perform market mapping and other specialist work to support sourcing candidates. Agencies will generally work on multiple companies' roles at same time.
- **Recruitment process outsourcing (RPO):** these are recruitment companies that will complete the entire hiring process for permanent positions in the organisation. Unlike a recruitment agency which works with multiple organisations at one time, an RPO contract will work exclusively on your roles. The team may sit on-site with

the inhouse TA partners or may be offsite. The tool used for these positions is usually the organisation's own applicant tracking system (ATS) and HR information system (HRIS).

- **Managed service provider (MSP):** similar to an RPO contract, an MSP can complete the full recruitment campaign for our organisation for their contingent workforce (e.g. temporary hires, agency workers, consultants). The tool used in support of this type of hiring is usually the vendor management system, as opposed to the company HRIS.

In cases when the above types of partners are used, your TA partners may like to own these contracts and become relationship managers – another skill that may be helpful for their wider careers.

Finally, your TA team will need to build strong cross-functional relationships. Whether you have a small TA team of recruiters, a significant team led by senior managers or have outsourced the service to an agency or other provider, it is important for the talent acquisition process not to operate in a silo, away from the rest of the People team and away from other business stakeholders.

For the TA process to be successful it needs to be seamless, and for it to be seamless the TA team will need to work in close collaboration with several key stakeholders. Many of those stakeholders will have a very different perspective on the TA process: HRBPs (for allyship and to get deep understanding of the team being hired into); remuneration and benefits (to execute their strategy and seeking additional support if needed); people operations (who will likely send the contracts, complete background checks and field pre-day one questions); legal (for immigration / visa / right to work support, for hiring into new /

difficult locations, or for protections for the most senior hires); finance business partners (who have ultimate ownership for the hiring budget); technology, for employee setup and payroll (who need to have the right processes and systems to pay your new hires). Encourage your TA partners to cultivate deep relationships with these key allies for when hiring becomes complex and hard, as it often does.

Source and attract

Once you have your workforce plan, confirming what and how much external hiring is required, your philosophy, confirming how hiring is to take place, and your tools to support it all in place, the next step will be to build your hiring plan. As we saw earlier, the annual workforce planning process culminates in hiring managers being given a headcount number or headcount budget to spend in the calendar year. Sometimes Finance may also stipulate when and even how the headcount budget is to be spent through that following year, which is important information for the TA partner. If there is an 'internal first' talent management philosophy, the workforce plan will seek to match the current workforce to the skills gaps first. After that, the TA process fills either remaining skills gaps and / or if the organisation is growing, finds more of the skills the organisation already has.

At the intake meeting with the hiring manager (HM), the TA partner sets the expectation that the sourcing net will be cast widely using the most generic skillset needed for the role, that they therefore may see unusual candidates put in front of them, seeking their buy-in early to think in a new way about who to hire. Similarly, the HM may be asked to evaluate candidates who do not have the traditional educational backgrounds they are used to seeing. The TA partners should ask the HM who is not currently represented on their team from a DEI perspective. Writing in *Harvard Business Review*, Ryan Roslansky, CEO of LinkedIn says sourcing and evaluating candidates on *"their skill sets instead of their work history can help level the playing field"*.[73] It can be helpful to have the HRBP at this meeting to help cement commitment to the process.

The following are the main sourcing channels may be used by the TA partner:

- **Existing candidate database:** low cost, immediate access, limited talent pool;
- **Company website career page:** low cost, wide talent pool, huge opportunity to stand out but needs quality investment to sell the company potential;
- **Job boards:** low cost, quick access, wide talent pool, difficult to stand out;
- **Employee referrals:** low cost, relatively quick access, increased chance of culture fit, limited talent pool, may result in bias and lack of diverse candidates; and
- **Social media channels**: instant and direct access, low cost, significant talent pool, crowdsource candidates asking employees to reshare and elevate roles. Check out how Twitter used its own platform to run a #OneTweetCV competition, which led to quality hires while encouraging candidates to consider writing super-short CVs.

Make sure the company EVP is prominent when making connections through all sourcing channels, but in particular at the point human contact is made with potential candidates.

In keeping with the most up-to-date practice of hiring for broad organisational capabilities and culture fit, job descriptions and job ads should have a broad job title to attract people of different backgrounds and experience to the position. The body of the job description should reflect the general accountabilities and responsibilities of the position rather than a list of prior experience and educational qualifications that are a prerequisite for applicants.

Link the job description to the company career framework in the background, as this will help the TA partner to sell the broader opportunities that will be available to successful candidates, and make sure it focuses on skills required for the position rather than prior experience of tasks required for it. From a DEI perspective, make sure the job description is written objectively with no bias. Statistically, women will only apply for a role if they can do pretty much all of what's on the job spec and are less likely to apply for a stretch role – that is one broader or more senior than the role in which they are currently.[74] Some companies place the caveat 'You don't have to have everything on this job description to apply – if you like the position and the company, send in your CV', or similar wording, to entice candidates from underrepresented populations who may not traditionally apply for such a role to do so.

Source accessible not just available talent. Active candidates are open to new roles publicly, and may or may not be currently employed, although usually are not. There is an interesting phenomenon at play following the 2022/2023 wave of redundancies in the technology industry where colleagues and ex-colleagues of those made redundant are sharing lists of their names widely on social media advertising how great these people are and how they would be super additions to other companies hiring. Gone are the days of being embarrassed to be not working – social media instead has created an extraordinary source for personal referrals.

Passive candidates are those that are employed currently and not looking for a new role. While they are quality candidates, the TA partner needs to approach them with sensitivity and discretion. There are candidates in the middle of the spectrum, who LinkedIn calls 'candidates on the cusp', who are networking quietly to find out what opportunities are out there – another valuable source of accessible talent.[75]

The TA partner can further expand the talent pool by intentionally sourcing other non-traditional candidates for specific roles. For example, neurodiverse candidates are excellent hires for cybersecurity roles. In fact Robert D Austin and Gary Pisano, writing in *Harvard Business Review*, go so far as to suggest candidates with autism can be excellent in positions that require attention to detail.[76]

Sourcing and hiring neurodiverse candidates successfully requires a very specific set up. Link up with 'social partners', for example As I Am, for expertise. Upskill those involved in the process, including TA partners, HMs, interviewers and others involved in using the necessary non-traditional, non-interview-based assessment and training processes required to level the hiring playing field. For example, reduce sensory cues by holding in-office interviews in a quiet environment; ask interviewers to wear dark, subtly coloured clothing; ensure there are no strong perfumes or scents either from anything in the room itself or from the interviewers.[77] It may help level the playing field by sending interview questions in advance. Don't forget that successful candidates will need a specific support ecosystem once they start in their positions as well including, for example, noise-cancelling headphones, anchored desks in particular areas of the office, potentially access to work more from home and / or indeed tailored career paths for long-term success in the organisation. Accenture is particularly progressive in all things DEI related[78]. In particular, the consulting firm's Neurodivergent Internship Programme is designed specifically to *"create a barrier-free and disability inclusive workforce, making it more accessible to a critical talent pool of high-performing people".*[79]

In the event that the talent pipeline is small after sourcing is complete, consider 'renting' in talent temporarily to get the skills in house quickly and avoid delaying important work getting done. There is a phenomenal source of professionals, growing by the day, who want to continue to deliver great work but in a way that they control their career more, which is the 'gig economy' workforce. There are 7 million professionals across all organisational functions who have signed up to global apps that match their skills with temporary roles. Other more traditional methods of temporary talent include using a consultancy or hiring fixed term contractors.

Finally, a word on measuring the success of your sourcing strategies. There are a number of metrics that can be used to monitor the success of each channel, including number of candidates per role, ratio of candidates to final hires, time to hire, cost to hire, quality of hire (measured by the percentage of new hires who pass probation), and ultimately employee tenure by different sourcing methods. Irrespective of which metrics you select, make sure you know which strategies work best for which hires, to ensure the time and money you invest in sourcing new candidates is making a return for the organisation.

Recruit and select

Recruiting and selecting the right candidates is all about assessing a small group of candidates for position and company fit. There are a multitude of approaches that can be taken, the choice of which will be dictated by:

- **Who you are hiring:** cohorts of college interns or annual apprentice programmes will likely follow structured hiring programmes rolled out annually. Hiring a vice president of sales will be very different and likely bespoke to each position every time.

- **How many you are hiring:** recruiting a group of new service team members is likely more successfully done via a day-long assessment centre where offers are given on the day. Hiring for a newly created head of the Data Protection Office will require a process, which is much more nuanced involving a cross-functional team of senior executive interviewers.
- **Where the company is in its lifecycle:** a hiring process for steady linear growth annually over a medium-term period for a mature, profitable organisation will be very different from one that needs to deliver in a hypergrowth scenario, which requires a significant increase in numbers over a couple of years to maximise a private equity investment quickly.
- **How quickly you need to fill the position:** if you need to get a key skill into the organisation urgently, external hiring may not be the most efficient method. However if this is still the chosen method, consider placing a person or team full time on the process. If it's a complex project, for example standing up a new sales team in Spain, consider creating a temporary team with representatives from TA, legal, people operations, remuneration, immigration and HRBPs, led by a project manager to focus the team on deliverables, dates, milestones, risks and other issues.

It is beyond the scope of this handbook to detail every type of recruitment technique available. Suffice to say there are many; each delivering for different scale, budget, skill being assessed, time and position type. A non-exhaustive list of interview techniques, still the main assessment tool used in most industries, include:

- **Phone interview:** often used early in the process to screen the initial candidate list;

- **Video interview:** an emerging type of interview technique, an 'on-demand' interview is when the candidate pre-records responses to interview questions;
- **Competency-based interview:** structured interview assessing for skills and behaviours needed for the role;
- **Role play interview or presentation:** more interactive interview technique, which prompts two-way communications and assesses the candidate against a particular scenario or situation; and / or
- **Culture fit interview:** structured interview focusing on the organisation's core competencies to assess how they can add to the company's values and culture.

There is increasing interest in the use of assessment techniques which have been made scalable through online tools. Whether you are assessing for coding skills or publishing skills, there is likely a tool that can assess ability in a non-biased manner, which will test candidates reliably for the skills, behaviours and competence that the position requires. Every recruitment project will still – at a minimum – need to assess for company fit (behaviours, values) and technical ability (skills, knowledge) in some capacity.

It was noted earlier that the TA strategy should have DEI checks throughout. If you have agreed a diverse slate, ensure there are checks for compliance to the slate throughout the process. If the agreed slate is proving hard to meet, escalate it at the time the challenge rises, not at the end of the process. Equally, an agreed ratio of diverse interviewers will be more complex and potentially time consuming to plan for. Don't leave it too late to book in the required diverse interview panel – start planning early to get into the right diaries for the right time in each process to ensure there is never an interview that does not have the agreed diversity ratio of interviewers on it.

A successful recruitment process should result in a small number of diverse final candidates from which final selection is made and job offers extended. As with all elements of the TA process, this step should be seamless, efficient and timebound. The final offer may go to an agreed candidate, however there may be a backup candidate who will be offered if the first offer is rejected. The offer should be made verbally initially, and include information on the salary, variable compensation (e.g. performance bonus or commission target), and any long-term incentive (e.g. equity in the organisation). If needed, the TA partner can have a pre-agreed sign on bonus ready to offer, but strict governance should be agreed for this at the start of the process.

The candidate should be asked to accept the offer within a short time period – this can be negotiated if necessary, however an elongated process may indicate the candidate is trading your offer against another and the TA partner will want to surface that as soon as they may have an inkling that this is happening. In the unlikely event that the organisation needs to rescind an offer, the TA partner should seek legal guidance from the outset to ensure it is done in a compliant manner.

When the candidate verbally accepts the offer, the written contract of employment can be sent for signing. This is likely to be done electronically, however some jurisdictions still require a wet signature, and this will be organised by the People Operations team. The people operations team will have a databank of contract templates to use and will require certain information from the TA partner in order to create it – a standard form should be used for this process to ensure all relevant information is supplied in a timely manner. There may be a degree of two-way communication at this point that clarifies the offer, which may be answered by either the TA partner or the people operations team, ultimately resulting in the contract being signed.

Once signed, the background screening process – which will include reference checking and confirming right to work – can commence. This may be done by the organisation itself, however many companies will outsource this process to a specialist provider. In a relatively recent trend, many candidates are choosing not to resign their current position until the background checks have been completed and the offer is unconditional. This means that the notice period for the candidate can only commence when the background check is complete, likely resulting in a later start date with your organisation. Occasionally the candidate can negotiate a shorter period than is contracted, however this consideration should be built into your TA timelines.

The period of time between the offer being signed and the new hire's start date can be long, usually at least one month but it can be up to six. Use this time wisely to stay in touch and build excitement with your new hire. Send swag with the company logo on it, have the HM invite them in for lunch with the team, and request for them to provide pre-hire information in a manner that befits the company culture. Where resources permit, build up to day one with increasing connections to build the excitement.

Induct and onboard

The purpose of onboarding is, according to Sinazo Sibisi and Gys Kappers of Wyzetalk, *"setting new hires up for success and decreasing the time it takes for them to become comfortable in their new roles"*.[80] Also called orientation or induction, a great onboarding programme boosts confidence, decreases time to productivity and increases retention. Like all learning and development (L&D) programmes, onboarding in particular was impacted negatively by the Covid pandemic. However, this has also provided the opportunity for organisations to re-build from scratch.

Onboarding is the first opportunity employees have to experience the culture of the organisation – that is, it's the first time they will get to see if 'what they said about working here' during the hiring process and in the EVP really happens in reality. A great onboarding programme will require significant cross-functional commitment, investment and effort for success. Likely owned by the L&D team, the other programme collaborators and deliverers include: talent acquisition, people operations, HRBPs, DEI , IT, analytics, facilities and security, communications, information security, payroll, and representation from ESG and CSR teams. Hiring managers of the new employees will also need to be present, available and invested in the company onboarding programme – visible executive support for the programme is always therefore helpful in that regard.

There is no ideal onboarding programme – the best ones will be those that are bespoke to each organisation. Here are some general considerations to give to (re)creating yours:

- Make sure, in general, that it does not overload new hires with information. Work out carefully what they need in each phase of the programme to avoid them feeling overwhelmed.
- Consider making the process as self-managed as possible. Give your newest employees responsibility for completing the actions themselves, while giving them the access, tools and support to do so successfully. In a prior organisation, we created a new joiner passport for new hires which empowered self-driven onboarding through task lists to be completed during specific timeframes.
- **Pre-day one**: activities may include requesting HR information (ideally submitted directly by the new hire to the HRIS), taking receipt of a laptop and other necessary equipment, and an offer to meet the others starting on the same day via an online or in-person social event. This

is also the opportunity to send swag, watch videos of different personas from the organisation, and provide a welcome pack clarifying what to bring where on day one, listing the first week's onboarding activities.

- **Day one**: activities will likely be limited to a few actions: welcome by HR and if possible, an executive; complete work authorisation checks; get photo taken for company badge; provide a more detailed breakdown of the rest of week one activities. If there is time, laptop set up can be completed.

- **Week one (general)**: often called induction week, activities should focus on providing the very initial information your new hires will need to get started. This includes core contact information, key intranet sites and company information. Meetings and other agenda events should be pre-populated into the new hires' diaries, to make it seamless for them to attend and to reduce any risks of getting lost – either virtually or in person depending on how activities that week are being delivered. Remember that if you are doing onboarding virtually, some countries like Ireland, Singapore and Australia require a virtual work from home (WFH) assessment early in the employee's tenure.

- As well as having practical presentations from teams such as facilities, security, IT and payroll, use this week to cultivate your new hire's sense of purpose. Put in presentations from the DEI team to introduce the communities and other employee resource groups they can sign up to. These presentations may also include educating new hires about how we speak with each other: for example, encouraging use of pronouns and how to create theirs, use of greetings like 'hi folks / hi all', addressing groups of colleagues with gender-acceptable terminology such as female / male rather than women

/ men and ability-focused phrases such as people being differentially able. This week's agenda should also include introductions from the those involved in ESG matters to showcase what is done at an organisational level to benefit the community.

- **Week one (manager):** activities should include welcome meetings between the new hire and their manager, as well as with their wider team. The focus of these sessions should be sharing information about who everyone is, how the work is delivered, how the team works together, including for example when team members are usually in the office, and how to contact each other through various asynchronous methods such as internal messaging tools.

- If appropriate for your industry and company, at the 1:1 meetings, managers can set early expectations around how performance will be assessed during the new hire's initial months. This should be done by taking a positive approach that encourages the employee to show their skills early, building their confidence. Make sure the manager creates a safe space for the new hire to learn – establish psychological safety intentionally from the outset. If possible, introduce a buddy relationship in this initial week also.

- **Month one:** It's difficult to capture a fulsome list of what to cover in the new employee's first month in one paragraph. In general, the content provided and the meetings set up should be more bespoke to each new hire: it may include further functional and team information; it will likely include certain mandatory training but also provide elective training options; there may be specific onboarding modules for particular roles (e.g. how we code for engineers; how we bring in revenue for sales teams), for particular offices or even specific geographies / jurisdictions. Build in as many human connections as you can during this period – in particular, if your organisation offers hybrid and remote working, using a network list to be provided by the manager (being the person who is best positioned to know who the new employee needs to meet at the earliest opportunity).

- From a performance perspective, the new employee should be given a clear list of tasks and deliverables (rather than goals) to complete during their probation, along with plenty of manager time and support to set them up for successfully achieving them. This is crucial in month one as it provides the manager, and the employee, with plenty of time to correct any potential concerns with what work the new hire completes and / or how they complete it before the probation period runs out.

- **Months two and three:** Many onboarding programmes will run for three months, dropping in more business, team, people and other content and introductions in a structured manner throughout. Crucially, as will be discussed later in the talent mobility section in chapter 8, use this period to gather information from your new hires about what skills they bring to the organisation, what skills they would like to learn next and what their career aspirations are for the next number of years. Consider celebrating the end of onboarding with a meeting with the CEO, with a graduation ceremony, and / or with a social event. Encourage the graduating cohort to create an alumni group and to stay in touch.

Decide what portion of onboarding will you complete live virtual, live in person, or through asynchronous activities. Make sure it is an equitable experience for everyone. Challenges with the new ways of working include everything from social isolation, to not connecting with culture, to learning at different speeds, to having technology access issues. Make the experience equally exciting and immersive for all your hires, particularly if you have a hiring programme for differently abled people. It may be prudent to have these early weeks of onboarding mandatory in-person, such is the importance of human connection and culture connection at that pivotal time learning about the organisation.

Make your onboarding programme memorable. Work with the marketing team to brand it, so each activity, training course and meeting resonates with your new hires as being linked to their onboarding. Have fun with it too – gamify onboarding content, create fun league tables of completed tasks and give out prizes. And, in case it has not been mentioned enough, use this time to create as many human and physical connections as possible for your newest employees – in an increasingly hybrid world of work, building robust relationships early will make later challenges easier to surmount and later successes more impactful to celebrate.

The organisation should consider a supplementary onboarding programme for new employees who will manage people, upskilling them on this element of the job from the earliest opportunity. New people managers hired externally can be onboarded with employees in the current workforce who are transitioning into people manager roles for the first time – onboarding the two cohorts together will likely create a strong manager community, where they support, lean on and learn from each other in a safe environment.

The same principle of dropping information in a timely manner still applies. Therefore, while some manager onboarding activities may take place at the same time as general onboarding, some will take place later as the manager experiences some people manager activities for the first time in real time. For example, if a new or existing person starts in a people manager role in May and they are expected to complete performance ratings at year end, then have a 'new manager rating training' in November, not in May.

Equally, for new managers staring in May who have to do a mid-year goal check-in in June, complete that training during general onboarding. Some further best practice advice for onboarding a new leader:[81]

- Be crystal clear about short-term objectives to help create value quickly.
- Provide a structured learning process offering virtual briefings and documentation to read in their own time or at set meetings.
- Build a robust stakeholder engagement plan defining how each of their roles relates to that of the new leader, prioritise them by importance, and intentionally put in meetings.
- Assign a virtual-onboarding buddy to help orientation, making early connections, navigating the organisation and accelerating acculturation.
- Facilitate virtual team building led by someone outside the team, with the goal of assimilating the leader into the full team expediently and building trust.
- Consider hiring a coach, creating a safe learning space for the leader become fully effective.

Measure the success of the onboarding programme with those who partake in it, those who collaborate on it and those who deliver it. Take quantitative and qualitative feedback after week one, month one, month three and after probation is passed (likely after month six). Sample metrics include the following: new hires passing probation, number of people that go through the programme and get promoted / move to other internal roles / become managers during their tenure, and other engagement and performance metrics from those who went through the onboarding programme from employee surveys.

Consider listening events from alumni groups, asking them how good the programme is, how much they still interact with each other as a group, and whether they would recommend the organisation to a friend to work here. Onboarding is a really important part of the employee experience and journey. Research has proven it binds them to the organisation tightly when done well.

HubSpot is a company known for being one of the happiest organisations in the world. Its EMEA Senior Manager Recruiting, Supriya Panje Iyer, explains in an exclusive interview:

"In 2013, HubSpot's co-founder Dharmesh Shah created the HubSpot Culture Code, a 120+ slide deck that highlights what we value, how we work, and who we aspire to be. The Culture Code captures our commitment to creating a diverse and inclusive organization and operating with HEART, an acronym that stands for the core values we admire: Humble, Empathetic, Adaptable, Remarkable and Transparent. The Talent Acquisition team plays an integral part in defining the recruiting and selection process at HubSpot to help assess competencies and candidates that align with these values.

"Frequently during interviews, I get asked, 'Is what I hear about HubSpot's amazing culture real?' And I always happily share an example or two that helps them understand why I think HubSpot is a great place to work. One reason is that HubSpot's leaders do a great job of modelling our Culture Code every day at work, even in the smallest things. And when leaders lead by example, teams automatically are influenced to model those behaviours. In fact, I bet most HubSpotters have an example of how another HubSpotter went out of their way to help a co-worker or how they championed a colleague when they were experiencing imposter syndrome.

"In addition to leading with HEART, HubSpot is extremely intentional about Diversity, Inclusion and Belonging and always tries to embed it

*in all of our processes. Our 2023 DI&B report speaks to our commit-
ment and accountability on this front. When you feel like you belong and
are accepted the way you are it's easier to do your best work.*

*"I believe in the values and mission of the company. When you believe it
yourself, it is very easy to sell it to someone else because your passion and
enthusiasm are genuine."*

Questions for a new CPO

- Is your talent acquisition strategy created directly from the business goals and captured clearly in your People strategy?
- What is the company philosophy around hiring internally first based on potential, versus hiring externally first based on prior performance?
- How well is your talent acquisition team set up for success in terms of processes, systems and other tools and information needed to execute the hiring strategy?
- What do your current metrics tell you about how well or otherwise the talent acquisition process is working? Where is it falling down?
- Does your talent acquisition team have the technical skills as well as the influencing, collaboration and networking skills to get the right level of commitment from hiring managers to a great process?
- What digital transformation needs to happen to create a best-in-class process, which will elevate your team to completing value-added work, and which will minimise the time and effort hiring managers need to invest in it? Do you have commitment from your CEO and CFO to prioritise this investment?
- How exhilarating is your onboarding process?

Summary

'It takes a village to raise a child' as the saying goes , and it certainly takes a significant amount of people, processes, tools, systems and effort to work in lockstep in order to find and onboard great new employees for the organisation – employees who will be excited to come, who will thrive when they get here, and who will stay for a long time, taking up numerous roles during their tenure. This all starts with getting the right people into the organisation in the first place. Spend time on creating the company TA philosophy with the executive who leads the business function; create a robust, unfailing strategy and a seamless execution process that changes only with the different hiring campaigns required in any given year. Don't underestimate the power of your current workforce in finding the next workforce – crowdsource new hires with a lucrative referral process and remind them why they joined in the first place by re-sharing and re-evaluating the EVP regularly with them.

Hiring new talent is exciting for everyone involved – take every opportunity to share and celebrate this great process.

Chapter 7

Talent assessment – performance management

TALENT MANAGEMENT				
Talent acquisition	**Talent assessment**	**Talent mobility**	**Talent development**	**Talent offboarding**
Recruiting new employees into the organisation	*Assessing employees in current and for next positions*	*Moving current talent around the organisation*	*Developing employees into the workforce of the future*	*Exiting employees from the organisation*
Talent acquisition strategy	**Performance management**	Promotion	Talent development strategy	Voluntary leavers
Source and attract	Talent planning	Internal talent marketplace	Learning and development curriculum	Regretted leavers
Recruit and select	Succession planning		Leadership and management training	Re-hiring
Induct and onboard			Building organisational capability	Retirement

Career framework
Employee value proposition
Feedback culture
Recognition culture
Employee:manager relationship

Figure 7.1: The position of talent assessment (specifically performance management) in the talent management framework

Introduction

At its most basic, talent assessment activities focus on measuring the performance of your current workforce, and planning for what the workforce needs next for future success. The ideal scenario is that the organisation, driven by the People team, thinks about how next to utilise the current employees' knowledge skills and competence before the employee starts to think about 'what's next for me?'. Talent assessment (chapters 7 and 8), talent mobility (chapter 9) and talent development (chapter 10) are some of the most powerful tools the organisation has to motivate employees to become the best versions of themselves, deepen loyalty to the organisation, and ultimately future-proof business success.

In this chapter we will focus on how to assess employee's current performance, that is, the performance management process and in the following chapter we will focus on the other two talent assessment processes: talent planning and succession planning. Both chapters together create a framework for the organisation to capture the information needed to check that the current goals of the organisation are being met, while gathering the information needed to build the workforce for meeting the organisation's future goals.

What are we solving for?

In the immortal words of Josh Bersin,[82] "*flexibility matters*". Talent management is no longer about vertical career ladders that are climbed methodically; it's no longer about being 'hired for', assessed and rewarded for doing a single job; and it's no longer about looking backwards to figure out what's next for talent in the organisation. The new vision of work requires organisations to double down on re-designing work around team outcomes rather than inputs. The People programmes need to provide the conditions for talent to be available to make this happen efficiently and effectively. Sounds easy. It won't be, but there is sufficient research that shows people want a vibrant career that they can control, where they grow and develop and carve out a customised career for themselves; organisations want employees who are highly motivated to do varied and interesting work, to work and stay in organisations that offer them the opportunity to do that and who do that in a way that rewards and recognises creating great outcomes.

So, where do we start with managing the talent in the current workforce? We start with the performance management process, that is, assessing employees' performance in their current positions.

What does success look like?

Once the employee has joined and been onboarded into the organisation, they spend most of the rest of their journey performing in their 'current position'. Performance management is about assessing ability and competence in that current position, often on an annual basis although more recent research advocates for ongoing performance management.[83] The performance framework must resonate with and motivate everyone in the organisation. A person's performance in their current role will change over time from learning in-role, to being fully proficient, to becoming an expert. The task for the organisation is to build a performance framework that talks to all of it.

The objective with managing performance is to ensure employees and leaders know what they are to work on, why they are working on it, are equipped to successfully complete their work and get clearly rewarded for that current work. At its most fundamental, your framework to achieve this includes the following:

- Articulate clearly how performance links to the continued success of the business; if we don't perform, the business could fail to achieve its goals.
- Describe in detail the agreed performance philosophy of the organisation (see below), especially why that particular philosophy has been chosen; if we perform in this particular way consistently and transparently, we know we will meet our goals as an organisation.
- Translate the multi-year business strategy into annual goals, measured by robust key results that aim high, and include behavioural markers; doing this means we know what we are aiming to achieve, to what level, and how we are to achieve it.
- Support leaders, managers and employees to crystallise the relevant organisation-wide goals into functional, team and individual actions; so they feel empowered to achieve these goals and targets in the way they know best.
- Keep the eyes of leaders, managers and employees on the bigger picture; ensure that good performance is in fact resulting in business successes, and that this good performance is personally rewarded, publicly recognised and expected consistently across the organisation.

We know what we want to achieve with the performance management framework: business success and employee retention. A robust performance management process will have a philosophy, a framework of policies and procedures that brings the philosophy to life, and a set of outcomes that ensures performance is delivering on business success and employee retention. Let's look at each element in turn.

Performance management philosophy

A philosophy about a people programme is simply deciding guiding principles around how the programme with work. In the case of the performance management philosophy, this is deciding how employee performance will be considered, measured, recognised and rewarded. The senior executive must align on their performance management philosophy before the People function transforms that philosophy into a framework. Aligning on a performance philosophy starts with aligning on a business strategy – what the business will achieve and how they will achieve it. The CPO must be involved in the business strategy discussions, so they not only know what the long-term vision of the organisation is but, more importantly, how the strategy was created, what was included not included and why, and how leadership spoke to the importance of each element of the strategy. A philosophy of performance management can be defined as *"the organisation's belief about how people should be managed to achieve the performance that the organisation needs to succeed"*.[84]

It is the responsibility of the CEO and their direct reports to create the philosophy, which should then be approved by the non-executive Board of Directors to ensure it will take the company in the appropriate direction for success. The CPO will guide the discussion on the performance philosophy given their expertise in this area. They may also lead the Board presentation when it goes for discussion and approval. There are any number of websites and books that discuss how to create the company performance philosophy, most of which include the following:

- Do we want a very prescribed, conventional performance management framework, of set steps, dates, roles and responsibilities, outcomes and deadlines or do we prefer the more recently accepted fluid framework, in which managers and employees have more autonomy on achieving business success and achieve it through regular, less formal 1:1 and team meetings?
- Yinjie Sheng describes this as moving performance management models *"from accountability to development"*,[85]

including the advantages of the current thinking around the more fluid, employee-driven model. Other recent research, including that proposed by HRLocker[86] and Josh Bersin[87] agrees that the need for agility, collaboration and employee development creates a strong case for less formal approaches. Choosing the right one depends on factors such as the industry, the location, the size and complexity of the market, the size and shape of the organisation, the culture and the maturity of the leadership.

- How will we do goal setting? Will we use a traditional top-down process, or will we grant teams, managers and individuals more autonomy in what they prioritise to work on and how they achieve success? Will we weight achievement of certain goals? How and when will we track achievement of them?

- How are we delivering the high-performance strategy? Does the organisation want to be a meritocracy, in which only a small number of those deemed to be the strongest performers get rewarded and recognised? If not, how will the organisation ensure that with broader recognition of performance, we are setting the bar high enough? Whichever is chosen, the other HR programmes like talent and succession planning, and internal mobility and promotion, must align to the same standard.

- Will we have ratings, and if so, will we rate what is achieved, how it's achieved or both? How will we accomplish that somewhat elusive employee perspective that a middle rating is great? How often will we assess performance with a rating – mid-year, end of year, more than that? How will we rate performance if we choose not to have ratings and move to a more manager / employee driven 'always on' performance measurement?

- How do we manage the people that are performing under the required standard? How and how quickly do we raise the matter with them? Does it depend on how long they are doing the role? How many chances do we give them before formally performance managing them?

- What is the reward differential between the best and average performers, the CEO and a junior employee (see also remuneration on this)?
- How many ratings do we have – three for simplicity, four to ensure no-one sits on the fence in the middle, five because we want more granular categories?

You can see how important it is to have top leadership, including the CPO, aligned on the philosophy of performance before going any further. Failure to align on this will result in tension and frustration among leaders, confusion and concern among employees and generally a fundamental flaw in how business success will be achieved. A great performance management framework can become an exemplary, illustrious example of a strong culture within the organisation – how we said we'd reward and recognise performance is how we really do reward and recognise performance.

Finally, while it is necessary for top leadership to define performance philosophy, is it sufficient? Current thinking spotlights greater involvement by employees and managers on influencing it.[88] Senior leadership should be tasked with defining the philosophy on the grounds they know what success looks like, and therefore are well placed to define how to achieve it; however, as is the current trend in so many areas of people matters, managers and employees can be empowered and encouraged to challenge and build on it, especially where they believe performance is not resulting in business success, explaining why, and proposing new or adjusted models.

Our view is that leadership should be open to trusting the workforce with this – otherwise you run the risk that your best people will lose motivation, vote with their feet and leave, resulting in the organisation failing to meet the second objective of performance management, that of employee retention.

Performance management policy and process

Once the philosophy is agreed, the CPO and People team create and oversee the framework of policies and procedures that execute on it. Chapter 12, on people policies and procedures, outlines the key elements for writing any policy. All are relevant for the performance policy, with the following key additional tips:

- **Simple and clear:** the framework should be free of HR and management jargon. Every single employee, manager or leader should be able to find what they need quickly, be able to interpret what they find effortlessly, whether it's a step in a process, a deadline, an action or an outcome. Where possible, they should be able to complete their action autonomously, in their own time, on their choice of devices.
- **Consistent execution:** the policy should stipulate which elements of the entire performance management process are mandatory and which are optional. Oftentimes, for example, individual managers are not comfortable having performance conversations, in particular when they are focused on the employee not meeting the required standard – therefore a mandatory step in the process may stipulate how and when to deal with underperformance so it is done equitably across the organisation. The objective is that the process is followed consistently so the experiences and behaviours of individual managers do not result in differential treatment of performance.
- **Eligibility:** it is important to state who is not included in the performance management process and why. For example, the contingent workforce is generally not in

scope for this process as it raises a risk of co-employment (i.e. when non-employees believe themselves to be an employee and claim employee rights). New employees are often not in scope for goal setting or a rating depending on when they join. For example, goal setting may only be completed after probation is passed. However, some form of written expectations of deliverables during probation is prudent. Finally, certain employees may not be eligible for a rating if, for example, they joined on / after a certain point in the year. In this case, the employee may attract a pro-rated average merit increase automatically, or perhaps no increase at all in that first year.

- **Objective and unbiased:** no performance framework is without natural bias. Managers will operate under a number of biases when reviewing performance, usually with no mal intent. These include: halo or horns (overly influenced positively or negatively based on one interaction); recency or primacy (overly influenced by a very recent or their very first interaction); stereotyping (having preconceived ideas that generalise cohorts of employees); leniency or severity (having an overall bar that is too low or too high compared to peers).[89] The most robust performance reviews will minimise personal difference, offer equal access to successful assessment, and reward achievement of the task. The DEI chapter in Section 3 will offer further advice on managing equitably in the workplace.

- **Tested and validated:** the performance management framework should have examples of where it has worked; this could be where an organisational goal was achieved by the accomplishments of these teams over the performance period, or by transparently sharing where a goal was not achieved and why. Another test case could include describing where a goal changed and illustrating how the accompanying team pivoted to successfully achieve the new goal.

- Change in organisational 'goal posts' are frequent, and the leadership should not shy away from being open about this, and indeed celebrating where the workforce succeeded in being agile to adapt to change. Goals and key results should be shared openly, especially within teams, so everyone is aware of what others are working on.

- **Link to the bigger career picture:** while most policies do not necessarily need to show any link to a bigger picture, it is imperative that the performance management policy is clearly and regularly linked to building a successful career in the organisation. It should point to where consistent performance in role leads to growing into new roles or to the next level of the existing role, being supported with learning and development, and ultimately having bigger impact.

A business strategy will be multi-year but the performance management framework, used to underpin achieving that business strategy, is usually created around the financial year. This is because the performance year culminates traditionally in a financial reward for achieving goals, thereby easily aligning it to when the company knows what profit it can plough back into the business. We will discuss the technical framework for compensation rewards more deeply in the remuneration, benefits and wellbeing chapters later.

Setting goals

Traditional performance management frameworks will take the annual goals, which are set at the start of the year by top leadership. Their role is to filter the goals down through their different functions (e.g. sales, technology, research and development (R&D), finance, risk, HR). Functional goals, or 'what' goals (i.e.

what we are going to achieve) are translated into regional / team goals, which are subdivided into manager and individual goals. In addition to functional goals that are focused on what the company will achieve, many organisations adopt organisation-wide goals that focus on how they are to be achieved. 'How' goals are generally based on the behaviours that the organisation wants to see in place as organisational goals are achieved. They are often based on the company's values.

Goals should follow the SMART model:

- Specific;
- Measurable;
- Achievable;
- Relevant; and
- Timebound.

They should also be aspirational, especially when the philosophy is focused on achieving high performance. Goals must also reflect the level of the employee. In chapter 5, we saw that a comprehensive career framework will inform the skills and behaviours expected for someone operating at each level of a job family. It's often useful to have a 'running the business' goal to capture the 'day job', which may not align directly to an organisational goal.

For consistency, it can be useful to capture criteria for what exceeding on the goal will look like, as often the goal setting activity can be subjective where one manager describes how a goal needs to be 'met' where another describes how a goal needs to be 'exceeded' (i.e. a stretch goal). Another tip for building consistent goal setting is to ask managers within a function to share their team's goals with a view to calibrating them and sharing best practice. It's imperative from a trust perspective that goal setting is carried out consistently and transparently across the organisation.

The advantage of this type of traditional framework is that all goals, irrespective of level or function, are ultimately tied into a visible organisational goal. It also helps to set and align on expectations between manager and employee and is important for employee motivation as they can see where they will have impact. However, this traditional top-down approach is being challenged. Current thinking on the future of performance is to facilitate employees writing their own objectives, working on what they believe is most beneficial to work on.90 There is little doubt that this model would positively impact tenure and retention. However, it would leave a great deal to chance in terms of whether the right work gets done, by whom and to what standard.

Would a blended approach to goal setting work best? Our most experienced leaders provide top-down, strategic, prescribed direction and targets, which if achieved will result in the organisation succeeding and thriving. Within the boundaries or guardrails of that direction and those targets, each function, team and individual then create their own set of activities which will result in the achievement of those aspirational goals. Co-creation of goals and the activities to achieve them may just produce the best outcome of all.

Many organisations ring-fence a portion of employees' time to work on a specific project or a goal that individuals believe in personally and feel passionate about. This can be effective – particularly for the younger workforce who feel strongly about working for organisations with purpose. Regardless of where and how focus areas are defined, everything should be measured against a set of targets. What gets measured gets done, and this is absolutely valid in terms of performance. The use of tools like Key Performance Indicators (KPIs) and Objectives and Key Results (OKRs) are helpful measurement tools to ensure the right outcomes are being measured and are resulting in business success.

Finally, on goal setting consider including development goals, DEI goals or Environmental, Social and Governance (ESG) goals, in addition to business goals. All such additional goals should be uploaded to the same system that is capturing business goals for visibility and tracking, but may be measured differently.

- Development goals are goals written by the employee to help them achieve better success in their current goal or, more broadly, help them have impact beyond their current role. When setting business goals, its useful to dovetail this process with writing development goals as it can be efficient to get any related training signed off early in the year. It also gives the manager sight of projects that employees wish to get involved in during the year, and / or get them thinking about a good buddy or mentor to work with. Development goals should usually not be measured or used as an input to the performance rating.
- DEI goals are imperative for organisations and, as we will see in the DEI chapter later, it can be rewarding and purposeful for employees to be allowed to insert related personal goals as validation that these goals are important and play a significant role in facilitating an employee being able to bring their full authentic self to work. ESG goals are becoming more important to organisations and are also a very useful attraction tool for candidates who are equally excited about organisational purpose as much as personal purpose. Companies could consider mandating the addition of a DEI goal and / or ESG goal at goal setting time which may or may not become part of the employee's performance review.

Reviewing and rating goals

As with goal setting, the question is whether or not to have the traditional model of a fixed, clearly defined, prescriptive cadence of meetings between manager and employee where goals are reviewed against target. A defined set of meetings helps to ensure this action gets done, identifies performance issues early (if there are sufficient meetings in the model), and provides a regular opportunity to review completed goals and / or change active goals. The outcome of the meeting is to achieve clarity between both parties as to the current status of each goal, and where a goal is not on track for completion on time / on budget / in full, a set of remediation actions are agreed. If the company decides not to have these prescribed goal check-ins, the expectations of all the above remains valid – the difference is that it will be the responsibility of the manager and employee to drive them. Consideration should be given to the level of maturity of the manager cohort in deciding which approach to take, as having prescribed wording, terminology and structure can help those managers who are less experienced or not naturally good at giving feedback.

The aim is to always have a healthy conversation, from which the employee leaves in a positive frame of mind, even when the discussion has been focused on where they are not meeting performance standards, as we saw in the feedback culture section in chapter 5. Suffice to say, managers must be great coaches to manage performance successfully within the non-prescriptive approach. As with goal setting, an organisation can put both models in place, to suit the varying skills of the manager cohort.

When it comes to assessing goal achievement, 'to rate or not to rate?' – that is the question. If the organisation decides to have ratings, you need to help determine what will they be, how are they defined, how often are they captured, and whether they are directly linked to performance outcomes like merit increases or not. Other considerations include:

- If the organisation has committed to a meritocracy philosophy (when the best performers are awarded the highest ratings and awards), how acceptable will a forced distribution curve be to employees, and will it actually drive better business outcomes?
- How do we ensure ratings are consistently applied? Will calibration meetings help (where the managers of all those in the same job family or team discuss grades and promotion opportunities, to drive consistency of standards and transparency)?
- How well are our managers skilled and equipped to have year-end discussions using ratings as the anchor point?

The advantages of ratings are that they give a quantitative measure of performance, which may be more powerful than qualitative feedback; they help the manager anchor the discussion generally around whether the employee is above, below or at average performance; it can help minimise any miscommunication or lack of clarity that the discussion might otherwise result in.

From the organisation's perspective, ratings allow true differentiation of performance (when done well), identification of individual and organisation-wide skills gaps, and facilitates performance trends across teams and the company. A rating can be assigned to employees' task-related goals (i.e. what they delivered) with a separate rating for their behaviour-related goals (i.e. how they delivered), or a single rating can be applied to both, indicating that both are weighted equally in the organisation. The organisation should define what each rating means, including specific examples.

It is prudent for consistency, transparency and ultimately the trustworthiness of the ratings process to use distribution curves and calibration sessions that hold managers and leaders to account. Distribution curves have unpleasant connotations in many businesses, when badly applied. However, they can be a useful tool to focus on what true 'above average' performance means. Communicating why a distribution curve is used, and what it is not used for, is important for manager and employee trust in the process. Where a distribution curve is used as guidance for managers, as opposed to for a forced distribution, it can be helpful to share curves with managers. For example, where a particular manager has a curve that is skewed to the right when compared with peer teams, with their overall function or when compared to company as a whole, this may warrant further challenge from their HRBP.

An organisation can opt not to have performance ratings in place. The main disadvantage of this – mirroring the goal setting and review processes – is that less experienced managers and leaders, and / or those who are less strong at having difficult conversations can result in ambiguity and uncertainty in how well or otherwise and employee is doing in relation to meeting their goals. This can impact both objectives of performance management negatively, that is achieving business success and retaining employees. Unlike goal setting and goal check-ins, a blended approach, in which some employees have a rating and others don't, will not work. If ratings are to be used, they are to be applied consistently across all employees without exception.

The goal of the year end performance discussion is for the manager to confirm to the employee how well or otherwise they did in terms of achieving their goals over the course of the performance cycle. Depending on the model used by the organisation (i.e. prescriptive, discretionary, blend), the manager will proactively request and receive written feedback from the employee and their colleagues and assimilate that feedback into their own perspective. This will allow the manager to decide whether the employee performed at, above or below the expected level. The content of this meeting should never be a surprise – it is the job of the manager to keep the employee informed on how well or otherwise they are doing against expectations throughout the year, regardless of the model being followed.

Traditionally the manager does the majority of preparation for this meeting; gathering feedback, assessing goal success, applying a rating and / or creating a qualitative narrative. However newer models advocate the employee completing a self-review, rating their individual goal achievement and providing an overall rating and / or summary of their performance ahead of the manager submission. Ideally the manager would not see the employee submission until they have made their own, to reduce bias. In terms of timing, this meeting should take place as close to the end of the performance year as possible, ideally within a month of it closing.

Performance management is one of the most challenging, most complex and yet most important processes in the organisation. During the past 20 years, several models have come and gone, from rating everything to rating nothing, and everything in between. A recent Gartner paper[91] confirms what many leaders, employees and CPOs feel about the process now – that it's not working due to requiring too much effort and not being sufficiently useful. They advise that to make the process more useful, it needs to be:

- Business-driven: customise components of the process to business units, functions, or groups;
- Employee-owned: empower employees to adapt the process to their needs; and
- Work-centred: modify the process to enable collaborative work.

None of these are surprising, in fact they cover four of the strongest themes throughout this book: aligning HR to business goals, customisation and personalisation, empowering employees to have an impact, and greater team collaboration. One of the organisations leaning heavily into these themes for its performance management process is Netflix. Its process involves a real-time review where any employee provides feedback to anyone else in the organisation in a freeform text box.[92] Feedback is not anonymous, and the feedback window opens between April and May, crucially well away from the annual salary review cycle. While this model certainly appears to hit some of the utility elements called out in the Gartner report, it remains to be seen how well this process works over time.

Performance management outcomes, including underperformance

The desired outcome of the performance management process is that the overall organisation is performing at a level that will result in business success and employee retention. The culmination of the process is the final year end performance discussion; however, the work is put in throughout the year to set and reset expectations of performance levels. As well as reviewing performance at that final review meeting, the manager may use it to share the impact of the employee's performance level on a salary increase in the following year, and / or use it as an opportunity to discuss career growth and / or promotion opportunities, which we will discuss in the next chapter on talent mobility.

A company with a high-performance culture means the manager and employee continuously align on whether agreed, ambitious goals are met, and calling it out clearly when they are not. The link between performance, reward and recognition cannot be underestimated. We discussed recognition in chapter 5. Acknowledgement of performance is recognised in its reward policy, which we will discuss in chapter 14 on remuneration. Most companies will have a 'pay for performance' philosophy, and therefore high performance will usually result in a financial reward when achieved, either in the form of a base pay increase and / or a performance-related bonus, either at the same time as the annual pay review or through the performance year (see chapter 15 for more on this). Whatever model is selected, it should be crystal clear to employees what elements of their performance are being recognised by base pay changes, bonus payments or by other recognition programmes. Public sector, charities and other industries may not have this philosophy, and instead will provide set salary increases based on meeting a fundamental standard of performance or occasionally tenure. However, they will still insist on adequate performance, and any underperformance issues will still be proactively managed.

Managing underperformance

Crucially, the performance management process identifies when an employee is not meeting the required standard of performance, either in what they are delivering or how they are delivering it. As we've said, discussing underperformance should not be left to the year-end discussion, rather it must be caught as the employee is trending towards not meeting the standard. In capturing performance issues early, the manager is on the front foot to help the employee address the matter before they are deemed to be formally underperforming. This is also required legally in many countries, whereby the organisation is required to give the employee notice of underperformance, with specific responsibility for creating an action plan to bring the employee back to the performance standard.

This action plan, often called a Performance Expectation Plan or PEP, captures the specific area(s) where performance is dipping, the measures by which the employee will be deemed to be adequately performing again, and the support (e.g. training, mentoring, shadowing) that will be put in place to aid them. The PEP will also have a very specific review schedule and should be as short as possible while being adequate for the person to show improvement. For example, if the employee needs to improve on how they run a quarterly business review, the PEP will at least need to be a full quarter long to allow them show that improvement.

Where an employee fails to meet the requirements of the PEP, they will be moved onto a formal Performance Improvement Plan – or PIP. This formal step in the performance management process is when the employee is put on official notice of not performing to the required level. The documentation for a PIP is similar to that of the PEP, indeed the former can form the basis of the latter, with revisions for new dates and additional measures and supports if and as needed. The manager and the employee should both sign the PIP (although not signing it does not usually result in the document and ensuing process being invalid). So long as the employer can prove that the employee had notice of the underperformance (PEP) and clarity on when the formal (PIP) process for improving performance commenced, that is sufficient to meet their obligations.

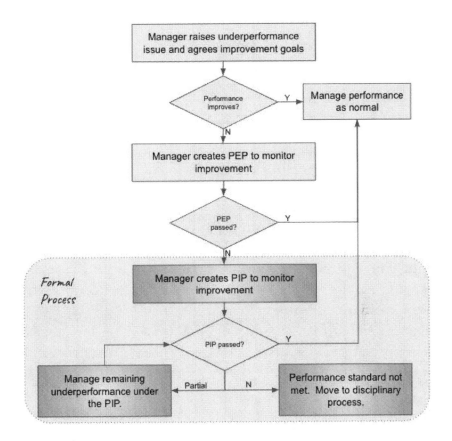

Figure 7.2: The performance expectation and improvement process

The other matter for which the employer is responsible is proving that, over the course of the PIP process, there were regular meetings with the employee which captured progress against each area of underperformance. At the end of the process, there can be one of three outcomes: the PIP is passed, meaning that the employee has reached the performance level required for each area described in the plan; the PIP is partially passed, which results in a further short period being given to the employee to meet the remaining performance standards; or the PIP is not passed, if the majority of areas of concern captured in the plan have not been met.

The outcome of the PIP not being passed, at the end of either the initial or the extended PIP end date, is that the employee is placed into a disciplinary process, covered in chapter 12.

Once a PIP has gone to the disciplinary process, the underperformance does not need to be further debated. The objective of the disciplinary step is to apply a sanction. The severity of the sanction will usually be directly influenced by the acceptance of the employee to their accountability in whole process, the effort they put into improving, their aptitude to actually improve and their attitude throughout. The employee may go through this process up to three times, with verbal warnings leading to written warnings. A third sanction is usually dismissal, and the employee is managed out of the organisation. It is somewhat rare that this outcome will ever arise as usually by that stage the employer has found a more suitable, mutually agreeable role for the employee, or the employee will have resigned.

It is important to note the regional differences in the management of underperformance. In the US, while the process is similar in that expectations must be set and time given to improve, the formality and time given to the process is usually much less. On mainland Europe, the process is viewed more strictly than what has been described above, and much more responsibility is placed on the organisation to prove underperformance.

To finish on a positive note, a PEP / PIP process can of course result in the employee improving their performance to the required standard. This is contrary to popular belief that this process always results in the employee being managed out of the organisation. The other outcome from this process is that the employee realises their skills will be better suited to a different type of role, and they may subsequently move such a role, inside or outside the organisation, if the opportunity arises. The PEP / PIP process is truly a period of time to assess performance for a positive outcome and, while difficult, should be messaged consistently as such.

Questions for a new CPO

- How comfortable are you with the current performance management philosophy and strategy? Does it match the overall culture of the organisation? Is it assessing performance gaps accurately and in a timely manner?
- Where are the gaps between the competencies in the current workforce and those that are needed to achieve business success (1) now and (2) into the future that are appearing from your performance management process?
- Does the company have an agreed performance philosophy with clear standards for what is to be delivered by each function, and how it is to be delivered?
- Is the current performance management framework working? If not, what needs to change?
- What elements of the performance management process need to become more efficient?
- What technology is in place to better automate the performance management process?

Summary

Performance management is critical, and complex. Assessing the current performance of employees is one of the more significant and important People programmes for organisational success. Employee performance must always be linked to the goals of the organisation, whether those goals relate to financial performance, service levels or company purpose. Organisational standards for performance must be clearly defined by the Executive team of the company, driven by the CEO, supported by the CPO and approved by the Board. Employees must be made aware of what those standards for performance are so they can work towards them consistently. Performance may be categorised into what the employee achieves, as well as how they achieve it. In addition to articulating clearly what great performance looks like, the performance management policy will communicate what will happen when employees do not meet the required standards.

There are many models of performance management that can be used by the organisation, ranging from being very prescriptive and 'top down' led, completed according to a fixed schedule of activities across the performance cycle, to being less formally rolled out, empowering employees to drive their own actions. Most importantly, regardless of the model selected, performance must be rewarded consistently across the organisation, and it must feel like a useful process for both employees and managers.

Chapter 8

Talent assessment – talent planning and succession planning

TALENT MANAGEMENT				
Talent acquisition	**Talent assessment**	**Talent mobility**	**Talent development**	**Talent offboarding**
Recruiting new employees into the organisation	*Assessing employees in current and for next positions*	*Moving current talent around the organisation*	*Developing employees into the workforce of the future*	*Exiting employees from the organisation*
Talent acquisition strategy	Performance management	Promotion	Talent development strategy	Voluntary leavers
Source and attract	**Talent planning**	Internal talent marketplace	Learning and development curriculum	Regretted leavers
Recruit and select	**Succession planning**		Leadership and management training	Re-hiring
Induct and onboard			Building organisational capability	Retirement

Career framework
Employee value proposition
Feedback culture
Recognition culture
Employee:manager relationship

Figure 8.1: The position of talent assessment (specifically talent planning and succession planning) in the talent management framework

Introduction

While performance management is focused on assessing performance in an employee's *current* position, talent planning and succession planning are about assessing talent for the employee's *next* and *future* positions.

Up-to-date performance data is used as an input to both, which is supplemented with information about potential, skills gaps and future roles to inform the organisation about what the current workforce can do and wants to do next. These two processes also inform the organisation about what skills are missing from the current workforce, providing an opportunity to close the gaps with current employees while buying in those skills (permanently or temporarily) so as to continue to successfully meet business goals.

What are we solving for?

The pace of business change is such that organisations are required to constantly upskill and reskill employees for their next and future roles. A continuous cycle of performance management, talent planning and succession planning will provide the information to do this successfully. The insights that are generated from performance management can be input into talent planning – the people process which plots performance and potential to assess whether and when the employee will be ready to move to a new position.

Dave Ulrich and team, over years of extensive research, have mapped the organisational capabilities that have been shown empirically to impact on the success of organisations[93]. The latest iteration of this lists the following as truly making a difference:

12 well-studied organization capabilities

1. Talent
2. Agility
3. Strategic clarity
4. Customer centricity
5. Right culture
6. Collaboration
7. Social responsibility
8. Innovation
9. Efficiency
10. Accountability
11. Information / analytics
12. Leveraging technology

Ulrich et al

This is an incredibly powerful insight. Each of the capabilities above is effectively a muscle, one that can be honed and strengthened. The research indicates that, if you consciously devote time and effort to honing these capabilities, you can materially impact on the performance of your organisation. So, an investment in talent planning, talent development and succession planning can be an actual driver of tangible bottom-line results.

Outputs from talent planning can include further upskilling, additional education, exposure to stretch projects or expanding an employee's networks. Rich talent planning information is then used in the succession planning process. This is a risk-mitigating people programme that takes a snapshot of the strength of the bench for significant positions across the organisation with a view to ensuring every key role has an internal successor that can fill it when the role becomes vacant. This prompts further action around the internal mobilisation of talent and / or the activity of buying or renting in that talent until the current workforce is ready. These three talent assessment tools prepare the organisation for what will be needed next for business success.

What does success look like?

Let's look at each assessment tool in turn.

Talent planning

Talent planning is the process that measures an employee's potential for their next role in the organisation. The outcome of the process is an action for the manager, employee or both, which is focused on the employee continuing to grow and develop in preparation for their next position in the organisation. The main tool used is the talent planning grid, which maps employees based on current performance and future potential.

Assessing the performance and potential of your workforce at a given moment in time is an important task that informs where every employee is in their readiness for a new position in the organisation. Gartner[94] defines it as *"a tool that managers and HR use to evaluate employee performance and potential for advancement in the organisation…[and]… helps stakeholders to visualise an employee's effectiveness in their current role and likelihood for success in future roles"*.

We favour the 9-box grid for assessing performance and will use it going forward, but other formats (4-box, 6-box, 9-box, 16-box) are available for you to consider.

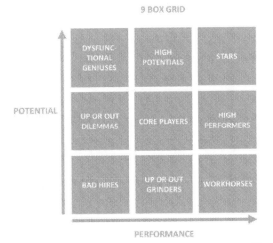

Figure 8.2: Sample 9-box talent planning grid[95]

The steps in this talent planning process include the following:

<u>Establish programme governance</u>

As always with a significant people programme, get the Executive team committed to the process, securing their buy-in to sponsoring and completing this action within their own function, within the required timeframes. Decide what grid you will use, and what the definitions will be for each level of performance and potential – there are many open-source models for support. Decide on whether the information you gather will be used purely for developmental actions or also for assessment (e.g. for performance, promotion, internal hiring, succession). If you do decide to use the information you gather for assessment purposes, make sure the related processes are clear that this information is to be an input and why.

Decide how often and when this activity should take place. It is not an action that is linked to the annual performance management cycle nor the annual goal setting cycle, so can and should be undertaken during a quiet period outside of those activities.

Depending on the size and maturity of your organisation, it can be done in a matter of a week or a month. Any longer than a month and it may lose its significance. Talent planning conversations should be interesting and energising. They are an opportunity for the CPO to take leaders aside, maybe even offsite for a truly focused and in-depth discussion about the organisations brightest stars and lead a future-focused conversation steeped in positivity and with a bias for action.

Next, decide who is in scope and not in scope for each review: for example, you may likely decide that anyone new to the organisation (past six months) or anyone new to a role (past three months) are not to be included in this round. Equally, you can elect to run a talent planning project for a selection of your organisation, for example to include all managers only or for selected functions. If there is time pressure, the discussion may be solely focused on those in the top and the lower boxes, being the employees needing the most immediate action. Be aware that any reduction in scope will of course raise challenges from those not involved.

Another alternative is that you could complete a formal talent planning process (i.e. completed by the full project team with formal meetings set up throughout the process to work with leaders ensuring all actions are taken) while offering a self-service option to those managers of teams who are not in the formal process.

One of the most important aspects of creating your talent planning project is to decide with your executive on what information is to be shared with whom. This information is sensitive and needs to be treated with the highest degree of respect. Research has changed over time on whether to share talent data with the employee or not, with most (such as a 2023 Korn Ferry report) agreeing currently that it's the right thing to do to.[96] Most astute employees will know that this type of assessment is being or should be completed by an organisation. It is therefore credible for you to be reasonably open about this assessment being run and that it is part of the overall talent management programme. Talent management includes talent assessment, talent mobility and talent development: talent planning is merely one activity under the talent assessment element.

The two most important outcomes of this work are for the manager to have a two-way conversation with their employee about what skills and roles to seek out next, and for the organisation (managers and HR) to fill any skills gaps that are emerging. These two things are not mutually exclusive and the information that emerges from this assessment fulfils both. Therefore, the manager can – and should – share that having completed this talent planning activity, they would like to create a focused action plan with the employee, working towards moving to a new level or position in due course.

The manager should not share specific information about what box the employee is in (an astute employee will possibly figure it out from manager conversations which is fine), and certainly not any calibration information or data on others. We've seen throughout this book that newer employees to the workforce demand openness and transparency – so stand over this work proudly rather than be opaque about it and instil confidence in your managers in how to share this important data appropriately with their team members. Roleplays in your pre-launch training and education sessions are a great way to practice this conversation.

Programme execution

For medium to large organisations, set up a team to execute the process in a disciplined, project-managed manner. The team should be made up ideally of a project manager (to oversee the work efficiently and effectively), HR Business Partners

(HRBPs) (to collaborate with leaders on completing the process consistently), and representatives from the DEI team (to ensure the process is robust, equitable and captures the right information for successful outcomes for all), the talent development team, the systems team, and analytics. A smaller organisation can equally successfully roll out this programme with a HRBP, an excel spreadsheet and support from the L&D team.

Every single time you run the project, offer pre-launch briefings or self-service training to the managers and leaders who are in scope to complete a review. This is important for consistency as every time this programme of work is completed, there will be a new manager doing it. Make the time to upskill them for consistent execution, done in a manner that is in line with the programme philosophy. Your pre-launch knowledge sharing can be a mix of online or live and can be self-service depending on each manager's comfort level with what is expected of them. Make sure pre-launch training covers the governance of the process, where it fits into the broader talent management ecosystem, what the overall programme looks like, the definitions they will need to understand and use, and the particular steps they will need to complete.

Talent assessment

Send each manager a list of their direct teams to complete the talent information on all their direct reports, ideally in a tool that is linked to your HRIS, but it can be done manually on spreadsheets if necessary. Pre-populate the grid with as many of the following data points as possible but leave others blank for subjective assessment by the manager. Use as many dropdown options as possible for the blank subjective fields – it helps in collecting consistent data from which useful metrics can be captured. Here are some of the most common talent planning data fields:

- **Employee details:** employee ID, name, team, level, title, total tenure, time in current position, time since last promotion, most recent performance rating (all pre-populated).
- **Performance level:** this is the current performance level of the employee, which is their demonstrated skills and behaviours over approximately the last year. This can be pre-populated with the performance level from the previous year's talent planning process but should be amendable by the manager. It could also be pre-populated based on the employees most recent performance rating for efficiency, as its unlikely the employee's performance level will have changed significantly since that last performance rating. So for example, if you have a five-point performance rating scheme from low to high, and you have a talent planning grid with a three-point performance level (low, medium, high) you could pre-populate this field for your managers with 'Low' (if the most recent rating is 1 or 2), 'Medium' (if the rating is 3) and 'High' (if the rating is 4 or 5). The dropdown options provided will be dependent on the definitions you use for your talent grid (options: low, medium, high if you have three performance levels; low, high if you have two levels in your grid).
- **Potential rating:** this is the likelihood an employee is ready to move into a new role in the organisation: that is, how likely they are to be able to make a bigger impact in the organisation at this point in time, either through a promotion within their current job family or with an internal move to another area. This can be pre-populated with the level from the previous year's talent planning process but should be amendable by the manager. The dropdown options will be dependent on the definitions you use for your talent grid (options: low, medium, high if

you have three performance levels; low, high if you have two levels in your grid).

- **Attrition risk:** how likely an employee is to leave within the next six months (options: low, high).
- **Promotion readiness:** how ready an employee is to be promoted within their current job family within the next two years (options: next six months, 6-12 months, 12-24 months, not ready).
- **Strengths:** short open comment field for the manager to complete. Set the expectation that managers should complete a maximum of two strengths. Provide a cheat sheet to help guide managers towards selecting from a finite number of options. These options can be provided via dropdown options.
- **Development areas:** short open comment field for the manager to complete. Set the expectation that managers should complete a maximum of two development areas and provide a cheat sheet to help guide managers towards selecting from a finite number of options. These options can be provided via dropdown options.
- **Talent actions:** based on the strengths and development areas, the manager will select three-to-four talent actions for the employee to complete. Ideally this should be a list of dropdown options. Sample options include learning programmes (technical, leadership, targeted training), gaining broader experience (shadowing, temporary project), or building network (sponsorship, mentor).

Managers should be guided to take a short period of time, say five minutes per assessment. The managers of the managers who complete these grids should check them for alignment and consistency, all the way to the top of each function – you may decide that the most senior leaders only need to check a level or two down to make best use of their time on this activity.

Talent review

Depending on the system used to capture the data, you may be able to create every talent grid at the push of a button, which will have the names of each employee appearing in the relevant talent planning box on your grid. If you don't, your project team can create them for the managers manually.

If you are running a formal process, this is the point your HRBP team will meet with the leaders to review their talent grid. The programme may elect to do this review only at the most senior levels, or only in the team with the highest attrition / retention risks. If the project is a self-service one, make sure there is robust support documentation to help managers correctly understand and interpret their talent grid and make good decisions on what to do next. Self-service managers should be offered HRBP office hours or other face-to-face options when they feel further HR support is needed.

The analytics team should surface and collate important themes from this data, including what skills gaps are prevalent, is the process fair and equitable across all employee cohorts, and what L&D themes are emerging that the talent development team can action. HRBPs should be given sight of the data after the analytics team has surfaced the themes and insights, in order to validate it. HRBPs should also be tasked with auditing the data for accuracy, consistency and fairness.

Once the data is ready to share with leaders, HRBPs should schedule talent review meetings to discuss the following themes. Self-service material should also be made available to lead managers through analysing the data themselves:

- **Talent grid:** look at the overall populated talent grid. Ideally there should be a mix of people in the middle and middle-high boxes, with a small number in the high-high and low-low / low-middle boxes. Those in the high-high and high-middle boxes will need actions that help them grow and move into new roles or projects imminently. Those in the low-low and low-middle boxes should be moved to a more aligned role or project, receive support to improve or be considered to move on from the organisation. Every 12-24 months, employees should be moving around the boxes. Verify the outliers – make sure the leader can stand over them to their own manager if needed. And finally, robust challenge may be needed to ensure the manager is completing their assessment consistent with the organisation-wide definition of high performance and high potential. Equally, if the leader genuinely has a high number of people in the high-high or low-low boxes, immediate and significant people actions will be needed to either retain high performers, or support and manage underperformance.

- **Promotional readiness:** does the grid match the promotional readiness list – are those that are listed as ready for promotion within the next year appearing in the top-right boxes? How big is that list? If it's large and accurate, the leader will need to prepare your promotion business cases for the next opportunity, as well as begin to consider how to backfill this group. If there is no opportunity to promote any higher due to lack of business need, the leader needs to think about what alternative projects or experiences they can be offered in the short term. If there are no people ready for promotion, is that accurate? If yes, who are those with the highest potential that need particular skills or experiences to be ready as soon as possible so employee potential is being reached, and leaders are not missing out on achieving a business goal.

- **Attrition risk:** how does the grid match up to your attrition risk list? If those that are high attrition risk are in the lower boxes, then these people have skills that you may not need in your team right now, and they may be able to find other roles in the organisation, provided they are a good culture fit and have potential. If there is high attrition risk in the people in the top boxes, immediate action is needed to retain the high performers including, for example, reward, promotion, position change, interesting projects, mentorship or helping them build their network.

- **DEI and hybrid working check:** if you have the DEI data, the leader should review the talent grid against employees in underrepresented populations. Where do the females in the team sit? Where are those that have identified as LTBTQ+, or those that have cultural backgrounds that do not represent the majority of the team? The grid should also be reviewed through the lens of where employees are working from: home, office or both; and indeed those working in headquarters versus those working in smaller offices. Talent planning is an area that is prone to natural bias, even with the best will in the world of the leader involved. Make sure that leaders who have made poor decisions that do not 'level the playing field' are treated with respect, are taught how to do talent planning, and understand that their natural bias is something they constantly need to be aware of in all people-related matters. Monitor that this improves over time.

- **Talent actions:** the most important goal of reviewing the talent data with the leader is to ensure they do something with it. The relevant follow up action may relate to building skills within the team, filling a skill gap from a source outside the team, moving a person to a new level or a new role, or building a better network. The outcome of the review may even be a risk-mitigation action of focusing attention where there is a high attrition risk team member without a clear successor, by ensuring they document and share their knowledge immediately.

A couple of final things to consider. Depending on the leader's talent planning ability and the maturity of the organisation, it's likely that some form of follow-up with managers will be required, to ensure they complete the agreed talent actions. The follow-up actions can also be shared with the relevant employee, to ensure they own the action too. Second, the time frame individuals need to master their role differs with role level, complexity and skills, where the more senior the role, the more time generally needed in it before a new or elevated role should be considered. Finally, proficiency in the current role is usually necessary before upskilling into the next role – however, be cognisant of the fact that sometimes a great employee may simply be in the wrong role and will perform better in a role more suited to their abilities.

From an organisation-wide perspective, the data collected from talent planning should be mined for identifying broader skill gaps, not just those that appear with each individual employee. It's likely that the skills gaps that emerge at the most senior levels of the company will attach greater risk. The talent development team should complete a SWOT analysis of competencies, ensuring they will meet current and imminent business priorities. These gaps should be monitored over time and be seen to be closed.

Succession planning

Succession planning is the process that highlights gaps in the skills or knowledge needed in the organisation for the future. It creates a bench of people to be ready to step into key organisational positions, either now or within a fixed window into the future. The positions that appear in the succession planning process are usually high level or specialised, where there is a scarcity of people and / or competencies available to be successful in the role or indeed where a particular position is being filled by the only person in the company who can do it – a Single Point of Failure (SPoF). While this usually applies to senior positions, lower-level roles can also appear on the list, in particular where there is a scarcity of general talent in teams that are core to organisational success (e.g. data scientists, storytellers, AI engineers).

In carrying out a succession planning process, think about it from a risk management perspective. Succession risk is the risk of not having a sufficient bench of talent in the organisation to meet business goals. It is appearing more frequently in the people risk register, and often makes it to the list of organisation-wide risks to be monitored, such is the impact it can have on business success and organisational survival. Gartner[97] summarises the five key succession risks that HR need to address as:

- "Vacancies mean neglected time-critical leadership responsibilities;
- Successors are often under-developed;
- Focus on existing roles leads to misalignment with future business needs;
- A homogeneous pipeline can damage company culture and performance; and
- Lack of transparency around succession management disengages employees."

The above list illustrates what succession planning will solve for your organisation and hence its criticality. On a very practical level, the steps to complete this exercise are:

- **Identify the key positions:** select positions that are crucial to business success, that currently are a 'single point of failure', that are highly specialised for the industry or sector the organisation competes in, and / or positions that are new or require a long lead time to become proficient in. There is no right or wrong list – it will depend on the organisation, its maturity, its workforce and its industry at that moment in time. Importantly, collect the broad skills and behaviours needed to be successful in this role, as opposed to prior experience, educational or specific functional skills.

- **Identify the successors:** the current role holders in the positions identified are the primary identifiers of potential successors. To avoid tunnel vision and any natural bias, the HRBP and skip level leader (i.e. the manager of the current role holder) should review the proposed successors. Ideally there will be a bench of three successors: one ready in case of emergency, someone ready now (in zero to six months) and ready later (6-24 months). Other informed parties should add to this initial list of potential successors, such as peer leaders, adjacent functional leaders and / or HR Business Partners – they may well identify a successor from an unexpected source.

- **Collect the successor information:** collect the following information on each potential successor: name, ID, job title, level, current manager, current role, current skill set, time in current role, last promotion date, current performance management rating, current talent grid point (potential / performance), and any other pertinent feedback to help identify gaps in the employee's current skill sets to meeting the proposed future role. Ideally the HRIS will accommodate succession planning and auto populate a list. If not, the information can be manually collected on a spreadsheet.

- **Create a succession map:** create a succession map that identifies bespoke development plans for successors to close their gaps to these roles. Ideally the system will also have reporting functionality that creates a list of roles at risk with no immediate successors, which will kick off a talent acquisition strategy to buy or rent the skills in that are immediately required and who have no immediate or imminent successors.

Similar to talent planning, succession planning is likely a project you will run annually or every 18 months. Like talent planning, this is an important business planning tool that forms part of a bigger talent management framework that future-proofs the organisation for ongoing survival and success. While it does not need to be headlined on the organisation intranet site, it can and should be spoken about in a way that employees understand it is carried out regularly, why it's important, why it's not a process that requires wide employee input, and why the outputs from it are not widely shared.

Finally, consider the following principles when preparing succession planning to ensure it meets its key objective of being a risk mitigation tool:

- **Prepare leaders to participate:** as always, start with getting executive commitment to the programme. Successful succession planning requires open and vulnerable leadership, where the most senior people in the organisation commit to intentionally creating a group of people who will take over their role. The right culture needs to be in place for this to be successful.
- **Align the programme with business objectives:** throughout this book it has been highlighted that all the HR programmes and initiatives need to align to business goals, and succession planning is no different. The People strategy must link clearly to business goals – that is, the roles elected to be in-scope for the succession plan must be those that drive and are central to business success.

- **Look beyond the obvious:** use the organisation-wide career framework to consider the potential bench, not specific job families or simply those from within the same function as the position. This will broaden the succession talent pool.

- **Promote a long-term view:** ideally succession planning will have the luxury of taking a 12-36 month horizon, during which the succession bench can be developed. However, there may need to be an 'emergency list' for a small group of imperative roles, while those in the 'ready soon' and 'ready later' list buckets are prepared.

- **Think of succession planning as creating a 'farm team':** (a US term for sports teams who have a feeder system of developing players) – every team will turn over in time and, in keeping with the sports analogy, build depth in the squad consistently to ensure there is a strong bench to pick from when needed.

- **Look at succession planning in layers:** not only should a bench be created for specific people to find successors for, but a 'shadow pool' of candidates for broad organisational competencies should be created from the following generation of successors. This next generation of successors should be developed now by building out their experience and knowledge in all the key organisational competencies.

- **Incorporate into performance management:** succession planning goals can be incorporated into the annual performance goals or development plans of both leaders and identified successors, ensuring the building of key knowledge and experience is constantly top of mind.

- **Plan for knowledge transfer:** succession planning is about transferring institutional knowledge to others in the organisation. This process should seek to identify that critical corporate memory and transfer it effectively to successors.

- **Job development is not limited to promotion:** when considering how to give your successors the exposure to and experience of the competencies they need to build, think about not only the traditional promotion process, but also expansion in their current positions with temporary work assignments, and / or moves via the internal talent marketplace to adjacent roles.
- **Use a variety of methodologies:**[98] use a combination of learning, development and growth techniques to fill competency gaps in successors, including coaching, mentoring, training programmes, job enrichment, shadowing and temporary assignments.

Questions for a new CPO

- Do you do regular talent and succession planning, to inform the organisation whether or not the current workforce can – or has the potential to – achieve business success?
- Where are the gaps between the competencies in the current workforce and those that are needed to achieve business success (1) now and (2) into the future?
- Are there patterns to the succession gaps, e.g. leaders who are not sharing knowledge?
- What elements of the talent planning and succession planning processes need to be more efficient?
- What technology is in place to better automate the talent planning and succession planning processes?

Summary

Assessing the performance levels of the current workforce (previous chapter) and using the data from that process as an input into talent planning and succession planning (this chapter) are possibly the three most important programmes of work in the HR toolkit. Why? Because these three programmes of work inform the organisation what actions need to be taken now to meet current business goals and what actions need to be taken next to grow and develop employees for their next role. The outputs from these programmes therefore protect the organisation from losing current knowledge and future-proof the organisation by planning what skills need to be taught next.

By running these programmes with the current workforce, the organisation gets ahead of attrition and maintains employee motivation, in highlighting roles they may consider moving into next. However, these programmes are necessary but not sufficient. The rich information that results from assessing talent must be actioned into talent outcomes. From here, we look to how we can move talent around, keep our people engaged and keep serving the evolving needs of the organisation.

Chapter 9

Talent mobility

TALENT MANAGEMENT				
Talent acquisition	**Talent assessment**	**Talent mobility**	**Talent development**	**Talent offboarding**
Recruiting new employees into the organisation	*Assessing employees in current and for next roles*	*Moving current talent around the organisation*	*Developing employees into the workforce of the future*	*Exiting employees from the organisation*
Talent acquisition strategy	Performance management	**Promotion**	Talent development strategy	Voluntary leavers
Source and attract	Talent planning	**Internal talent marketplace**	Learning and development curriculum	Regretted leavers
Recruit and select	Succession planning		Leadership and management training	Re-hiring
Induct and onboard			Building organisational capability	Retirement

Career framework
Employee value proposition
Feedback culture
Recognition culture
Employee:manager relationship

Figure 9.1: The position of talent mobility in the talent management framework

Introduction

In this chapter we consider two potential next steps that use the information from talent assessment activities in order to retain current skills, maximise employee potential, and ultimately achieve business success; promoting employees to a higher level within their existing job family so they can have greater impact, and moving people to new positions within the organisation so they continue to have impact in a new team or function.

What are we solving for?

All the great work carried out under the Talent Assessment programme will be for nothing if the organisation does not use the performance, talent and succession information to move employees ready for new challenges around the organisation. Organisations need to have proactive, intentional programmes of work to intercept employees feeling that they need to go elsewhere to get this challenge, by either promoting them within their current function or creating opportunities for them to move to adjacent roles, creating new opportunities elsewhere in the company. Retaining employees is simply an imperative – the Irish Business and Employment Confederation (IBEC) *HR Update 2022 Workplace Trends and Insights* report has placed retention as top of the HR priority list, stating:

> *"Greater focus on existing workforces is also a key aspect of talent management strategies, with basic pay increases (77%) and additional upskilling within current career path (64%) being prioritised ahead of other Pay & Benefits and Career Development initiatives."*[99]

An anecdotal look across several HR publications highlights the importance of retaining employees above hiring new employees, and for many reasons. It costs something in excess of 160% of a new hire's salary to find and onboard them for one, to say nothing of the increased loyalty an existing employee will feel from being offered the opportunity by their manager to grow consistently and have impact. Finally, there is the retention of corporate knowledge that comes from longevity. Organisations need to flip the emphasis from focusing on investment in hiring new employees to obsessing over retaining the ones they have.

At any moment in time, more than 90% of employees are performing at the required level. The issues of talent wars, great resignations, skills availability and tight labour markets can all be solved by working harder to retain the current workforce. Getting a promotion and getting a new role in the organisation are two of the best ways to retain a valuable employee.

What does success look like?

There are numerous ways to move around an organisation. Often a lateral move or even a move down a level is an important step in a person's career, linked to learning a new skill or getting exposure to a particular team, leader or way of working. From time to time, an internal move downwards may also be needed due to redesign of work or workflows, employee competence, or organisation redesign. For the purposes of this chapter, we will focus on the two core aspects of internal mobility which can be facilitated by the People function: a well-executed promotion process, and the creation of a vibrant internal talent marketplace. Both processes are opportunities for leaders and managers to ensure they are placing the right people in the right positions at the right time.

Promotion

Promotions elevate employees into the next level within their existing job family when there is a robust business case to do so. A promotion can be defined as an increase in job level within the same job family, that may also come with an increase in salary.

Promotion must always be aligned to performance (specifically as a performance outcome), to ensure it reflects either existing or future ability consistently, to operate at that next level. Crucially, a promotion must always be aligned to a business need – there must be a tangible increase in work and in the performance level required to meet the new business need. It is usually appropriate to promote a person when the current role has increased in scope, for example through greater complexity, increased remit or responsibilities, higher revenue targets or bigger geography.

As with all people programmes, the promotion process should start with a clear, well-defined, well-communicated philosophy, policy and process. There are some of the considerations that may be given to putting these in place:

- Who has what role in the process, and who is accountable for what? When creating the promotion policy and process, be crystal clear on who does what, when and why at all points in the process. Share the policy widely and publicly so there is trust in it and ensure all people managers in particular are well versed it how it is to be followed.

- What is the organisation's philosophy on promotions? Organisations can decide on having a leading philosophy (where employees are promoted into a role based on potential) or a lagging philosophy (where employees are promoted based on proven experience) for promotions. If there is an 'internal first' hiring philosophy, it makes sense to have a leading philosophy – moving employees to roles in which they have the potential to excel, as opposed to having experience in them already, in order to maximise the opportunity for existing employees to enhance their impact.

- Who drives the promotion process? An organisation may have self-managed promotions (by either team lead or – for the very brave organisations – by employees themselves), formal processes run by the People team or indeed something in between. For example, for lower-level roles or for certain job families, where you can identify the promotion criteria sufficiently, the business case for promotion is clearly defined and the employee's ability to elevate into the next level is objectively assessable, a self-managed process may work well.

- How often should promotions happen? Promotions can be run according to a particular set cadence through the year (e.g. annually, biannually, quarterly, monthly) or can be 'always on'. In a set cadence, the promotion process is run during a fixed window or windows during the year. Often it is aligned to year-end and mid-year review and ratings processes as those are the times that feedback is gathered and salary changes take place anyway. However, they do not have to take place during those times. In fact, managers are likely to be busy with those other people matters at those times and may thank you for taking one process out of the mix. An alternative is to have an 'always on' process in which managers can request and process promotions at any time. The decision will depend on the maturity of the organisation, the philosophy decided by the CPO and Executive team, the degree to which people processes are systems-led and automated and the resources available from the People team to support.

- What data is gathered and how? The promotion documentation should be captured on the HRIS. Standard data inputs include: employee id, name, team name, level, title, total tenure, time in current role, time since last promotion, most recent performance rating, the employees' current position on the career framework. Talent planning data (i.e. the employees' current position on the talent planning grid) may be used but only if it has been decided at organisation level that it can be an assessable input into a promotion decision, and not just captured for development purposes. The HRIS should automate the pre-populating of promotion documentation at this part of the process. The manager (or employee) seeks to supplement that objective data with subjective feedback from a selection of colleagues. This can include direct reports (if they are a people manager themselves), team members, peers, cross-functional colleagues, project team members and / or anyone else with whom they have worked over the previous year or so. The requests for feedback should be associated clearly with promotion feedback, should be short and prescriptive and ideally captured on the HRIS. For example, the requestor could ask, referencing the promotion criteria for the role: What has this person done well? What could this person have done better? Do you have any concerns about the person operating at Level X of the ABC job family?

- Who makes the decision? Generally for a promotion, the person best placed to make the decision is the employee's manager. It's likely the manager is functionally aligned, and therefore can stand over the business case for elevating the employee, as well as the skills required for it, and testify that the employee has – or has the potential to develop – the required skills. It is useful to have a more open discussion around promotions, in particular once those being promoted are at more senior levels in the organisation. Calibration meetings, where all the promotions for the same job family or team are discussed together by all the managers of that job family provide a valuable check and challenge for consistency and quality. The People team can, and should, facilitate calibration meetings with agendas, timings, inputs and outcomes, to ensure they are completed to the highest standards and result in the right decisions being made for the individuals involved and for the organisation.

- How are promotion decisions validated and checked for consistency and equality? There must be transparent pathways to and criteria for promotion as part of the programme governance, as well as clarity on who makes the decision and when it's made. The HRBP team, with the support of the analytics team, can complete promotion decisions audits, validating that diversity representation is met, that those working remotely or via hybrid working are fairly assessed, that there truly is an additional scope and remit at the next level and that there are no unexplainable outliers either not promoted or not considered for promotion.

- How should promotion outcomes be discussed? Promotion outcomes should be shared by the manager to the employee as early as possible after approval and the completion of the final check. Sharing a promotion outcome before final approval can have horrible consequences, including breaking the trust between employee and manager. If the organisation philosophy is for the manager to share with the employee when they are submitting a business case for promotion, and approval is not given to go ahead with it, the manager must share equally transparently that the decision was not approved and why. It's important the manager provides autonomous feedback on why, based on objective criteria, without oversharing who approved or did not approve it through the process. The focus of such discussions should be on how to close the gaps that will bring success the next time.

- Should promotions be publicly celebrated? Yes, absolutely. Promotions are indicative of a growing business and a developing workforce. When top executives celebrate promotions, it shows transparency of and commitment to this important process. It also provides another opportunity to have positive conversations across the workforce about what good looks like. In a world of increasingly complex hybrid working, this is another important opportunity to elevate and celebrate the performance culture in the organisation, virtually and in real life. On the flip side, not sharing promotions transparently may unnecessarily breed mistrust in this important process.

As with many people processes, there is no right or wrong way to set up your promotion framework. Success will come from how it aligns with organisational values, how well it is designed, committed to by the Executive team and executed. Seek to build trust in this process – from a retention perspective, it's an important one to get right.

Internal talent marketplace

Creating a vibrant internal talent marketplace is an alternative way an employee can gain new experience within the organisation. Prioritising the retention of the existing workforce is fast becoming a higher priority than hiring new employees. Having an active internal hiring process that offers new and backfill roles to existing employees first is the tool to achieve that. An 'internal first' philosophy has the double impact of lowering the time and costs associated with talent acquisition, while increasing retention by elevating existing employees to higher and / or more interesting positions. The added bonus is that the organisation is therefore hiring externally for fewer, more junior positions, for which there is likely a bigger talent pool available. Having an 'internal first' hiring philosophy needs the right framework, mindset and process build around it to be successful. A strategy to build this internal job framework needs consideration around the following:

- **'Internal first' philosophy:** management genuinely prioritising matching the current workforce to new and backfill roles will indicate to employees how valued they are, shows investment in them, and ultimately lengthens how long they will wish to stay at the organisation.
- **Reskill and upskill:** linked to the 'internal first' philosophy, existing employees may not have prior experience in a role but have the potential to succeed in it. Upskilling and reskilling, before and after a person moves into a new role, will reduce the need to acquire new talent elsewhere, keeping your workforce lean and engaged.
- **Executive support:** it is difficult for managers to let great team members go. Visible executive support will be needed for success, including seeing the most senior leaders role modelling the right behaviours. One of the biggest failures of this process is talent hoarding. Incentives such as rewarding managers for exporting talent may help encourage the right behaviours.
- **Governance:** who can apply for internal roles? How long do they need to have been in their current role? Does there need to be a minimum performance level to apply? Does the successful employee's current manager have to let them go, and / or within what timeframe?
- **Permanent and temporary positions:** The internal talent marketplace should not only include the filling of new and backfill permanent roles, it should also include opportunities to step into temporarily vacant roles (e.g. family leave) and project roles, via secondment, rotation or just open applications. Adding these roles will truly create ongoing opportunities, bringing the current workforce back constantly to see what and who they can learn from next. In considering moving to temporary projects, it should be clear to employees that such moves are linked to learning and growth opportunities and not necessarily

to level or salary changes. In return, crucially, internal candidates must know they can and will return to their 'permanent' role when applying for temporary projects. All these questions must be answered and articulated clearly for a consistent and successful process.

- **Provide a white-glove service**: deliver the internal marketplace programme with all the care and support needed to elevate current employees as often as possible. Upskill the TA partners who work on this programme to deliver a service that includes everything the candidate needs to support a successful application, including getting into the right mindset to apply, CV refresh, coaching, creating an elevator pitch , practicing interview technique and mentoring.[100]

- **When to go external**: the programme governance should also be clear about the circumstances in which hiring managers can hire externally. The bar should be set high; external hiring should take place only after due diligence has been completed on current workforce potential and possibly should only happen for hard-to-fill roles, or in a hypergrowth situation. It should never be done just to save time – and it's rarely successful in this regard anyway! For example, if a hiring manager wishes to hire in a team lead externally to avoid having to make two separate moves, they should be encouraged to first elevate an existing team member to the team lead role and then subsequently backfill for their current role.

Make the internal talent marketplace philosophy crystal clear across the entire organisation. Show intent by dedicating a team of TA practitioners to this programme of work. Increase the success of the programme by providing a full 'white glove' service to internal candidates. The internal hiring process should broadly mirror that of the external hiring process in terms of consistency and efficiency. However, there will usually be a much richer database of candidate information available to the TA partners delivering this programme, to help them identify and make the strongest hires available in the organisation.

Employees' current skills and future position aspirations should be captured on the HRIS, initially as part of the onboarding process and subsequently updated at least annually by employees or their managers. Marry that with performance, talent and succession data, and an intentional internal recruitment process pre-empts the next skills gaps in the company by providing those opportunities to current employees in the first instance.

A successful internal talent marketplace is going to need resources, of the human and IT kind. It's unlikely your applicant tracking system (ATS) will be sufficiently effective given they generally do not capture the necessary information on current employee. Consider acquiring a talent mobility platform that connects both the HRIS and existing ATS functionality to create a full end-to-end technological solution. In general the system needs to:

- Track the current company organisation design, ideally identifying vacant and new headcount via position management;
- Capture the skills and competencies of the current workforce;
- Track the future competencies required by the organisation (we'll look at how to do a competency audit in the next chapter on talent development);
- Have a 'wish list' database of other areas of work the current workforce would like to get involved in (again this can be captured originally during onboarding and updated annually by employees);
- Create job descriptions that describe both positions that are permanent in nature as well as temporary ones that

will appear (hopefully more and more) designed to get specific pieces of work done. Employees can apply for these 'temporary project teams' in the same way they would apply for a permanent internal move;

- Match the permanent positions as well as the temporary project work to the best pipeline of current employees, including nudging and encouraging specifically those in under-represented populations to apply for the work; and
- Capture feedback on how well the person has done the work when either the temporary team wraps up or at the end of the standard performance year.[101]

Finally, if an 'internal first' talent marketplace is set up intentionally, measure its success. Capture the financial cost, time and other savings that were achieved tangibly. Track the increase in tenure, numbers of roles held, employee motivation and employee satisfaction that increase as a direct result of this retention process. Brand it for the Employee Value Proposition, recognise those who make it a success (especially the managers who give up team success for organisational success by sharing their talent) and sell the stories of those who benefit from it internally and externally – they'll be delighted to see their names in lights. A prosperous internal talent marketplace will be a true organisational differentiator.

Questions for a new CPO

- Is there an agreed promotion philosophy, with clear steps on when they happen, who is involved, and what the governance is?
- Have you prioritised internal hiring above external hiring? Do you have an 'internal first' philosophy, where current employees are intentionally interviewed for vacant new and backfilled roles? Is that philosophy based on hiring

for potential rather than experience? Do you have an internal hiring talent acquisition team?

- What elements of the talent mobility processes (promotion, internal talent marketplace) can be made more efficient?
- What technology is in place to better automate the talent mobility process?

Summary

Taking the previous two chapters together, talent assessment and talent mobility are the HR processes that plan strategically for investment in people. They focus on retaining current talent, intentionally moving that current talent around the organisation first, before buying or renting remaining skills. Talent assessment is a fixed set of finite tasks that are executed in agreed windows across the year, however talent mobility needs to be an intentional, measured, ongoing process of elevating current employees to new and vacated positions as often as possible.

Finally, plan for *all* your talent – this includes everyone, not just the 'superstars'. An important story resonates with Anne from when she worked in her first ever role as a banking assistant in a high street bank in a working-class area of Dublin. A very clever assistant manager asked who the most important person in the branch was, and after many incorrect guesses was told that it's the person who cleans it. This person arrived in the morning before the branch opened and came back in the evening as the employees were leaving, and whose work ethic and performance level were undisputable. The branch would simply not be able to open or function without them. In the words of Dave Ulrich,[102] *"everyone matters"* – keep that front of mind as you mobilise as many people around the organisation as much and as regularly as possible.

Chapter 10

Talent development

TALENT MANAGEMENT				
Talent acquisition	**Talent assessment**	**Talent mobility**	**Talent development**	**Talent offboarding**
Recruiting new employees into the organisation	*Assessing employees in current and for next roles*	*Moving current talent around the organisation*	*Developing employees into the workforce of the future*	*Exiting employees from the organisation*
Talent acquisition strategy	Performance management	Promotion	**Talent development strategy**	Voluntary leavers
Source and attract	Talent planning	Internal talent marketplace	**Learning and development curriculum**	Regretted leavers
Recruit and select	Succession planning		**Leadership and management training**	Re-hiring
Induct and onboard			**Building organisational capability**	Retirement
Career framework				
Employee value proposition				
Feedback culture				
Recognition culture				
Employee:manager relationship				

Figure 10.1: The position of talent development in the talent management framework

Introduction

Talent development is the area of talent management tasked with growing and developing the skills of the workforce to meet both organisational business goals and personal career aspirations.

It's well established that learning and development (L&D) (now more commonly known as talent development) is core to business survival: the old adage 'what happens if we train people and they leave? Worse, what happens if we don't train them and they stay?' still rings true. It's also well established that employees stay in companies in which they learn new skills, feel invested in and get exposure to new situations.

For a long time, L&D was one of the few areas of the people team that provided tangible return on investment figures for their offering. In many ways, the objective and passion around talent development has not changed. A quick glance across HR publications for the 2023 priority lists indicates either organisational capability and / or leader and manager effectiveness are at the top. Safe to say, talent development is going to be high priority for the people team for some time to come.

What are we solving for?

Talent development focuses on future-proofing the organisation by upskilling and reskilling employees relentlessly and can be defined by Tess Taylor, an HR consultant and former Managing Editor of *The HR Writer* as:

> *"the efforts to build upon employees' existing skills while identifying new skills and opportunities to help achieve organizational goals. It ensures that an organization remains competitive in the ever-changing global market."*[103]

Talent development needs to meet two objectives:

1. Supporting the achievement of business goals by continuously identifying the skills and competence strengths and gaps in the workforce (business success).

2. Facilitating the employee continuously meeting their career goals (employee retention).

Proactive management of the employee's career is the responsibility of both employee and employer. The organisation needs the workforce to be open to upskilling and reskilling in order to meet future needs, often for work that is not even defined yet. Equally, no longer satisfied with simply moving up a career ladder within a job family defined by the organisation, employees want the freedom and flexibility to craft bespoke, nuanced careers that suit where, when and how they want their lives to be at any moment in time.

Linear vertical career paths are going to be a thing of the past and supporting employees in shaping their own career journeys will be a differentiator. Astute companies will find a way to facilitate people moving seamlessly around them as they build experiences that will ultimately take them to the next step on their personal professional journey, thus staying with the organisation, while in parallel ensuring the achievement of organisational goals.

What does success look like?

A successful talent development plan will start with a strategy, including a philosophy describing how growth and development will be prioritised in the organisation. Emanating from the strategy will be the core of talent development – the suite of learning offerings for employees, managers, leaders and Executive team. There should also be programmes for under-represented populations in the workforce to support levelling the playing field. The suite of talent development programmes will likely be broken down by mandatory or self-selected, by function, perhaps even by geography, and should be offered across a number of different channels. Finally, your talent development programme should include investment in organisational capabilities, which – according to HR guru Dan Hawkins – are *"the collective skills, expertise, and alignment of the people in your company....Organization capabilities are critical yet intangible assets that cannot be duplicated"*.[104]

Let's look at each in turn.

Talent development strategy

The talent development strategy will be unique to each organisation because it must be inextricably linked to the business goals. However, there are a number of things that should be considered as the strategy is devised or refreshed.

As always with a significant people programme, ensure there is commitment from the CEO and Executive team to the strategy, including adequate financial and human resources allocated to execute it successfully.

The Executive team needs to commit to financial investment as well as creating the time and space to get involved in upskilling and reskilling, and who will role model the agreed philosophy to which they sign up. The strategy and underpinning philosophy require the following considerations:

- How much will be invested per employee? Research from HR consultancy Workhuman suggests that the current average L&D investment is approximately €1,200 (£1,100) per person, getting just under 35 hours formal training per year.[105] This will not include the traditional on-the-job observations, 1:1 training, or the knowledge acquired by osmosis just by sitting among experts.

- What are the current skills gaps in the organisation? Ideally the HRIS will capture current individual employee skills, which they will enter themselves during onboarding and update annually. It will also host performance, talent planning and succession planning data. The talent acquisition and / or career planning systems should be able to create an inventory of current skills that are sought in job descriptions and aligned to various roles within the organisation. The analytics team should be able to complete a gap analysis that highlights where the current gaps are between the two data banks of information.

- More importantly, what are the future skills gaps in the organisation? More on that in the section on building organisational capability below.

- What is the current learning management offering? Ideally, it will provide end-to-end support on everything the organisation needs to deliver in terms of training (mandatory, self-selected), across all channels (live in-person, live online, via laptop or smartphone), all locations (in the office, at home, external providers), during desired timeframes, and by required team, function or group (sales only, all managers, all of finance). Do the learning systems talk to the HRIS to marry the data required to carry out a cost-benefit analysis of talent development investment, as well as to create the correlations necessary to assess if your training programmes are achieving the desired outcomes? Does the LMS need to support developers, authors and facilitators of training within the business, and not just those within the Talent Development team? There are many vendors providing learning platforms available today, meeting the differing needs of organisations at all levels of maturity, size and budget.

- What is the governance around access to and responsibility for paying for and completing learning? Who is in-scope for what programmes? Is there a chargeback to the business unit for programmes signed up to but not completed? Is there a chargeback to the employee if they leave within a certain period after receiving certain training programmes? What is the policy around study leave?

- How will the impact of the talent development strategy be measured? Using a KPI model, consider measuring how well the programme met a strategic goal, to what extent it closed an organisational capability gap, or how it impacts the 'internal first' talent mobility goal in terms of cost and time savings compared to external hires?

The talent development strategy will be complex and given the pivotal role it plays in continuously closing skills gaps for future success, it's important this strategy succeeds. The following HR data points provide inputs into your strategy: career framework, job descriptions, job advertisements, performance management outputs, and talent and succession planning outcomes. When these inputs are collated, along with the organisation-wide requirements to understand strategy, culture, legislation, DEI and the wider environment, the resulting suite of programmes to educate the workforce is significant. Suffice to say, the talent development strategy will require significant investment from a human, financial and time perspective but remember to outsource, rent, build and invest training resources smartly – let technology and external experts do the heavy lifting.

Learning and development curriculum

The majority of organisations will have a suite of learning and development programmes. Usually accessed via an online intranet page or in-house application, this is where employees come to find everything – whether it's basic compliance training or access to university programmes, the full curriculum should be available in one place, easy to access from multiple devices, and efficient to use. Given the proliferation of development offerings available, and the fact that every organisation's offering is likely to be different and regularly change, this section is best served by outlining the main elements of programmes that you might consider offering in your organisation.

One way to categorise the curriculum is into the following three core areas:

- **Personal capabilities** derive from building individual and interpersonal skills;
- **Professional capabilities** come from building professional knowledge and skill related to developing people and helping them learn; and
- **Organisational capabilities** affect an entire organisation's ability to drive results and mission success.[106]

Programmes are also likely to fall into one of the following categories:

- **Mandatory learning** required to be completed by all;
- **Role-based learning** required to be successful in a role; and
- **Personalised learning** differentiated by an individual's career aspirations.

Any given programme is likely to be delivered by one or a mix of the following:

- **Stand-alone event**, either self-completed, live virtual or live face-to-face;
- **Learning journey**, continuous programme with a mix of workshops, mentoring, pre / post coursework, experience; and

- **Learning persona**, series of skills to be gained to be fully proficient in being able to complete a certain type of work.

Development opportunities should be offered across the entire employee journey, so employees feel like they are learning and growing constantly, even if some of the courses are less exciting mandatory requirements. Development opportunities should be offered:

- As part of onboarding and new hire induction;
- As outputs from a promotion, internal hiring, talent planning or succession planning cycles;
- Upon change of role, move from being an individual contributor to a people manager, or from a manager to a senior leader (more about this in the next section in this chapter);
- As part of ongoing learning about of culture of the organisation, DEI, company values, ESG and Corporate Social Responsibility (CSR) offerings; and
- As part of a long-term career objective following a conversation with a manager.

The long-standing ratio of how much of each type of learning is optimal, 70:20:10, where 70% takes place on the job, 20% through intentional interaction and collaboration, and 10% through formal training, still stands. However, what has changed in recent years is the expectation that the talent development function will deliver more than the formal 10%. With technology and the support of external and internal expertise as well as cross-functional collaboration with the business, the talent development team can play a role in supporting the rest.

Manager and leadership training

While all learning and development is important, it is worth highlighting manager and leadership training for the positive impact it has when an organisation gets it right, and more importantly, the outsized negative impact of when it is not provided to the level needed.

As with the learning and development curriculum in general, it's useful to capture why this part of your curriculum is so important, and what you might consider when you are putting your programmes in place.

The roles of manager (mid-level people managers) and leader (senior-level people managers, likely managers of managers) appear consistently throughout this book. Organisations place extraordinary pressure on this cohort of employees to complete a suite of people-related actions, often on top of the day job, sometimes providing services to their team members for which they are not trained – all the while expecting them to do it really well.

It's true – we know the employee:manager relationship is one of the core reasons why people join and stay in organisations, and indeed why they leave. However we need to invest more in our managers to prepare them to be the best they can be in this pivotal position. One of the most urgent focus areas for the CPO and their Executive team going forward is to unburden managers, maximising automation and digitisation of people-related activities, and giving them time back to spend with their team, teaching them, elevating them, recognising them, and getting on with meeting business goals. More about this later in the book. For now, let's capture some key talent development elements to support them in this challenging part of their work.

General manager / leader skills

There are a number of other general skills that we know are needed for our managers and leaders to be successful in the world of work. Gartner places leader and manager effectiveness in its top five HR priorities for 2023, such is its importance, and describes how managers need to be role models, supportive and empathic and deliver results.[107]

Dave Ulrich describes the key traits needed as *strategist* (shape the future), *enabler* (executor, make it happen), *talent manager* (engage your team) and *human capital developer* (build next generation).[108]

We need to ensure our managers can build teams that will deliver outcomes by creating a space where team members feel safe, are empowered to deliver how they see best, and celebrate success. Any manager / leader curriculum should provide for building organisational muscle in these core skills.

Trust and empathy

Managers and leaders need to create trust in their direct teams and with any cross-functional teams they get involved with. Manager training should include building competence and confidence in creating positive relationships, using good judgement and expertise to make decisions, and being consistent[109]. This part of the manager persona is associated with building a cohort of humble coaches, or servant leaders who, according to Dan Cable, Professor of Organisational Behaviour at London Business School, *"serve employees as they explore and grow, providing tangible and emotional support as they do so"*.[110]

This is not solely about creating managers who are in service to their team members. On the contrary, the manager's role is to *"increase ownership, autonomy and responsibility"*[111] of their teams, while they continue to guide, advise and lead them. Remembering the importance of creating psychological safety being crucial to talent management success from chapter 5, the manager / leader curriculum is where they are taught to create it – ask "how can I help?", listen carefully, and give credit when it's due (remember recognition in that same chapter – managers can't give or get enough of it). If the management and leadership cohort is creating this trust across the organisation, the organisation is going to be onto a winner.

Managing for performance

We see in the general skills above that there is a mix of a focus on outputs and on having the right 'smart skills' (we prefer that to soft skills) to achieve them. However, finding that sweet spot between actually delivering outcomes and *how* you deliver them is not easy. Journalist and business author Tony Schwartz[112] advises that we focus on people growth and not be obsessed with performance: build safety first, which leads to working authentically and honestly, which builds trust.

Don't stop there – develop managers who embrace healthy challenge. Give them the confidence to welcome challenge for the betterment of the work, to allow tensions to be surfaced and worked through in a healthy way. Similar to creating the robust feedback culture discussed in chapter 5, managers should not be conflict-averse nor insist on playing 'happy families'. Healthy tension will create a more productive, higher performing team, as long as there is a culture of openness and a shared goal of finding solutions.

In thinking about the ability of managers and leaders to facilitate great career conversations, current thinking is that they should aim to operate as performance coaches. Author and coaching expert Timothy Gallwey[113] describes this coaching as "*unlocking a person's potential to maximise their own performance. It's helping them to learn rather than teaching them".*

This takes place over time, where the coach seeks and monitors continuous improvement via regular feedback, towards specific career or other business objectives. Coaching is a key skill for managers.

The Coaches' Journal ✅
@TheCoachJournal

Real Coaches:

1. Lead with love
2. Act with integrity
3. Set high standards
4. Build real relationships
5. Develop the person and player
6. Focus on process and preparation
7. Teach life lessons and leadership
8. Stress teamwork and toughness
9. Make a difference
10. Make it fun

2:04 AM · Dec 8, 2022

168 Retweets   **14** Quote Tweets   **655** Likes

Figure 10.2: Managers as sports coaches[114]

<u>Executing on the new business operating model (ways of working)</u>

Another core element of the curriculum will focus on teaching how to lead and manage in the evolving world of work. We know managers and leaders are involved in most activities relating to talent management. They need to be able to execute these activities in a way that levels the playing field for all, which will equip them to lead multi-generational workforces, and to elevate under-represented populations. Whether they are onboarding, assessing, moving or motivating a team, they need to do it in a way that fosters equality, ensuring no potential is left unturned.

Part of this upskilling needs to focus on empowering managers and leaders to say *No*, particularly to work requests that do not meet the needs of the organisation. Managers are on the front line to respond to a plethora of requests to work in a variety of ways. Their upskilling needs to provide them with the policies, processes, cross-functional support and platform to say no to a request when needed, and to explain why. Supporting managers to make their decisions, fairly, efficiently and effectively will build trust in these processes.[115]

<u>Inclusive leadership</u>

Build a cohort of inclusive leaders and managers. Organisations need to intentionally elevate particular groups, whether that is based on where and when they work, how they work, or being from a particular under-represented cohort. Teach leaders and managers about the natural bias they will have in how they select, coach and elevate different team members. Regardless of whether an employee is an introvert, in a particular age group, or from a particular cultural background, or is hesitant about elevating their potential, everyone deserves to be coached and invested in. Teams, and organisations, cannot be run successfully with conventional 'A-team players' and there will always be a mix of abilities and confidence among team members. Managers need to get to know where each of their team members is, appreciate their individual talents and *"intentionally support them to be their best"*.[116]

Deloitte[117] captures what it calls the six traits of inclusive leadership; Commitment, Courage, Cognizance of bias, Curiosity, Cultural Intelligence and Collaboration, and notes that all these traits are *"very tangible and developable"*. Formulating an inclusive leadership programme around these traits will set managers on a path to success.

Finally, remain sensitive to the enormous ask that organisations place on their managers. They are expected to be technical experts, teachers, coaches, mentors, networkers, career managers, financial advisors, wellbeing gurus and psychologists. Treat them with the empathy and respect they deserve for doing this difficult job; understand their natural limitations and provide touch-of-a-button solutions for them to get more specialist help when they, or an employee, needs it. Some people do this role not because they crave it, but because the organisation left them no other career option but to do it. Elevate the role of manager within the organisation – call out and celebrate the extraordinary job they do, day in, day out.[118]

In upskilling them on all the above, give them a safe space and time to learn and improve. You need broad shoulders to be a manager and a leader – let's not forget that and provide support for every step on this part of their people leader journey that we can.

Building organisational capability

The latest thinking on talent development encourages the building of a skills-based organisation.[119] Norm Smallwood and Dave Ulrich discuss intangible assets in the organisation in an article for *Harvard Business Review*, defining these assets as *"the collective skills, abilities and expertise of an organisation… the outcome of investment in staffing, training, compensation, communication and other human resource areas… [and] …they represent the ways that people and resources are brought together to accomplish work".[120]*

Rather than being focused on the skills and competences needed to succeed within a particular role at a particular level of a job at a particular time, a skills-based organisation will articulate the broad skills, knowledge and competences needed for the *organisation* to succeed. Innovation and technology render the life span of specific skills very short. When an organisation focuses on broader skills, it really does set itself up for success, and in doing so, creates a truly differentiated employee value proposition that is only its own at that moment in time.

Start with a capability audit to surface the organisational capabilities that the company is known or wants to be known for. The Smallwood and Ulrich article referenced above[121] lists the following examples of organisational capabilities:

- **Talent:** good at attracting, motivating and retaining people;
- **Speed:** making important changes rapidly;
- **Shared mind-set and coherent brand identity:** ensure positive and consistent experience of our organisation;
- **Accountability:** getting employee high performance;
- **Collaboration:** working across boundaries for efficiency and leverage;
- **Learning:** generating ideas for impact;
- **Leadership:** embedding leaders through the organisation;
- **Customer connectivity:** building enduring trusted relationships;
- **Strategic unity:** articulating and sharing strategic viewpoints;
- **Innovation:** doing something new; and
- **Efficiency:** managing costs.

An additional organisation capability to highlight is social skills. Gartner reveals that the pandemic has caused young people to miss out on building smart skills such as *"negotiating, networking, speaking confidently in front of crowds, and developing the social stamina and attentiveness required to work long hours in an in-person environment"*.[122]

Paying attention to this critical interpersonal factor will reap rewards.

The capability audit should start at the top with the C-suite. It starts by capturing a list of all the things the organisation wants to be great at, which is then narrowed down to focus on a small number of capabilities that are inextricably linked to the company strategic objectives. From there, the talent development team builds capability academies around them. The Association for the Development of Talent[123] describes a capability academy as *"an architected collection of programs, content, experiences, assignments, and credentials based on a functional area"*.

A Capability Academy is still somewhat functionally aligned, and still delivered via a blended learning approach, what is different is that the objective is to upskill the entire organisation, albeit to different levels, to become a true differentiator in your industry or sector. Many companies could consider building academies around currently important and scarce capabilities such as cybersecurity, digital selling and supply chain for example.

Ideally, members of the Executive team will each sponsor the academy most closely aligned to their function, and the talent development team provides the academy content to the organisation as a whole.

Talent development outcomes and outputs

Pulling it all together, the outcomes of a robust talent development framework should be:

- A competent manager who knows what skills gaps they have on their team and how they can fill those gaps by developing their own team, or by permanently or temporarily buying in the skills, to achieve business goals; and

- A motivated, high performing, engaged employee who is aware of and has actions to close their current skills gaps, build new skills, and plans to have a long career with the organisation.

An employee learning and development plan and a career plan are the two tangible outputs from talent development. Training provider Get Smarter[124][123] defines each as follows:

"an employee development plan is one that immediately focuses on up-skilling for a current personal or business need, usually created by the employer and employee together; a career development plan is a long-term strategy, created by the employee themselves, focused on the skills and knowledge they want to build to shape their career".

Depending on the maturity and needs of the organisation, as well as on the individual experience of the manager and employee, these conversations can be held more or less frequently. What is key is that they happen at the right cadence for both parties involved. There is shared responsibility for manager and employee to have the conversations. The manager creates the platform and culture for the growth to happen. The employee captures their skills or knowledge gaps and their career aspirations and owns their own development. Ann Hiatt in the Harvard Business Review suggests that the employee can achieve that by answering three questions:

- **Purpose:** who do you want to serve and empower, and by what method? What captures your attention, what drives you to act, how do you want to spend your time?
- **People:** who do you want to work with, align with, brings out the best in you? What mentors and sponsors do you need to uncover opportunities?
- **Pace:** this is determined by your goals and current life circumstances – be aware of both. How often do you

want to be upskilled given the stage of your career you are in? What contributions do you want to make in your role?[125]

Questions for a new CPO

- Is the talent development philosophy clear, including how investment in growth and development will be resourced financially?
- Is your talent development strategy articulated clearly, and is your talent development team set up for success to deliver it? Does the team have the right skills to execute the strategy, and have you empowered them to execute it?
- Do you have the right technology to deliver your learning and development curriculum in a manner that is modern, efficient and effective, and which offers choice to employees on when / where / how to engage with it and complete their learning?
- Does every employee have access to a career map that shows them where they are and options on where they can take their journey next?
- Have you created the conditions for your managers and employees to articulate current development gaps and to find the right solutions to fill them?
- Have you created the conditions for your managers and employees to co-create bespoke careers at the organisation?
- Are development and career discussions held at the right cadence, and resulting in minimising attrition?
- Does every employee have a learning and development plan and a separate career plan?
- Where are you on the journey to creating a skills-based organisation, that focuses on building organisation capability around a small number of core competencies?

Summary

The talent development strategy must deliver the following: attract and retain talent, motivate and engage employees, build an employer brand, create a values-based culture and develop people's capabilities.[126] Employees need to know where they stand and where they are headed, in service to the organisation's success. They want to do impactful work that is interesting to them, learn new skills, and create a successful career. Organisations want employees to have impact, to meet business goals, and to stay. Creating a vibrant and varied talent development offering is a win for employees and employers alike: employees feel valued, trusted and in control of their careers and organisations future-proof themselves with tenured skilled employees who carve out a career with them.

Talent development is not a process for only the 'superstars' – it supports every employee at every part of their career journey, whether they are getting better at what they are currently doing, struggling, preparing for what they will do next, or creating a vision for their future. The employer who is serious about retaining its people as an enabler for business success will make this happen. Employees need to not to just turn up and perform; they need to strive, flourish and seek to achieve their wildest career dreams. Companies should ensure every employee has a path to advancement, that they see it, and they are facilitated to work towards achieving it.

According to McKinsey: *"Many people are no longer interested in or inspired by climbing a career ladder that someone else has built."*[127] The new career development question is 'Who do you wish to be and become?'. Employees no longer want to climb up a ladder that is fixed and leaning stationary against a wall – they want to be intrepid mountaineers crafting their own squiggly journey to the apex of their career.

Chapter 11

Talent offboarding

TALENT MANAGEMENT				
Talent acquisition	**Talent assessment**	**Talent mobility**	**Talent development**	**Talent offboarding**
Recruiting new employees into the organisation	*Assessing employees in current and for next roles*	*Moving current talent around the organisation*	*Developing employees into the workforce of the future*	*Exiting employees from the organisation*
Talent acquisition strategy	Performance management	Promotion	Talent development strategy	**Voluntary leavers**
Source and attract	Talent planning	Internal talent marketplace	Learning and development curriculum	**Regretted leavers**
Recruit and select	Succession planning		Leadership and management training	**Re-hiring**
Induct and onboard			Building organisational capability	**Retirement**

Career framework
Employee value proposition
Feedback culture
Recognition culture
Employee:manager relationship

Figure 11.1: The position of talent offboarding in the talent management framework

Introduction

When an employee leaves an organisation, that is usually the end of the relationship... usually, but not always.

In the majority of cases, a person exiting the organisation will do it on good terms, in that they have delivered good work, experienced growth and learning, created a good network, and are leaving because there is a pull factor that they cannot turn down. Occasionally, the relationship between the company and the employee leaving can be strained. In all cases, the organisation should seek to ensure the leaver moves on with the relationship as healthy as possible.

In this chapter we will investigate how well or otherwise an employer can influence the final stage of the relationship with their employees who wish to move on. Ideally the organisation should seek to maximise what was a great relationship as a talent attraction tool for other candidates in its network, as well as to leave the door open to have the right employees return. At a minimum, the company should mitigate the risk of the leaving employee negatively impacting the company's reputation.

What are we solving for?

Many of us are influenced by our parent's relationship with their work. Anne's father joined Dublin Port (then called the Dublin Port and Docks Board) when he was aged 16 and left when he took early retirement at aged 55. Most of his so-called Baby Boomer generation, also called the 'silent generation', took a job for life and exited when their tenure was up, based on a statutory retirement age. How different it is four working generations later for our employees, Generation (Gen) Z!

The generation that came after this 'silent generation' of Baby Boomers, Gen X, is a mix of people who have had one job, like many in more traditional industries like the public sector, and those who have had numerous work relationships, like the authors. The expectation is that by the time most of the global workforce is Gen Z, those with a job-for-life will be few. Certainly the current trends with the voluntary workforce in the gig economy, married with employee expectations to create their own personal career journey, are an early testimony to that. How organisations therefore think about attrition must be cognisant of this current workforce makeup, given that those currently in executive positions in an organisation will often be from Gen X and earlier, and those making up the majority of the workforce being Gen Y / millennials and Gen Z employees, who are more comfortable with moving reasonably regularly between employers.

Managers and leaders who are further into their careers need to get more comfortable with attrition, not be hurt by it or take it personally, and need to refocus leaders on enhancing their team skills and knowledge to match their current business needs and finding new team members who have the strongest skills and behaviours to achieve them. However, those in executive positions are running a business and may not view employees leaving the organisation as being important. Time will tell.

What does success look like?

One of the most powerful predictors of low attrition will be executing, and measuring the success of, everything articulated through this section on Talent Management. The data will help leadership understand which elements are working well and which elements are not contributing to longer tenure and business success. What is the overall attrition rate, and of those who are leaving, how many are regretted? For those whose time is coming to an end with the organisation, how can organisations elevate the memory of all leavers to ensure they leave with as positive a perspective as possible? Let's look at each group in turn.

Categories of attrition

It is important for the CPO to understand why employees leave the organisation. There will usually be 'pull' factors, that draw the leaver to another position, organisation or total change of career or life direction. Sometimes there are 'push' factors, where the employee cannot get what they want from their career in the current organisation.

The organisation will usually have more control over the push factors than the pull factors, but equally should try to influence the pull factors also. Let's break down the categories of attrition a little further to see where the organisation can influence attrition in order to retain the capability needed for ongoing business success.

Overall attrition

Total attrition is the number of employees leaving the organisation in a given period divided by the average number of employees in the organisation over that same period. That definition alone raises questions, given the myriad of worker types currently in organisations. Many organisations will now not only have permanent employees but will have agency workers (i.e. workers employed by another company, who likely do similar or related work to employees), contractors and other non-employees who do work on behalf of the organisation. Let's assume the total attrition figure is reasonably representative of an organisation's full worker population (i.e. the employee cohort represents the vast majority of those doing work on behalf of the company). In this case the total attrition figure should be representative of the industry and geography that the organisation is operating in.

An attrition figure higher than the industry and location average, unless a conscious choice by the organisation, should be a red flag and be investigated, unless of course the organisation is seeking to be a differentiator in the sector or at a different point in their organisational journey than their competitors. A figure lower than the industry and location average is not always a good thing and should also be investigated, to ensure people are staying for the right reasons and that the organisation isn't going stale.

Voluntary, involuntary, regretted and non-regretted attrition

Total attrition is a helpful start to understanding why people are leaving your organisation, but it's not enough. The organisation should be clear on which employees they would have liked to keep, and which they are happy to let go through attrition. The answer will lie in the skills, knowledge and behaviours that are required to maintain business success and help it reach its future potential. Leavers should be categorised as voluntary or involuntary leavers, and regretted or non-regretted leavers.

Voluntary attrition is the number of leavers who are leaving of their own volition, usually through resignation or retirement; involuntary are those that are not leaving through their own choice.

Regretted leavers are those that the company would prefer to retain; non-regretted leavers are those whose capabilities are not required for current or future business success, those capabilities including skills, knowledge and behaviours.

Let's have a look at some examples of each:

- **Voluntary / regretted:** these are performing and engaged employees who elect to leave the organisation and who have capabilities that are needed for current and future business success. Organisations should seek to retain this group and dissuade them from looking elsewhere for their next role, ideally before they even begin to think about leaving, by continuously being developed and offered great opportunities. When the leaver genuinely does not want to leave, the organisation can seek to find a new learning opportunity, a new permanent or temporary position, an exciting project or a financial award to stay (see retention bonus later in chapter 14). Take the time to fully understand the situation holistically to ensure that enticing a 'good leaver' to stay is done only where the outcome is likely to be a success. This will include considering their prior reasons for leaving organisations, their alignment with the values and culture of the business, their 'pull' factors for moving and their 'push' factors for leaving.

- **Voluntary / non-regretted:** these are employees who are voluntarily leaving the organisation but may not have a skill or competence that the organisation currently needs or will need into the future. These leavers may be excellent people, who are fully engaged and doing their best for the organisation, however they may not be having an impact now, nor have the ability or appetite to be reskilled or upskilled into a position that is important for the current and future success of the organisation.

- **Involuntary / regretted:** this situation arises when employees who do not elect to leave the organisation by choice, but who are valued and engaged employees who are having an impact. This situation, often in a layoff or redundancy situation, can arise when an organisation is downsizing (for example through automation), is outsourcing a service (for example, due to it being not core to business success) or due to a change of strategy. This situation usually gives rise to multiples leavers from a single process; however it can happen in single employee scenarios. A specific type of redundancy situation arises where the organisation is selling a part of their business, where the employees in that business are transferred to the new employer without breaking their service. Redundancy and TUPE processes are further explained in chapter 13.

- **Involuntary / non-regretted:** involuntary attrition of a non-regretted leaver is where the company elects to exit an employee from the organisation as they do not have the skills or behaviours needed for the current or future success of the business. This situation would usually arise with individual employees as opposed to with a full team. Examples of this type of attrition, sometimes called 'termination for cause', include where the person does not meet the required performance standards for their role and has not successfully come through the Performance Improvement Plan (see chapter 7) and the follow-on disciplinary process (see chapter 13), or where the employee has breached policy.

Retirement

In the EU there is no law mandating a statutory retirement age, except for mandatory retirement for a small number of occupations that have physical fitness requirements such as military and airline professions. However, given the state pension currently commences at the age of 66 in the UK and Ireland, it has become common for workers to retire at that point in their career. This is the subject of some debate in recent years however, in particular in relation to age discrimination. In addition, a small number of countries have legislation that prohibits mandatory retirement, including UK, Denmark, Poland and the US. Previous generations of workers have sought early retirement, often paying into their pension over several years to provide for this financially. It is prudent for the CPO to consider retirement legislation considering current pension legislation, as one may directly impact the other. Equally, an organisation should encourage its retiring employees to seek specialist advice to confirm they can adequately finance their retirement.

<u>Dignity</u>

It should be remembered that there is a person behind every leaver and organisations need to treat all leavers with respect, regardless of how long they have been with the company, how many goals they have achieved or how positively engaged they were while they were there.

As with any relationship, there are two sides to every story and when someone walks away from an organisation, they should be allowed to do so with dignity. Even under the most challenging circumstances, the organisation should try to ensure that each leaver will feel they left with their heads held high as they said their goodbyes. This can be done in a number of ways. First, time is often the most appreciated benefit that can be afforded to a leaver – time to find a new role, time for a difficult situation to be digested, time to tell whomever they need to tell that their situation is going to change. In the most challenging and complex situations, time can be the window that is given to a particularly dissatisfied leaver to process a situation that they fundamentally do not agree with, so that by the actual exit date they are leaving on a more composed basis. When the leaver is exiting involuntarily, and assuming there is no serious breach of contract, it is greatly appreciated when leavers can be given financial support to bridge the gap between leaving the current organisation and starting in a new one. Some processes require the organisation to provide a minimum amount of financial support, for example in redundancy situations. A further support that may be offered to leavers, particularly in redundancy scenarios, is an outplacement service. This service helps prepare the leaver for finding a new position and may include updating their CV and interview skills practice. Whether any or all the above supports apply, the organisation and everyone in it should be humane in its interactions with anyone leaving it. No matter what the reason, it is never a decision that has been taken lightly.

In terms of process, there are two important wrap-up steps that the organisation should take: completion of a leaver checklist and an exit survey or interview. The leaver checklist should be provided to the employee close to their final day, and should include the following:

- What the employee needs to return to the company and where to hand them into. For example, a laptop and phone should go to IT, a badge to security and desk keys to facilities. With hybrid working, many organisations have needed to adjust this process for collecting these items from employees not working in the office at the end of their tenure;
- Confirmation of when access to company systems will be switched off;
- Confirmation of final pay date and outstanding commission payments dates;
- How to contact the company with any queries post-leaving date;
- Confirmation of final actions that must be completed by the employee before their end date, including outstanding expenses claims;
- Depending on the level and function of the leaver, a checklist may include a non-solicitation clause; this confirms the employee cannot take suppliers, external clients or employees from the current organisation for a specific duration; and
- If the situation warrants it, there may be a reminder around organisational expectations for the external

communication of the circumstances of the person leaving.

The second consideration to give to leavers is whether to complete an exit interview, exit survey or neither. In general there is rich information to be drawn from those leaving the organisation, especially regretted leavers, around what push and pull factors were at play in their decision. How the person is feeling about leaving will bias this information in a certain direction. For example, if the leaver feels positive about moving on because they had a great experience but needed to leave because the company did not have the next role for them, they will answer in a very different way from the employee who feels the organisation did not help them reach their potential and feel pushed out. This is when an exit survey sent a short period after the leaving date may result in more objective answers than would be otherwise given in an exit interview on leaving day. Either way, this data should be sought in some format and fed into workforce planning reports and processes that seeks to retain the current workforce and to potentially replace the leaver.

It would be remiss not to spend some time discussing The Great Resignation, also known as The Great Reshuffle and The Great Talent Swap among other things. There are many influences on the trend from a job-for-life to having a multitude of employers over the working life. At its very core is the mindset shift in the employer-employee psychological contract. The CIPD differentiates the legal employment contract, which provides a certain portion of the agreement between employee and employer from the psychological contract, which *"describes how the parties themselves understand their relationship, their own views of commitment and what they can expect to receive in return"*.[128]

While generally not legally enforceable, the psychological contract is still an important intangible bond that workers have with their employer.

For many workers from Generation X or earlier, the essence of this contract is that the employer will reward the employee with salary and benefits in return for work that is given to them to complete, in furtherance of the organisation's goals.

Fast forward to the newest generation of employees, the core of the psychological contract for Generation Z workers is that they will come and work for an employer provided the employer not only pays them a fair wage and provides relevant and bespoke benefits, but also allows them to work on projects and activities that are meaningful to them, in a location that works for them, at a time that suits them and for an organisation that has a purpose with which they can identify.

The proverbial shoe is on the other foot, at least in markets with scarce employment. With the benefit of 30 years working across all five generations of workers, the optimum psychological contract is one in which each party mutually respects what the other is seeking to attain, and the pendulum will settle in that middle ground in due course. The employee respects that the leadership is running an organisation that has goals, boundaries, guardrails, ways of working and lived behaviours that, when signed up to by the employees, results in a successful business.

Whether that business is being run for profit, for purpose, or something in between, employees must align on the company strategy and how to achieve it. In return, the employer (via its leadership) should seek to empower their staff, minimise those boundaries and guardrails and maximise the opportunity for its employees to work when and where they do their best work, in areas that they feel they can make their most significant impact.

When done well, the new psychological contract between employer and employee unleashes individual, collective and leadership power in one direction. As with all things, mutual respect of what each party brings to the table is the key.

Case study

In November 2022, several technology companies across the globe let significant portions of their employees go as part of a workforce adjustment, following significant hiring through the pandemic. Stripe was one such company, exiting 14% of its global population. The leadership at Stripe took responsibility for the over-hiring and allowed employees to leave with their heads held high, feeling valued and without blame; albeit frustrated and somewhat disgruntled given the financial success the company still enjoyed. The parting communications from their leadership read as follows[129]:

There is no good way to do a layoff, but we're going to do our best to treat everyone leaving as respectfully as possible and to do whatever we can to help. Some of the core details include:

- **Severance pay**: we will pay 14 weeks of severance for all departing employees and more for those with longer tenure. That is, those departing will be paid until at least February 21st 2023.
- **Bonus**: we will pay our 2022 annual bonus for all departing employees, regardless of their departure date (It will be prorated for people hired in 2022).
- **Paid time off (PTO)**: we'll pay for all unused PTO time (including in regions where that's not legally required).
- **Healthcare:** we'll pay the cash equivalent of six months of existing healthcare premiums or healthcare continuation.
- **Restricted stock units (RSU) vesting:** we'll accelerate everyone who has already reached their one-year vesting cliff to the February 2023 vesting date (or longer, depending on departure date). For those who haven't reached their vesting cliffs, we'll waive the cliff.
- **Career support:** we'll cover career support and do our best to connect departing employees with other companies. We're also creating a new tier of extra-large Stripe discounts for anyone who decides to start a new business now or in the future.
- **Immigration support:** we know that this situation is particularly tough if you're a visa holder. We have extensive dedicated support lined up for those of you here on visas (you'll received an email setting up a consultation within a few hours), and we'll be supporting transitions to non-employment visas wherever we can.

Figure 11.2: Best practice example of a redundancy communication

When it comes to the moment employees are walking out the door, particularly in a situation such as the example above, there is little excuse for not allowing them the space, time and – where possible – financial support needed. Most importantly, allow them to step away with pride in what they have achieved, feeling respected for having given their valuable time to our organisation. That costs nothing.

Questions for a new CPO

- What is current total attrition, what direction is it going, and how does it compare to the industry and the local geography?
- If it's higher than the average, why are more people leaving your organisation than others, using quantitative and qualitative data to get to the core issue(s)?
- If it's lower than the average, is this for the right reasons and is there sufficient fresh talent coming in?
- Are your leavers departing with pride and feeling respected, regardless of why they are leaving? If not, why not?
- Within your current leavers, are the right people leaving, that is, those who are not aligned with the strategy, direction and behaviours that make our business a success, or those who have a skillset that are no longer core to meeting our goals?
- How do you ensure that the organisation's leaders consider every leaver as an opportunity to provide an existing employee with a new skill and position, to bring in a brand-new skill that is not on the team, or to save a little of the payroll budget to use elsewhere to retain and grow employees?

Summary

Attrition, while expensive and time-consuming to address, is acceptable. The People function services a business with needs that are changing, adapting, refocusing, and re-engineering daily. The organisation has an opportunity to use attrition to ensure those ever-changing needs are met.

The global workforce is managed by senior, tenured leaders, many of whom had a job-for-life, and many of whom feel frustration with the less tenured workers who demand a different relationship with their employer. The CPO has the opportunity to change this leadership mindset to embrace the evolving nature of the employer-employee relationship and use it to the maximum to retain or buy in new, fit-for-purpose, agile, fully aligned, future-focused skills to the workforce.

Leaders must see attrition as an opportunity and the People function must build efficient, automated, nuanced processes to make backfilling for leavers a seamless operation.

SECTION THREE – PEOPLE TEAM: THE HR CENTRES OF EXCELLENCE

Chapter 12

Legal framework for people management

Note: Neither of the authors is a qualified lawyer. While we have taken care with the content, the below is not intended to be complete or accurate legal advice for all scenarios. Please consult your legal advisors before taking action.

Introduction

Sitting behind the employee's journey through the organisation is a cohort of specialist People teams who move in and out over the course of that journey, making it a success for employee and employer alike.

Chapters 12 to 18 capture the work of the various specialist People teams that make up this HR Centre of Excellence (CoE) as it is often called, and the chapters are loosely structured to begin with the most fundamental employee needs such as contracts of employment and pay and culminating with people analytics. In the first chapter of this section on HR CoEs, let's investigate the legal framework that needs to be in place from the outset of the relationship, to protect employer and employee alike.

What are we solving for?

There will be a legal framework in place to protect employee and employer no matter what location or industry a company sets up in. For the organisation setting up in a single geography, it can be relatively straightforward to meet these fundamental requirements, and there is usually legally accurate information publicly available to facilitate it: for example, ACAS in the UK[130] and the Workplace Relations Commission (WRC) in Ireland.[131]

For global organisations, in particular those seeking scarce skills such as machine learning engineers, meeting these requirements is exponentially more complex as it requires having employing entities in multiple locations, each with its own set-up, tax, legal and even language requirements. As a CPO, never underestimate the time and cost required of setting up in a new geography simply to chase talent. Build the muscle with your HRBPs to have robust conversations with their leadership about the cost / benefit of hiring into a new geography and create a location strategy playbook for hiring managers to facilitate this process happening efficiently and effectively. The outcome will be good decisions being made about who to hire from where, while meeting the organisation's tax and other legal requirements.

You must put the fundamental legal framework in place before moving onto more enticing areas of people success like performance, motivation and engagement. The regulatory requirements of all jurisdictions will differ, and you should always seek employment legal advice to ensure you meet those specific to where you choose to operate in.

What does success look like?

Contract, terms and conditions of employment

An employer is usually (not always) legally required to set out in writing certain minimum terms and conditions of employment, relating to pay, role, location, working hours, and other basic provisions which will govern the employer/employee relationship.

In most countries, the most important action to complete is to provide your employee with a contract of employment. While a 'contract of service' (as opposed to a 'contract for service' which does not result in an employer-employee relationship being created) can be created verbally, it is common practice and indeed best and safest to create a contract of service in writing. Usually such a contract will be required to contain the following information.[132]

1. The full names of the employer and the employee;
2. The address of the employer or of the principal place of business;
3. The place of work, or where there is no fixed or main place of work, a statement specifying that the employee is employed at various places or is free to determine their place of work;
4. The title, grade, nature or category of work for which the employee is employed or a brief description of the work;
5. The date of commencement of the contract of employment;
6. The duration and conditions relating to a probationary period, if applicable;
7. The expected duration of the contract, in the case of a temporary contract, or the end date if the contract is a fixed-term contract;

8. The remuneration, including the initial basic amount, any other component elements, if applicable, indicated separately, the frequency and method of payment of the remuneration to which the employee is entitled and the pay reference period. An employee may also have the right to a written statement of pay;

9. The pattern of work, including the hours the employer reasonably expects the employee to work per normal working day and per normal working week; where variable, the number of guaranteed paid hours and how additional hours are to be remunerated;

10. Any terms and conditions relating to hours of work (including overtime);

11. Terms or conditions relating to paid leave (other than paid sick leave):

12. Terms or conditions relating to incapacity for work due to sickness or injury;

13. Terms or conditions relating to pensions and pension schemes, if in place;

14. Periods of Notice or method for determining periods of notice, including minimum notice periods in accordance with the relevant law;

15. A reference to any collective agreements which affect the terms of employment;

16. The training entitlement, if any, provided by the employer; and

While most countries will have specific employment legislation, in the absence of having country-specific information, putting these terms and conditions into a written contract will put you in good standing legally from the outset.

Further additional clauses may be added to a contract of employment, including shift work / overtime requirements, data protection and restrictive covenant clauses. More robust confidentiality provisions and the protection of intellectual property are always good to have too in certain sectors such as technology. Whether you choose to include these or not may depend on the seniority of the role, the type of role and the nature of your industry, among other considerations.

A contract of employment may also include certain policies and procedures such as grievance, disciplinary, absences, leaves and dignity at work. However, it can be preferable to place as many company-wide provisions as possible into a company policy and procedures handbook and reserving the right to change or update these policies and procedures, without updating contracts.

Terminating a contract is equally important to do well, and to do so within the relevant jurisdiction's legal framework. We looked at the leaver process and the importance of doing that well from a psychological and reputational perspective in chapter 11. Now let's focus on the legal aspects associated with this. A contract of employment will usually be terminated in the following circumstances:

- **Mutual agreement:** contract ended by agreement with both parties, e.g. on the end date on a fixed term contract;
- **Operation of law:** contract ended automatically, e.g. when a fixed term or specified purpose contract comes to an end;
- **Termination for or without cause:**
  - Termination for cause: when the employer terminates the contract due to particular action or inaction of the employee. E.g. performance or conduct.
  - Termination without cause: also called a termination for convenience, this is when the employer has the right to terminate the contract for any reason. E.g. redundancy or reduction in force; and

- **Resignation:** contract ended by the employee, which is accepted by the employer.

Other legal areas where it is important to give some clear consideration include:

- **Health and safety:** most jurisdictions will have clear legislation defining how the health and safety of employees is to be managed by the employer. This legislation may be monitored by a particular expert body of the government, such as the Health and Safety Authority of Ireland[133], the Health and Safety Executive in the UK[134] or the Occupational Health and Safety Administration in the US.[135] It is prudent to make use of expertise provided by the local bodies where you are set up, to understand the key legislation in this area, and often to get guidance and templates on writing the relevant policy. In the UK[136] and Ireland,[137] all organisations are required to have a Safety Statement by law, which will include the specific risks and mitigating actions for their specific industry or sector.
- **Working time:** working time is a much bigger issue in Europe than it is in the US, with most European jurisdictions placing caps on the number of working hours employees can do, legislating for rest breaks, making statutory provisions for holidays and requiring employers to record working time. The EU Working Time Directive (which has been implemented into domestic law by all member countries of the European Union) governs working time, including how employers are required to capture working hours for employees, which is actively monitored in many jurisdictions. As with all elements of employment law, ensure you check and adhere to the statutes required in the countries you are operating in with internal and / or external legal counsel.

- More recently, the UK and Ireland have introduced a Code of Practice on Flexible Working. Employees, who meet certain criteria including having six months service and being classed as an employee of the organisation, can make a flexible working request from their employer, who must consider the request under certain principles. Additionally, codes around the Right to Disconnect are being put in place in many jurisdictions, outlining the employee's right to not perform work outside of their normal working hours.

- **Data protection:** employers across the EU are required to meet the obligations of national privacy laws and the General Data Protection Regulation (GDPR) legislation. This requires employers to take care in how they capture, process, update and delete employee information. An individual has the right to request access to the personal data held relating to them and can have this information deleted or corrected if it is incorrect. Non-compliance can result in severe consequences, including a substantial fine as well as reputational damage to the organisation.

- **Protected disclosures:** EU law protects employees who disclose breaches of laws and regulations. The EU Whistleblowing Directive requires employers to establish procedures that facilitate employees being able *"to raise concerns confidently without fear of retaliation, by ensuring anonymity"*[138] and provides for the protection of whistleblowers from penalisation. As with data protection obligations, the company's legal team will be an important collaborator to ensure this important legislation is complied with.

- **Employment Equality:** the employer is required by law to protect its employees from being discriminated against. Every jurisdiction will have its own bespoke list of grounds for discrimination, and most will include gender, sexual orientation, age, race/nationality, religion, and disability at a minimum. The employer is required to ensure that these groups are not directly discriminated against, indirectly discriminated against, discriminated by association, or excluded. Company policy should include identifying the types of discrimination that will not be accepted (including specifically victimisation), as well as the process that will be followed when allegations of discrimination arise. This dispute resolution process should include mediation, redress, disciplinary action, appeals and enforcement elements.

- **Grievance, disciplinary, bullying and harassment:** in many countries, employers are obliged at a minimum to have a grievance policy, a disciplinary policy, and a policy covering harassment, sexual harassment and bullying. A grievance procedure is the process by which the organisation will deal with a dispute. This may be when an employee has a concern about a term or condition of employment like pay or promotion but can arise when there is a concern about the conduct of someone in the organisation. A disciplinary procedure is the process by which the organisation will deal with matters relating to the capability, competence or conduct of an employee. Across Europe in particular, organisations are required to follow very strict guidelines to ensure employees are disciplined in a fair, consistent and dignified manner. Harassment, sexual harassment and bullying policies relate to expected behaviours around employee conduct and dignity at work and how to deal with complaints.

- **Dismissal:** when an employee's capability, competence / performance or conduct have been deemed sufficiently lacking, an employer has the right to dismiss an employee. Legislation covering employee dismissal in many European jurisdictions will require the employer to carry out clear steps to ensure the employee has had notice of the employer's concerns, has had sufficient time to address them if appropriate (if the breach is not at the more serious end of the spectrum) and ultimately only dismisses an employee in limited and well-investigated circumstances. An employee usually has several channels of recourse under employment legislation in such jurisdictions, most commonly under a form of unfair dismissals' legislation. Contrary to this, in the US (excluding Montana) and in a small number of other global jurisdictions, employment is considered 'at-will' which is defined by the National Conference of State Legislatures as being when *"an employer can terminate an employee at any time for any reason, except an illegal one, or for no reason without incurring legal liability"*.[139] Therefore, the employees' right to raise concerns about an unfair dismissal are limited, and usually fall under some exceptions provided by case law and statutory legislation.

- **Transfer of Undertakings (Protection of Employment) (TUPE):** Transfer of Undertakings legislation protects the service and rights of an employee where a business, or a part of a business, is being transferred to or merged with another business. This legislation also covers situations in which activities are outsourced to a contractor or insourced from a contractor or where there is a changeover in contractors. The legislation is complex and is nuanced by jurisdiction. However the general obligations under this legislation will include: a period of information and consultation; respecting current terms and conditions; recognition of service; and justification for terminations. Expert legal advice should always be sought by a CPO where a decision is made to transfer out or in, elements of its business.

- **Redundancy:** redundancy legislation specifies the circumstances in when an employee may be made redundant and may be entitled to receive a redundancy payment. Given the complexity of this process, you will be well advised to engage with expert legal advisors when the situation arises where employees need to be let go on the grounds of reduced work or a skill set no longer being required by the organisation. The legislation provides clear guidance on how to manage a redundancy situation, and we will look at the process for carrying out this activity in the next chapter. Similar to TUPE, the legislation generally includes obligations under process objectivity, notice periods, selection processes, payment calculation and taxation, and collective redundancies.

Questions for a new CPO

- Who completes the contracts of employment for new employees, and how mature, knowledgeable, supported are that team?
- How well-defined is the process between the Talent Acquisition team and those who complete the contracts for new hires working?
- How is the process for contract amendments working? Is the right information provided to the team doing the amendments, at the right time, to facilitate all employees always having an accurate contract of employment?
- How knowledgeable is the internal legal team on people legal matters? Do you need to secure expert external legal support in addition to internal support?
- At what point in the workforce planning process are you, as CPO, consulted on potential new jurisdictions? Do you have enough time to complete due diligence on new entities and locations from a people perspective?
- Who provides you with timely information on changes to employment law in your existing jurisdictions?

- What is the culture of dealing with breaches of contract? Will a candidate or employee feel safe enough to raise a concern with their Talent Acquisition or HR partner, or would they prefer to walk away or go straight to an external party? Accountability for making mistakes should be part of the organisation culture, including that of the People team.
- Are all policies clearly owned by a particular team, which may be the People team, the corporate security team, the facilities team, the finance team or others? If a policy is owned by another team, is the People team aware of it and have they collaborated on it, to ensure alignment?
- How do we ensure that, from the employee perspective, all policies (those owned by HR and other functions) are provided in a way that is simple, accessible and ultimately legally compliant to employees at any point in time?

Summary

Providing the legally-required terms and conditions of employment is the most fundamental responsibility of HR – it is the most basic layer of the service provided by the HR team. While this may not be the most stimulating and rewarding area of HR to consider, it is core to the function's success. It protects the employer and the employee. Always carry out full legal due diligence with your internal legal counsel, or external legal providers if you do not have a bespoke internal employment legal team, for all jurisdictions and you are working in. Your internal legal team and / or tax team may have some specialist knowledge relating to some areas of employment law, however ensuring that you meet all the legal requirements relating to employment is core to your organisation's success.

Reputational damage alone, especially in a world where millennial and Gen Z employees demand a respectful relationship with their employer and are not afraid to share when they do not get it, can bring a company down, over and above any financial implications that may follow when the HR function gets this wrong.

Chapter 13

People policies and procedures

Introduction

In the previous chapter we outlined the most common employment legal requirements that are in place to protect organisations and those who work in them. Those requirements are often translated into a framework of people policies and related procedures, captured in an employee handbook, and made available to the workforce to access.

A good policy framework will ensure the organisation does not breach its legal requirements; however, a great policy framework can demonstrate commitment to a strong people culture. For example, a good dignity at work policy will show where the organisation commits to zero tolerance of bullying, outlines clearly what behaviours are expected and not expected in the dignity at work policy, and ensures breaches of the policy will be dealt with under the Disciplinary Policy. A best-in-class framework will seek to invest fully in every employee's potential, making the organisation a truly wonderful place to work, and maximising organisational success.

What are we solving for?

A robust set of people policies and procedures protects everyone. The organisation's people policies and procedures should, at their most basic level, protect everyone legally, physically and mentally. On top of that, the people policies and procedures should offer growth opportunities and ultimately flourishing opportunities, where employees can have a long and successful career with the organisation.

People policies and procedures should be captured in the employee handbook, and written in a way that is clear, accessible, easy to understand, up to date, and regularly re-shared with the workforce.

A framework incorporating the following should cover most if not all of the organisation and employee needs:

PEOPLE POLICY AND PROCEDURES FRAMEWORK					
Health, safety and security	Respectful workplace	Leave		Communications	Ways of working
Health and safety	Dignity at work	Public holiday and annual leave	Bereavement leave	Social media, internet and email	Where we work
Drugs at work	Respect for property	Family leave	Mental health leave	Communications	When we work
Modern slavery	Respectful work attire	Sick leave	'Pawternity' leave / pet leave	External behaviour	How we work
	Relationships at Work	Jury / vote leave	Other leave such as sabbaticals, study leave		
Other people policies					
Talent acquisition (chapter 6)		Talent mobility (chapter 9)		Total reward (chapters 14 and 15)	
Talent assessment (chapters 7 and 8)		Talent offboarding (chapter 11)		Diversity, Equity and Inclusion (chapter 16)	

Table 13.1: Contemporary framework of people policies

This chapter will focus on all the policies and procedures in the top half of the above table. As specified, other chapters of the book have focused / will focus on the policies and procedures in the lower half of the table.

What does success look like?

As CPO, you may consider developing policies and procedures by thinking about what is required by law, what is best practice for the industry / geographies, how to report breaches of policy / procedure, and how to enforce them. There is no perfect taxonomy of policies, and how you ultimately capture and communicate them should be based on your organisation size, industry, geography and company values. Before we focus on the detail, however, there are a couple of high-level considerations to give to creating and maintaining your people policies and related procedures.

The most efficient, effective and transparent way to capture all your people policies may be in an online employee handbook. In that way, they are all in one place, accessible globally (with tailored links to different countries you operate in if appropriate) and can be updated efficiently by the People team. The introduction in the handbook should state that all policies and procedures captured within it are designed to be for personal reference only, are not contractual terms and conditions of their employment, and can be changed by the organisation unilaterally from time to time. As a People function, you can and should encourage comment and feedback on policies from your employees, so you consistently hear about what is working and not working well.

When writing your policies and procedures, always capture the following:

- Ensure the policy and procedures are readily available, online on the company intranet, and offline in paper form;
- Define clearly what the policy and / or related procedure is;
- State the relevant legislation if the policy is legally required to be provided;
- Specify the owner (role or department) of the policy;
- Describe what and who the policy covers as well as what and who is not covered;
- Outline eligibility for the policy or those covered by the policy;
- Clearly capture the individual steps in the procedure relating to the policy;
- Give examples of what great looks like;
- Give examples of what a breach of the policy looks like;
- Explain how the policy will be enforced, and who is accountable for enforcing it;
- Provide channels for reporting breaches; this can be captured in a single policy around reporting channels rather than in each individual policy;
- Describe how breaches will be addressed;
- Expressly reserve the right to change the policy and procedure;
- Give links to people and places where employees can read more about the policy; and related procedures, including where they can provide feedback on the policy.

Finally, before you launch or update your policies and procedures, seek support from employment legal experts, and indeed from your CEO and C-suite peers, for reassurance, buy-in and ultimately their success. Pre-launch involvement with employee groups is also advised for visibility or if you are open to it, for feedback and potential changes ahead of launch.

Let's look at the different categories in more depth.

1. Physical safety, health and wellbeing policies
   a. **Health, safety and security at work:** employers are obliged to manage and conduct work in such a manner to ensure the health, safety and welfare of their employees. Remember, in most countries this extends to anywhere an organisation's employees may be working in and from to include client sites and employee's own homes or remote work spaces. In some companies this policy may be written by the Facilities team or Corporate Security team. Regardless of policy owner, this policy, which is often captured in the company's Safety Statement, should include everything from safe systems of work, hygienic workplaces, office layout, access to workplace buildings, occupational health assessments, display screen equipment and visitor passes. It may also include if / when animals are allowed to be on work premises, as well as if or under what circumstances photographs can be taken of offices and the people working there. It may also include policy around travel and driving while working at the organisation. Specific information about how this policy will be enforced is required (in addition to wherever you decide to capture generically how policies are enforced). This policy should also include a clear procedure for how to report workplace injuries and the people to contact in the event of an emergency.
   b. **Drugs at work:** this is policy around the organisation's tolerance or otherwise of drugs, alcohol and smoking. Generally, there will be zero tolerance for intoxication at work. The policy in general should have clear guidelines about why it is in place, tolerance levels, acceptable conduct where

alcohol is allowed, and importantly how potential breaches will be investigated, given specific tests may need to be carried out to confirm breaches. The policy may also consider education of employees around the dangers of intoxicants at work, as well as support for those suffering from addiction (via for example a referral service). It is advised to develop this policy in consultation with employees in particular, as it is quite a sensitive matter. For the same reasons, providing clear visibility to employees to when it may change over time is also advised. Again remember, an organisation's work place extends beyond the four walls of the building and encompasses social activities, holiday parties, etc.

c. **Modern slavery:** in this policy, the organisation attests to its people management processes being designed to ensure that employees are legally entitled to work in the relevant jurisdiction and to safeguard employees from any abuse or coercion.[140]

2. Respectful workplace policies

a. **Dignity at work:** discrimination can be defined as the treatment of one person in a less favourable manner than another person for a reason connected with a protected characteristic. There are generally a number of codes of conduct in place in any jurisdiction relating to conduct, which can include harassment, sexual harassment and bullying. The organisation's Bullying and Harassment Policy, sometimes called the Conduct or Dignity at Work policy, on abusive behaviour, violence, bullying and harassment is an imperative, not least to meet legal requirements, but to ensure that expected conduct at work is clearly defined. Be clear in particular on what is defined as abusive conduct, as well as healthy conduct, in your organisation. Do not assume that anything is too 'mainstream' to not be explicitly named in the policy – definitions and examples including verbal abuse, exclusion, humiliation, intimidation, intrusion, gestures, pressure, innuendo, jokes, screen displays, posters, unwelcome advances, microaggressions, bullying, harassment, stereotyping, violence and any other types of conduct that you do not want in your organisation, can be called out explicitly.

- Many employee challenges that arise do so under this policy. Therefore you should be able to rely on a clear policy around employee conduct through the whole employee journey, including for example: how you hire and onboard, how you pay and promote, how you offer learning opportunities and how you facilitate employees being the best version of themselves in general. This policy is also particularly relevant to when an employee needs to be exited from the organisation.

b. **Use and Respect for property:** this policy may define what property will be provided to the employee, and how the employer expects that property to be respected. It can contain everything from the office workplace and all within it, to a simple piece of equipment to do a job, like a laptop or power drill. Expectations around theft in the workplace and related enforcement can also be captured here, as well as potential outcomes. This policy should also link to the 'bring your own device' (BYOD) policy, which is likely owned by IT. At the time of writing, there is an uptick in concern about the risk of particular applications being on devices that employees use for work purposes.

c. **Respectful work attire:** dress code policy is a common one in the employee handbook and should include expectations of how employees are to dress in different situations and different roles at work. A highly subjective area in general, a robust policy will give clear guidance on what is acceptable and what is not acceptable as possible to ensure the policy is readily enforceable when needed. Given the recent focus on when where and how we work, this may need to be revisited and updated.

d. **Relationships at work:** the two main areas this policy may cover are family relationships in the workplace and romantic relationships in the workplace. While this may be seen as a sensitive area, employers should set expectations around both and most importantly why the policy is in place. The key reasons for these policies usually focus on fraud, coercion and indeed many other outcomes that are linked to your ethics and compliance policies. Ensure that both HR and legal policies in this regard mirror and complement each other, to ensure clarity for employees and enforceability of all policies for employers.

3. Leave policies

a. **Public holiday and annual leave policy:** most jurisdictions will provide statutory leave provisions for employees for both. Organisations can and — in many ways — should provide additional annual leave provisions if they are affordable, to attract candidates and retain employees. The policy on annual leave will usually consider how many days are offered, whether that changes with tenure and seniority, whether more time can be bought, whether the employee must accrue the leave first (this is usually a matter for individual company policy except for a small number of jurisdictions such as France) and if more leave is taken than was accrued by an exit date, in which case the employer retains the right to recoup payment from final pay. As always, check with employment legal counsel in the jurisdiction in which you are operating, to ensure you comply. A traditionally attractive type of annual leave offering is a career break or sabbatical, which is an often unpaid (or increasingly paid) period of extended annual leave. Usually reserved for employees who have specific tenure and have demonstrated high levels of performance consistently, this can be a successful retention tool. Study leave is another option that can be provided to attract candidates, and to foster a growth mindset in employees. It is noteworthy that, like working hours, many jurisdictions require the employer to retain annual leave and public holiday records to prove compliance with the requirements under employment law.

b. **Family leave policy:** in most countries, there will be statutory leave provisions for maternity leave and paternity leave; some may also have provisions for various types of parental leave (e.g. ordinary parental leave, shared parental leave, parents leave), adoptive leave, force-majeure leave and carer's leave. In general, the spectrum of leave provided for under this category of 'family leave' is increasingly considering every type of family, every aspect of family, and leave that crosses the whole lifespan of the family – e.g. marriage leave, term time leave and fertility leave. Provide what is statutorily required at a minimum, and where affordable, consider providing more for attraction and retention purposes. In addition to the usual elements of eligibility and process for application, these specific policies should include clarity around statutory and (if offered by your organisation) top-up pay, impact on benefits, and the process and support provided for returning to work. Many of these statutory leaves have strict rules around how roles are to be protected during the period of leave.

c. **Sick leave policy:** Sick leave policy covers planned and unplanned absence from work. Legislation in most jurisdictions will provide for at least minimal protection for employees to cover them for when they are unable to work and will often be linked to a statutory sick pay scheme and associated process. Some companies operate discretionary or set contractual sick pay schemes, where the amount and duration of the benefit is linked to the employee's length of service. The associated absence management procedures should: outline how the absence is to be monitored; have clear roles and responsibilities for the employee, the manager and the people team; include practical requirements such as when to submit a medical certificate and when to use occupational health supports (i.e. when an absence is lengthy, complex or frequent); and include a robust, supportive return to work process after an absence. Governing absence requires continuous effort, much of which can be automated including, for example: informing new employees about the policy and procedures;

reminding employees with regular awareness training (including for example when employees can and should work from home if well enough to work but not well enough to travel to work); and accurate consistent capturing of absence data. Consistent application of the policy, in particular where it differentiates how the benefit is to be applied to different employee cohorts, is crucial to ensure there is no difference in where, when or with whom the policy is applied. Transparency in the application of workplace policies is usually encouraged, however care must be taken with absence due to the confidential nature of medical information, and due care and diligence must be provided to keep secure any medical data provided to the organisation and to only retain that which is relevant and necessary.

d. **Other leave:**

    i. Jury leave and voting leave: often provided for under local legislation, these situations cover leave to fulfil jury service or to fulfil democratic rights to vote.

    ii. Bereavement leave: facilitating the employee time to make any necessary arrangements for the funeral as well as the mental space to work through their loss.

    iii. Other mental health leave: covering for example miscarriage leave and leave related to the menopause and gender reassignment, or time off due to mental health issues.

    iv. 'Pawternity leave':[141] a more nuanced leave, allowing employees time off for tasks associated with their pets' needs, that is becoming more common in the tech industry in particular.

4. Communications policies

  a. **Social media, internet and email policy:** The objective of these policies is to ensure employees are clear about their responsibilities in how, when and where they use the company's internet and email facilities. The immediate and widespread impact of misuse of these policies cannot be understated and these policies should never be overlooked, especially given the newest generation of workers have not known a time before the internet. Sample templates of these policies are widely available. As long as the employee can be traced to, or associated with, the organisation, even personal social media posts have the potential to affect the reputation of the organisation. They should therefore be used with great care and discretion.

  b. **Communications policy:** this polices clarifies when, where and how employees can discuss the company publicly. As always, it is worthwhile identifying clear examples of what is acceptable and not acceptable behaviour. This should include detail around who is authorised to speak publicly, what media training is required in advance, what information and pictures can and can't be shared publicly, including when representing the company in presentations, networks and public speaking events. It can be useful to include in the related procedure that employees contact the Public Relations or External Communications team prior to accepting requests for public speaking events. It's also worth noting that this policy will need to link closely to a number of legal policies, including policies around ethics, insider trading and compliance.

    c. **External behaviours:** In organisations in which company representatives are active publicly, this policy should ensure they are adequately always protected personally and seek to keep as much of their non-public life private. A company public relations policy may also contain expectations around this.

5. Business operating model policies (ways of working policies)

    a. **Where we work policy:** the newest generation of employees will challenge employers to provide maximum flexibility in where they can work from. This policy must be considered along a number of levels, including the global location of employees; office (WFO) vs. home (WFH) vs. hybrid working where there is an office available; benefits being provided to each cohort of employees; taxation, setting up WFH and hybrid workers safely both from a legal perspective and to ensure they can do their best work in both. This policy should capture the considerations that the organisation will give to this policy, which is increasingly important for organisations to get right.[142]

    b. **When we work policy:** this policy captures the hours that employees will be expected to work. At its most basic, this policy will capture how it meets legal obligations around the maximum hours of working, including how it will capture and retain employee working hours records. However, it can also include guidance around core hours that must be worked during a working day (which should be captured on the employee contract also.), overtime, on-call rules, flexitime, job sharing options and part-time working. This policy can also include guidance around being timely for work (if you don't create an attendance policy described in the final section), as well as the employee's responsibilities for using the correct procedures for capturing their working hours and their non-working hours. For global organisations, this policy can capture expectations around how the company, and its employees, will work across time zones – it is important not only from a legal perspective, but also to prevent burnout and attrition. Some employees like working morning and evening, taking personal time in the afternoon; some like to start and finish early; others like to start and finish late. The key to the success of this is open and transparent dialogue around how personal employee preferences can be facilitated, so long as they meet legal requirements and support the business being as successful as it can be.

c. **How we work policy:** a policy focusing on how we work is a relatively new concept and is borne out of the move towards increased flexibility in where and when employees will work. In many ways, it is the glue that will hold this flexibility together, as the objective of this policy is to provide clarity, tools and processes to successfully work together asynchronously and geographically distributed. A 'how we work' policy will need to have strong links to the company's performance management philosophy, as its content will need to dovetail with how objectives are written, measured and rewarded – essentially success will lie in all these elements focusing on rewarding and recognising outputs and outcomes rather than time, effort and other inputs. Elements of this policy may include: defining a shared language for managing work and having consistent methodology for how work gets done; aligning on what internal collaboration and conversation tools to use such as Slack or Box; using a consistent decision-making model across the organisation;[143] writing team working agreements which clarify how teams will communicate and get work done; having meeting-free planning days or weeks each quarter; and agreeing meeting etiquette including for example having clear start / end times, using pre-reads and agenda, confirming the meeting type, and even giving license to checking if a meeting is required at all or could the work be done asynchronously. This policy should also link to a workplace policy on how the office is set up, where ideally there are quiet areas, collaboration areas and social areas so there is an appropriate spot for those coming to the office to get work done.

It may appear that some policies and procedures are missing from the list above; often what is thought to be the remit of the People team and function is, in fact, a policy that should be owned by other expert areas of the business. Generally, the People team can collaborate with other functions as they write their polices but each function should take ownership of their own policies. This ensures that the people policies facilitate enforcement of other functional policies and procedures.

Occasionally the People team may get involved in the investigation of a breach, however given the People team are not the subject matter experts of other functions' policies, it is usually not appropriate for them to get involved at the investigation stage. For example, the People team would not have the sufficient expertise to investigate a money laundering allegation or a potential breach of information security by an employee. However, the People team can support investigations carried out by the business to ensure the process is followed judiciously. Some of the more common examples of policies that do not fall into the remit of the People function include the following:

- o Expenses, mobile phones, travel and other related policies should be owned, written and monitored by the finance function;
- o Anti-corruption, gifts and hospitality, insider trading, conflict of interest, outside projects / work, data privacy and other related compliance and ethics policies should be owned, written and monitored by the legal / compliance function;
- o Business continuity, crisis management, incident management planning will usually be owned by the IT or operations teams;
- o Data privacy, data protection, data security should be owned, written and monitored by the Data Protection Office within the legal function; and
- o IT security, including acceptable use, systems access and BYOD should be owned, written and monitored by the IT function.

Reporting channels

All people policies should have a provision for how employees and managers can report breaches of policy. This may be called out in each policy, or in a single place in the employee handbook. The following are the common channels available for organisations, some of which will be required by law depending on the jurisdiction:

- **Manager**: ideally a breach of policy will be reported to the employee's manager in the first instance. Managers should be fully trained, and reminded regularly, on their responsibilities in their manager fundamentals training, including when to keep something confidential or not, especially when a disclosure may result in immediate harm to the employee or another party. Managers should have easy and always-on access to support for these matters. Managers are obliged by policy to take action around any concern raised to them. In the event they feel they cannot address the matter themselves they will need to inform someone on the People team (usually a HRBP or the Employee Relations team) for further support. Where the concern is conduct related, either the HRBP or Employee Relations team may investigate the matter. Where the concern is related to a business process, HR may advise a more appropriate team to investigate, with HR in support.
- **HR Business Partner**: an employee's HRBP is a trained member of the People team who will be readily available to discuss potential policy breaches and implications, where the employee feels they cannot report the matter to their manager. All employees should know who their HRBP is. Sometimes the HRBP will also become a member of a team investigating a potential policy breach, either as liaison with the relevant parties and / or as a confidential recipient of the outcome where they will have responsibility for administering the sanction for a proven breach. A HRBP is obliged to further investigate all matters raised with them.

- **Employee Relations team:** The Employee Relations (ER) team may have a number of responsibilities in an organisation. In some cases, they will take responsibility for collective bargaining and other industrial relations matters. In other cases, this team may investigate individual employee concerns around conduct. They are usually highly trained in negotiating, influencing, mediating and investigating. Where this team are set up to investigate conduct matters, they can be contacted directly by an employee, usually via a team alias for speed of action, and will revert to the reporter of potential policy breaches directly in the first instance. Often this team will lead an investigation of a conduct policy breach as an independent party and produce a report on the outcome, sharing elements of the report potentially with the person who raised the complaint; the alleged wrongdoer; the alleged wrongdoer's HRBP; the alleged wrongdoer's manager and potentially other stakeholders. The ER team may also have a role in proposing a sanction where the complaint is proven and will be obliged to investigate all matters raised with them.

- **Ombuds office:** a relatively new channel, increasingly organisations are putting in place an ombuds office in the workplace.[144] An independent person or team, usually hired into the legal team rather than the People team, the role of the ombuds office is unique in that it is not required to report a potential breach of policy that is reported to it, unlike the previous three channels. This uniquely positioned office can therefore have 'off the record' conversations with employees who are not sure they want their concerns to be reported formally initially. The ombuds office is allowed to keep all conversations private unless there is an imminent risk to the reporter or someone else. Rather, their role with the employee is to hear their concern, probe further to ensure the employee is thinking broadly about the issue and direct them – if appropriate – to the other informal or formal channels to progress their concerns. In addition, the ombuds office will consolidate all matters raised to them anonymously into reports for the highest levels of leadership, with a view putting in place or building on existing policies and processes to protect and prevent further organisational issues.

- **Ethics helpline:** this is an internal service, often owned and run by the compliance team, which offers the option to report concerns over the phone or online to someone outside the People function. The team will work with the person reporting the concern in the first instance, before reporting the concern to the relevant person in the people team as it is obliged to do.

- **Whistleblowing helpline:** facilitates employees making confidential, protected disclosures regarding a past, current or future concern. The whistleblowing helpline can be operated internally or externally. There is an increasing number of companies offering confidential helpline services that organisations can purchase to meet their requirements under this law. Employees should be provided with the details of the organisation's helpline, which should be accessible online and offline, by phone, email or a combination of both.

A final word on reporting potential breaches of policy and procedure. The employee handbook will have a clear, well communicated policy around zero tolerance of retaliation towards or victimisation of an individual who raises a concern, or in cases when an individual is participating in a workplace investigation on the back of a concern being raised. Such actions, which will also deal with vexatious claims (i.e. a claim brought solely to harass another person), will be dealt with under the full power of the enforcement processes used for all other People policies.

Enforcing policies and addressing potential breaches

As for reporting channels, the employee handbook can have a single place outlining how policy breaches will be enforced, as opposed to describing it in every policy – however, where a policy or procedure has specific actions around enforcement (e.g. testing for drugs, use of surveillance camera), these should be called out clearly within the relevant policy. Most jurisdictions will be required by law to provide robust processes for raising, hearing and investigating potential policy violations. Usually this will be captured in the employee handbook under a grievance policy (to report concerns), a disciplinary policy (to appropriately sanction proven policy and procedural breaches) and a dismissal policy (to terminate employment where the breach warrants it). Sample policy and procedure templates are often available on local governmental sites in the labour or employment sections. As noted previously, these processes should be adhered to closely by the People and legal teams to ensure fair process to the parties involved, and to protect the employer from legal, reputational and financial harm. When an organisation seeks to modify a legally provided template, it should get approval from its employment legal team.

Questions for a new CPO

- What is the aim of the organisation in executing its people policy framework; merely to meet legal requirements? To differentiate and delight? To save money?
- Do you have the fundamental, tier one policies and procedures in place to keep the company legally compliant? If not, what gaps need to be filled immediately?

- Do you have all tier one policies in place, and most of tier two policies, meaning employees are accepted, learning and growing? If not, which ones can you add on now and next?
- Do you have all of tier one and tier two policies in place, and some tier three policies? If not, which ones can you add on now and in the future?
- Are all relevant policies in place, not only those clearly within the remit of the people team, but those that may be under that function (e.g. health and safety, facilities) and those that are clearly within the remit of other functions (e.g. compliance, ethics, data protection, IT security)? How well are these functions collaborating on policy creation and enforcement, to ensure an overall robust framework for managing the people-related risks within the organisation?
- What's around the corner? How well equipped is the people team to get updated on the next employee legal requirements in all your jurisdictions, and to put new policies and procedures in place to meet them?
- How well equipped is the People team to research and ideate on creating a different offering, or be a first-to-market with a new policy that nobody else is offering, so you can be seen as market leading in terms of creating the best employee experience?

Summary

You will rarely need to write an organisational People policy and related procedure from scratch, as publicly available, trustworthy, locally nuanced, legally accurate templates will generally be available from local government agencies and / or employer bodies websites. People policies and procedures are the 'bones' of the People team – the basic skeleton that keeps all people matters running smoothly. The most minimalist 'skeleton' of policies and procedures will keep your organisation out of the news and will be the minimum that candidates and employees expect to have in place. The elite, best-in-class version will result in candidates climbing over each other to be offered a role with your organisation. When hired, they will not give a moment's thought to them, simply because they trust their managers, leadership and the People function to have them in place and are too busy working to bring the organisation to newer and higher levels of success.

All CPOs should strive towards offering the best version of people policies and procedures they can – the results will be seen when employees vote for them with their feet, or not, as the case should be.

Post-pandemic, the need for a much broader set of flexible work and work-life balance policies is one of the top priorities for People functions around the world. While this is challenging to get right, and may have been forced on us as a global workforce, it feels like organisations have finally met their people at their own level – offering true choices that facilitate employees positioning work, home, social and personal life as they see fit. Leaders should set clear boundaries around all employee policies. However, in return for offering as much flexibility as possible, and in the knowledge that the boundaries will ensure the business continues running successfully, this should result in a productive, happy, healthy and thriving workforce.

Chapter 14

Total reward – remuneration

Introduction

Often called total reward, remuneration and benefits are the financial elements of the employee contract. The CIPD[145] defines six components of employee experience, where total reward falls into the first component:

- Performance and recognition;
- Work life balance;
- Organisation culture;
- Employee development and career opportunities;
- Business strategy; and
- HR strategy.

The success of the total reward package will become apparent when nobody is talking about it, due to it meeting everyone's fundamental expectations of their employer. For those driven by monetary reward, pay and bonuses can be a differentiator. For those driven by a holistic benefits package, this too can set the company apart from its competitors. However, in the overall scheme of things, total reward is a hygiene factor for many –

especially those newest into the workforce. Employees expect it to be in place, and for it to be fair and equitable so they can focus on learning, growing and reaching their potential. They want to trust implicitly that it is fair. In this chapter we will discuss the cash element of total reward, that is remuneration or pay. The following chapter will discuss the non-cash element, the benefits and wellbeing programme.

What are we trying to solve for?

The total reward package is a fundamental layer of the psychological (and actual) contract of employment, ingrained in the entire employee experience. According to SHRM, it *"provides monetary, beneficial and developmental rewards to employees who achieve specific business goals. The strategy combines compensation and benefits with personal growth and opportunities inside a motivated work environment".*[146]

It is important to note how the above definition of total reward includes growth, development and recognition along with pay and benefits under the umbrella of total reward, as do many other definitions. That is how ingrained the entire EVP package is to employees. For the purposes of this chapter and the next, we will focus specifically on remuneration, benefits and wellbeing. It's important to note however that the total reward strategy must inextricably link to the entire talent management framework, in particular the talent mobility and talent development elements.

From a remuneration perspective, the organisation must in the first instance retain current staff through regularly assessing and benchmarking pay. Remuneration should at least match the cost of labour for similar roles in similar jurisdictions. From the perspective of new candidates, and with the increase in regulation relating to pay transparency the world over, organisations must create a robust remuneration strategy, decide the price that they will pay for each role, pitch the salary at that level, and stand over it. The objective of pay transparency is to create a more level playing field, where candidates and employees are better informed about the price that organisations are willing to pay for each position. It is not intended to be an opportunity for driving salaries upwards to the highest bidder.

The hiring manager and talent acquisition partner will work closely to ensure salaries offered to candidates are truly reflective of skills they are buying in, saving the highest offers for those skills and knowledge that are in short supply. Equally, it will be the CPO's role, with the support of the CFO and CEO, to create a robust strategy that will attract and keep people in the organisation, and to stick with that strategy – provided it is working. There is ample room for manoeuvre in the other elements of the remuneration strategy. Flexibility can come in the form of bonus payments, which can be fixed or variable depending on the position and long-term incentives. Indeed, a long-term incentive plan focuses current workforce around the achievement of a future goal, thus retaining employees, aligning incentives for success and maintaining salaries and bonuses at appropriate levels.

Remuneration is only one element of why people are attracted to and stay at companies, and provided it is at a level that is acceptable (not necessarily the highest possible level compared with everyone else), that will be sufficient for employees to move on to focusing on growth, development, community and career, which are often much more important to them.

What does success look like?

Total reward strategy

Before zoning in on the remuneration element of the total reward strategy, let's take a look at the bigger picture first. The total reward budget will form a significant part of the overall HR budget, and may include the following:

- Base pay;
- Variable pay (commission, performance bonus, retention payments, counter offers);
- Long term equity plan (LTIP);
- Retirement payments;
- Benefits programme costs; and
- Wellbeing programme costs.

There are a number of ways to approach the HR budget, including; incremental or 'last year plus', adjusting the previous years' budget for changes; zero-based budgeting, where all HR spend must be justified for the new year starting from zero; or flexible budgeting where the budget can be changed for transformation programmes. For incremental budgeting, the adjustments to last year's HR budget should include:

- Incremental and backfill headcount costs (salary, variable pay plus LTIP) based on approved increases in workforce plan for those hired *internally;*
- Incremental and backfill costs (salary, variable pay plus LTIP, plus recruitment costs) based on current or forecast attrition for those hired *externally.* This can be up to 160%+ of the new hires' salary, depending on what processes are used and how efficient they are;
- Current benefits programme cost adjusted for (1) incremental new headcount and (2) increases in programme costs; and
- Additional benefits costs for new programmes, adjusted for any programmes being wound down.

Another consideration to give the total reward strategy, before we focus on the remuneration element, is that it very likely needs to be updated. Hybrid working, pay transparency and work redesign may surface challenges with and gaps in many current total reward strategies. It will be a useful exercise to review the total reward strategy top to bottom and revisit the philosophy and governance around it. For example, will we change the base pay of fully remote employees? Are the lunch voucher and travel pass benefits equitable? How will hybrid working impact employee wellbeing if employees cannot create a boundary between work and home life? What contributions, if any, should we make to home workers? How does the change in focus from individual to team contributions and achievements affect our variable pay structures?

Hybrid working will also highlight how some benefits are no longer relevant or are now inequitable, as well as how pay needs to be linked to contribution and not where the employee lives.

As well as taking the opportunity to review your total reward strategy for recent global trends, consider taking the opportunity to tackle any historical compensation debt in your organisation; that is, where cohorts of employees are paid at different levels depending solely on when they started in the organisation. According to Kathi Enderes, Senior Vice President Research and Global Industry Analyst at The Josh Bersin Company:

> *"Every time you hire somebody, promote a person, decide on develop-ment opportunities, put people on projects, assign goals, or evaluate per-formance, you can introduce inequities that eventually show up as pay issues."* [147]

Build audit steps into your process that doesn't allow it to happen again. A review of the strategy using the following principles is a useful starting point:[148]

- Pay for capability, reward for contribution (e.g. employees log new skills and capabilities through the year for a market-rated pay increase). This requires a clear set of capabilities, skills and contribution for each role. Then reward the contributions as they happen, not just with base pay increases but using all the recognition tools and non-monetary perks in the drawer;
- Lean into team rewards. This drives better collaboration and teamwork. Re-design work around discrete outcomes being delivered by temporary project teams or working groups;
- Empower your people and create a culture of recognition (see chapter 5);
- Recognise the power of non-financial rewards. Time (to innovate or recharge or meet people) and opportunity (new role, challenging project, overseas posting, attended learning) are two of the most impactful tools that employees appreciate; and
- Build or re-build the total reward portfolio and tune as you go: test it, learn from the feedback, iterate the elements that are not working, and go again.
-

Remuneration

Remuneration, or the cash payment for work, can be made up of fixed pay (which is guaranteed and may or may not include allowances), variable pay (which is not guaranteed and usually comes in the form of overtime, bonus, commission or incentives) and a long-term incentive plan (also not guaranteed and usually provided in some form of company shares). Remuneration must be clearly defined, orderly, meet legislative requirements and be fair. It must also clearly link to the performance strategy.

The remuneration framework can be structured in a number of ways. Traditionally all three elements of pay are calculated on the value of completing a job. However, as we saw in the talent development chapter earlier, the latest thinking is that organisations should be retaining and hiring people around broad organisational capabilities rather than a narrow job they are fulfilling. The remuneration framework will need to change if and as organisations pivot to that way of designing work.

Structuring the organisation's remuneration package is complex and will require significant collaboration and alignment between the CEO, CFO and CPO. The core principles of the policy will include considering fixed pay, variable pay and long-term incentives. The policy should be measured for ongoing success, as with all people programmes, and needs to be particularly cognisant of meeting pay transparency and other new legal requirements.

Pay can be structured in a number of ways, including the following commonly used ones:

- **Spot rate:** this is one a number of methods for pricing a position in the organisation and is a fixed 'spot' salary for the work done. It could be an hourly rate, usually used for less complex work, or a price for a fixed piece of work, for example for a temporary contract to backfill a maternity leave.
- **Narrow pay grades:** typically used for public sector or government positions, this framework uses as its basis a job family (which will often be housed in a career framework, see chapter 5). A job family is a construction of roles within a particular function (e.g. within HR, there may be a job family for operations, HRBPs and the different centres of excellence), where each individual role is broken into a number of levels by education, experience

and skills needed for each level. A salary is then created around each pay grade. In this structure, the levels are very narrowly defined and there may be up to 20 points on the pay scale for any one role. Progressing through a pay grade framework is usually based on tenure and pay increments between each level are usually relatively small in value.

- **Broad salary bands:** while this framework also uses job families as their basis, there are wider descriptions for the education, experience and skills required at each level. This results in fewer levels, and larger increments are paid between them.

- **Salary ranges:** using job families with broad salary bands as their basis, the pay levels for salary ranges are structured based on the market value for the role. Often used by private organisations, the remuneration strategy selects a point on the market value for the role at which they are prepared for pay for the role. Usually referred to as the market positioning strategy, an organisation may, for example, decide to pay for a role at the 75th percentile of the market rate; that is, it elects to set the base salary for a particular role at the top quarter of what market participants pay. From there, the organisation builds out a salary band around their selected choice, usually 20% plus or minus the price. Each point on the job family therefore has a salary range associated with it. One of the main advantages of this framework is that employees and candidates can be placed along the range purposely, based on competency for the position: those in the lower third are usually new to the role and still learning elements of the role; those in the middle third are proficient and can do the full role; and those in the top third are experts in the role. However, placing someone in the range is both an 'art and a science'. Employees and candidates will have a history in how much they have been paid (the 'art') and may not sit perfectly in the appropriate of the band (the 'science'). Therefore strict governance, as well as an efficient exception route, is required to use them to their best effect.

An important formula for salary frameworks is the salary compa-ratio. This is the term used to define where an individual employee sits in relation to the salary band, either the company salary band or an industry salary band. It is calculated by dividing the employee's salary by the midpoint on the salary band.

For example, where an employee is paid at the exact midpoint of a company salary band, they are at 100% or 1.0 compa-ratio. Where an organisation builds out a salary band based on 20% plus or minus the midpoint, then it should be expected that most employees are paid between 0.8 and 1.2 of the selected salary point. The compa-ratio is used to establish fair compensation for employees, evaluating the annual payroll budget, determining rates for new hires and to identify inequality and outliers to the salary bands.[149]

There are several other considerations that will form part of the total reward strategy on pay. One such consideration is minimum wage legislation. Many governments set a minimum wage at which to pay employees. The cost of living is the amount of money a person needs to cover *basic* living expenses (food, housing and clothing) in a particular country. The cost of living is therefore dependent on the personal spending level a person somewhat arbitrarily elects to spend. It is also heavily influenced by the rate of inflation, which moves up and down in cycles. In an effort to protect those most vulnerable in society, many governments are introducing a legally required living wage. A living wage is the wage required for a person to achieve a *normal* standard of living, that is, above the basic standard of living provided for with a minimum wage. Defined in Ireland as 60% of the country's hourly median earnings, the minimum wage will achieve the level of a national living wage by 2026. Since 2022 the minimum wage has already been rebranded into the living wage in the UK and is based on a target to reach 66% of UK median earnings by 2024.

In contrast to the cost of living, the cost of labour is the sum of wages, benefits and employer taxes that an employer pays for having employees in a particular country. It is a cost that is somewhat more within the control of the organisation to use to help set a more appropriate level to position pay.

In addition to understanding the minimum legal requirements for pay, an organisation needs to know what its competition is paying for a similar position. Salary information may come from: external benchmarks from consultant companies, recruitment agencies, industry groups or other publicly available information; new hire salary information, including sign-on bonuses; exit interviews; and employee surveys.

In the event an organisation transfers employees across geographies, it will often do so using the compa-ratio to ensure these employees are paid an equivalent salary in the new jurisdiction. For example, if the employee is on 0.9 of their original salary band, they will be moved to that same ratio of the salary band in the new jurisdiction. This can often lead to confusion and frustration for the employee and their manager. It is prudent to explain this concept early and often throughout talent mobility transitions across jurisdictions, in particular if the employee is moving from a location where the role is in demand to one where it is less in demand, or where market rates are different, and therefore where the salary range will be significantly lower than a simple currency exchange rate calculation.

Organisations also need to create governance around how salaries will change when employees move up a level or grade within their current job family, or when they transition to a brand-new job family. There will be significant differences in how this is completed depending on the sector. For example, many public sector organisations use fixed salary points, described earlier in this chapter, giving a certain amount of certainty around annual pay increases. The magnitude of salary increases may also be subject to collective bargaining negotiations in organisations that have unionised employees. In non-unionised private sector organisations, in any given year, the CPO and CFO will decide a base increase for employees, based largely on the economic situation in the relevant jurisdiction. In addition, they may decide to allocate additional base salary increases to particular roles due to a lack of supply of core skills needed to be retained in the organisation. The CPO and CFO may also elect to rectify 'salary debt', where newer employees' salaries in particular roles are moving ahead of the salaries of tenured employees, whose starting salaries were lower but who have the same level of skills and experience as their colleagues hired after base salaries rose solely based on market dynamics; in these cases, cohorts of employees' salaries may be increased for salary equity purposes.

Very often, the promotion cycle will run concurrently with the annual pay cycle (see chapter 9). A salary increase following a promotion will usually be calculated based on specific governance set out in the promotion policy; for example, a promotion increase in a given year may be X%, or it could be increased in line with the minimum of the salary band for the new level – whichever is the greater. Governance such as this helps close 'salary debt' gaps. Whatever structure is in place, it should be well governed, with clear rules around when and why the person is in scope for a level increase.

In all cases, the core of progression expectations should be aligned intrinsically with impact on company goals, displaying company behaviours and being fair and equitable to all employees.

Let's move onto the second element of remuneration, which is variable pay. Like fixed pay, variable pay recognises past performance, and can be offered in a myriad of ways – each with its own advantages and disadvantages. The main tools used and considerations on how to use them include the following:

- **Performance bonus:** usually paid annually in the first quarter after financial close, when the organisation knows how much profit it has made the previous year. A performance bonus can be broken into an employee element (which is paid out at a level commensurate with their most recent performance rating) a team element, and an organisation element (which is linked to company profit). Therefore, a high achiever may benefit from both being paid out at a high level, whereas even a less stellar performer may benefit somewhat when the company is financially successful. For example, a performance bonus may be weighted by 75% personal objectives / 25% organisational objectives being achieved.
- **Sales commission:** usually paid to a revenue-generating team regularly throughout the performance year. Commission can be structured in various ways, usually along a mix of individual and team performance. Commission will be based on a target revenue figure and will often be paid quarterly. Senior sales leaders may have their commission calculated based on team targets only. The balance of fixed pay vs. commission is a hot topic for sales professionals.
- **Overtime:** usually paid when employees work more than their contracted hours. This can be paid at base rate or, often for night or weekend work, at a 1.5x or 2x rate. The

organisation should have a clear overtime policy, including what teams are in scope for such payments and how they are to be claimed and governed, and some limits on overtime from a health and legal perspective. If overtime is to be paid, the relevant clause will usually appear in the employee's contract.

- **Retention bonus**: this is usually a one-off payment, specifically used to incentivise a very high performer; an employee who has key skills and capabilities that the organisation cannot do without, and / or where there is a single point of failure in the workforce (i.e. where only one person can do a specific job).

- **Counteroffer bonus**: similar to a retention bonus to incentivise a high performer, this type of one-off bonus is paid to a specific employee to keep them in the organisation. In this case it is a retroactive tool, used only when the employee is going to leave to do a similar role for a higher salary. These should be used judiciously, and you need to consider the impact on the rest of the job family when you do this. Indeed, benchmarking against the market and adjusting salary may be a better tool than being held to ransom with one-off payments.

The key thing to be cognisant of with variable pay is that it can – and usually is – paid differentially to specific cohorts of the workforce. The overall bonus strategy should therefore be considered holistically to ensure it will be successful. In other words it should be designed to attract a candidate or keep an employee who is, or has the potential to, contribute to business success significantly. Some variable pay elements, such as bonus structures, can be transparently available for all employees to read on the company intranet site – John Lewis is an obvious example of this. Others however should be managed confidentially and sensitively. The amount of information shared in terms of bonus elements of pay will, like the other elements of reward, be dependent on the maturity of the organisation. Pay transparency and pay equity will certainly be a driver for organisations to consider increasingly how this type of information is shared, as well how much of it is shared and when it is shared across the organisation, and indeed beyond it.

A long-term incentive plan (LTIP) is an element of the salary package that is offered at the time of hiring but will be paid out in the future, provided the business and employee achieve certain business goals. An example is Restricted Share Units, which is a promise of company shares or cash in the future once a certain period of time and / or performance measure is achieved. These are complex and require specific expertise to be delivered effectively but can be very impactful in aligning incentives for the organisation and are worth consideration, especially when the company is in growth mode. An LTIP programme will often be offered only to more senior employees, who truly can impact upon the achievement of significant organisational goals.

A further consideration on pay governance and policy arises when some or all of the workforce is part of a trade union. While a union generally contracts with its members to negotiate on all matters related to the employee's contract of work, it is often in the area of pay negotiations that the relationship is tested to its maximum. That said, when both negotiating parties have a reasonably aligned view on a positive agreement, those outcomes can be powerful for all sides.

For example, the 1980s in Ireland was a decade of recession, emigration and peak trade union strikes; inflation was more than 15%, unemployment was 18%, and the national debt was at 115% of GDP.[150] In 1987, the first national pay agreement called the Programme for National Recovery between the government, trade unions and employers was agreed. Five more national pay agreements, over the following 20 years, contributed to Ireland having one of the strongest economies across Europe – collaboration and agreement between the employers and unions were a foundational building block for that change to occur. Ireland became revered for being a hugely successful small open economy, with unemployment reaching an all-time low of 3.9% in October 2000[151] unemployment (which it coincidentally also is in April 2023), historically low inflation rates and foreign direct investment flowing inwards, along with a multicultural workforce to supply it.

At the heart of successful union negotiations is a respectful partnership. While not always easy to establish or indeed retain, it will be in the organisation's best interest to do so. It is beyond the scope of this handbook to discuss union negotiations in depth. Suffice to say, there will likely be a reasonably well-trodden path in traditionally unionised sectors, where inputs to pay discussions will include labour market trends, industry-specific nuances (joint labour agreements), and the company's ability to pay. These are exactly the same considerations that are given to the pay framework for non-unionised employees, and both should be approached in the same vein. The relationship with the employees' union representatives is a really important one, that should be invested in. Both stakeholders have the same end goal – regard for the employees who are doing the work, while keeping the organisation open for business and competitive.

All remuneration awards are based on the company's ability to pay. This may be influenced by company profit, the cost of living and market rate fluctuations (which can happen for example when there is a particular skill shortage), all of which can change within a calendar year. Union pressure, public pay policy and industry competitors also influence how much a company will award its employees.

Remuneration is a hot topic for a number of reasons right now – the global recession driving up inflation and the cost of living, swathes of employees being made redundant from companies, and the desire for people to create their own careers outside of the control of organisations are just a few factors at play. It is therefore important for the total reward strategy to be adaptable to meet the fresh expectations arising from these global trends.

Pay equity is a highly debated element of the total reward arena and needs a clear plan of action in the strategy. Several jurisdictions already require mandatory pay disclosure by law, including gender pay and the inclusion of salary in job advertisements, and that number is increasing. The objective of pay disclosure legislation is to close the gender pay gap. The legislation differs by region with the following being the core elements in general:

- **Pay equity:** defined as equal pay for equal work, this meets a basic requirement for people doing the same job being paid the same. Pay equity needs to be in place across all elements of remuneration (base pay, variable pay, LTIP); and
- **Pay equality:** a more robust measure, this is the difference between what males and females are paid in an organisation. While there are specific definitions for each element of the calculation, it is generally measured by calculating the average hourly rate for all employees on a snapshot date and comparing the mean (average) and median (midpoint) pay for the males and the females in the organisation. The key to addressing pay equality is having a more balanced number of people in male and female roles, in particular in the most senior roles in the organisation, on top of fundamentally having pay equity.

Pay equality compares the pay of all working men and all working women, not just those in the same jobs with the same working patterns or the same competencies, qualifications or experience. A gap emerges when more females are in lower paid jobs and more males are in higher paid jobs. There are deep-rooted reasons for the current gender pay gap, which will take time to re-balance. Some of these reasons include: Executive teams being traditionally male; the marriage ban, leading to many Baby Boomers and some Gen X being legally required to leave the workforce when they got married, resulting in them falling behind their male counterparts from a career progression perspective; a lack of structural support for the Gen X and Gen Y / millennial workforce who are working, and women leaving the workforce after having children (e.g. due to personal choice or lack of affordable childcare facilities).

The gap is possibly going to get temporarily worse before it gets better due to the pandemic, which had a disproportionately negative impact on female and other under-represented groups. This however may be countered by recent reports of Baby Boomers (those aged 58-75 at the time of writing) who have been pushed out of the post-pandemic workforce due to planned retirement or redundancy, with many of this workforce cohort being male.[152]

The solution to closing the gender pay gap needs to be multi-faceted. We saw some of these solutions in earlier sections of the book: integrating DEI actions into the Talent Acquisition strategy; consistently and regularly educating managers on bias when making pay, performance and internal mobility decisions; providing bespoke training and community to elevate women and other under-represented groups; levelling the playing field with benefits (e.g. giving birth father as much time away as birth mother).

Each jurisdiction will have its own rules about what organisations are in scope for publicly reporting their gender pay gaps. It's safe to say the majority of organisations in most countries across the world will need to do this sooner rather than later. For most, there will be a gap, and for some, the gap will be significant. If you are not legally obliged to do it already, consider starting work on reducing the organisation's gender pay gap now and begin to tell the story of a downward trend over time as soon as possible. Comparisons with industry norms will also form part of the organisation's story, and whether its appreciated or not, it will form part of employee and candidate discussions around the company EVP. Be open, honest and credible with the organisation's gender pay gap report. Discuss it openly with employees – ideally before it is reported externally. One of the best places from which to crowdsource solutions, is your employees themselves. If there is an issue, own it and deal with it.

A relatively new field of thought on remuneration is real time compensation. This is where remuneration is given in real time to recognise work done in that moment. Many organisations do this already with performance bonuses: rather than paying an annual bonus long after the contribution has been made, this structure giving managers their bonus pot to use over a period of time (quarter, half year, annual) for on-the-spot financial recognition of an outsized contribution. This not only resonates with the recipient, when the employee's contribution (as opposed to the details of their financial award) is celebrated openly with the team, but everyone else gets to see what great looks like and what types of contribution get rewarded. The icing on the cake? Having a 'real time' bonus framework also takes one people-related action off managers at an otherwise busy time of the year, when we ask them to deliver year-end conversations, ratings, bonuses and goals a month after year end. And it should be a significant reward – we're not talking here about a small spot bonus to buy a coffee. This is the administration of significant financial bonuses at the time that the contribution is made. As with any bonus system, the organisation will need to create a clear policy around its use, who is in scope, how it will be governed, how managers will be upskilled to use it appropriately, and an audit step to catch any outliers. It should of course also be measured for success in actually attracting and retaining people in(to) the organisation. As Tamra Chandler, performance thought leader and CEO and cofounder of PeopleFirm, explains: *"Timely, bite-size rewards not only provide immediate feedback and reinforce desired behaviours, they also minimize the risk of recency bias and inequities that are often the product of annual review decisions."*[153]

Questions for a new CPO

- How does your total reward strategy attract and retain employees?
- When did you last review the total reward strategy?
- What do the relevant metrics tell you about the strengths and weaknesses of your strategy?
- Is the strategy fit-for-purpose for all cohorts of the workforce, or could a change in structure help attract / retain key cohorts?
- Do the pay and bonus elements both align with the performance strategy?
- Does the pay element of the strategy clearly align with the promotion process?
- Do employees understand all the elements of their pay?
- What does your gender pay gap report say about the pay and bonus structures in the organisation?
- If not yet in scope for gender pay gap reporting, are you considering measuring it early to begin to close the gap?
- Is the organisation doing everything possible to close the gender pay gap as quickly as possible? If not, why not?

Summary

Not surprisingly, remuneration has rapidly moved up the employee priority list over the last 24 months; covering monthly expenses went from number nine to number one in employee sentiment between 2021 and 2022 in one survey.[154] While it is really important, it is still one of the most basic elements of the employee contract. It needs to be acceptable to the employee so they can focus on growth, development and doing impactful work. The organisation is not in a good place if employees are having conversations about pay and bonuses – it means they are likely not fully concentrating on doing a great job for the organisation and reaching their career potential. As leadership guru Josh Bersin says:

> *"People are the one of the only appreciating assets we have in business, and when we continually think about 'minimizing labor costs' we think the wrong way".[155]*

Chapter 15

Total reward — benefits and wellbeing programme

Introduction

Most organisations will provide some form of benefits package to employees. Traditionally this may have included elements required by law as well as more discretionary items offered by the organisation to attract and retain employees: examples include healthcare, a pension, time away from work, salary sacrifice options for reduced cost travel and time off for community work. All those offerings remain relevant today. However, the expectations of the employer's duty of care have changed with the most recent generations joining the workforce, as well as due to global shifts in how where and when work gets done.

A benefits programme will need to evolve over time in line with changes in how, where, when and why we work. This represents a constant opportunity to make the company a really attractive place to spend time. Many expectations are centred around wellbeing. It is likely that the more traditional benefits programmes being offered already contain wellbeing offerings and have simply not been labelled as such. More needs to be done to keep the programme meeting needs and this chapter will take a look at all the offerings that the organisation might currently consider.

What are we solving for?

A modern benefits programme should embrace customisation, personalisation and choice. The current workforce – made up of as many as five generations in one organisation – will have broad and diverse needs. Where an organisation can afford it, the ideal programme will have some fixed elements to it to protect the company and employees (e.g. paid time off and pensions) with the majority of the remaining benefits allowances being offered to employees on a flexible self-selection basis. The benefits platform should be self-service, as far as practicable, offering employees basic information on all offerings with further education provided by the relevant external experts. It should provide robust data to facilitate measuring the ongoing success of every element of the programme.

Workplace wellbeing is going to remain a focus of employees for some time to come. The benefits programme will need to meet the current expectations for increased social and emotional elements of employee wellbeing, as well as the more traditional expectations of physical and financial supports. The programme offered will be dependent on organisation size, maturity and affordability, however the good news is that less is possibly more, from a couple of different perspectives. For example, some benefits will no longer be attractive to employees (e.g. travel discounts for remote workers); and in terms of overall workload, moving to a flexible benefits programme where employees are given a benefit allowance (usually a fixed percentage of salary) to select their own benefits from a set offering, can reduce the administration of the programme on HR and transfer control to employees. Regardless of the programme offered, it's crucial to communicate with employees regularly on how well the programme is meeting the workforce needs, to ensure that it meets the needs of everyone, and that it can be adapted to continue to meet those needs.

What does success look like?

Defined by the CIPD as *"non-cash provisions within the reward package, although they can have a financial cost for employers"*,[156] benefits are provided by organisations to meet legislation requirements, to attract and retain employees, to keep employees in good health, and even out of a moral obligation. Therefore, while it's crucial to have a great offering, it's important to realise that it will be impossible to have an offering that will suit every employee at all times over the course of their journey with the organisation. Additionally, as we will see later in this chapter on wellbeing benefits specifically, choice and customisation are key.

As with all people programmes, it's crucial to put robust governance and thought into your benefits programme. Some of the considerations that should be given to it include the following:

- **Aims of the benefits scheme:** depending on the culture, maturity and financial status of the organisation, what is management seeking to do? Meet minimum legal requirements and manage cost, or offer something market-leading that will differentiate it?
- **Scope:** who is in scope for each benefit? This includes worker type (i.e. permanent, temporary, full-time, part time), tenure (i.e. access on after probation or other initial period with the company) and employee cohort (although you would need a strong case to only offer certain benefits to certain employees).
- **Fixed or flexible:** decide what structure you want to put on your programme. A fixed benefit offering is a specific

list of benefits that employees are automatically given. A flexible benefits scheme is one where a certain percentage of employee's base salary, possibly differing by level, is paid to the employee on top of their salary to be spent on benefits that they feel best suit them. There will often be a fixed element even to a scheme that offers flexible benefits, to ensure the employer meets local legislation; for example an employee cannot elect to take zero annual leave days. The main advantage of a flexible scheme is customisation, which we have seen is becoming more and more important in every aspect of the employee experience.

The average benefit account works out at 30% of the employee's base salary, although the spread can be between 20% and 50% of salary. It's important to consider your benefits offering as part of the larger EVP.[157] Where a benefits allowance is not spent, it can be returned to the employee at the end of the financial year, subject to usual income tax deductions.

The downside of a flexible benefits scheme is the loss in savings for the organisation from group schemes, which will have a greater impact on the offerings that smaller and medium-sized firms can provide.

- **Inclusive and equitable:** the benefits programme must be inclusive and equitable for all – it must not only be fit-for-purpose for some of the workforce. This will require thought, possibly additional investment (i.e. to provide a benefit to a smaller, under-represented population of the workforce), collaboration with the DEI team and feedback from the workforce on whether it is sufficiently inclusive to meet the entire workforce's needs equitably.
- **Benefits platform:** as with all things people related, there is a proliferation of great platforms available to host the benefits programme. The platform requirements should

include the following: be available online or offline via a number of devices, so that employees can manage their benefits in their own time and space; be device-agnostic; be self-service, where employees can select and deselect themselves in and out of benefits as they need (and as the governance of the programme allows of course); be easily adaptable for the employer to add and remove benefits as they need; offer flexibility to the employee to make changes to their benefits at a time that suits them; and – crucially – have a platform that talks to the HRIS, so the flow of information between the two systems is seamless, accurate and where possible, real time.

The ideal platform will support the employee owning responsibility for selection and delivery of their own personal benefits package. The business case should also include the cost avoided of the people team completing manual benefits processes as well as the human time savings (by both the employees and the HR team) that a self-service platform offers.

- **Measurement:** benefits programmes have increased in cost over the last number of decades to more than 30% on average, an increase of 30% according to numerous sources.[158] Calculate the return on investment that the organisation's benefits package brings. A detailed cost-benefit analysis will not only compare offerings but will also provide you more broadly with the savings that are made by having particular offerings in place. Some will be financially measurable (e.g. the reduction in sick pay and absence days from providing the Employee Assistance Programme or the reduction in travel pass costs due to hybrid working) and some will be less tangible but worth estimating (e.g. the increase in tenure due to access to medical and dental healthcare). A bespoke benefits platform will provide the data, analytics and trends you need to stand over the programme offering. Close down those programmes that aren't being used but be sure to have transparent communication and discussion with employees on why this is happening and provide alternatives.

- **Communication:** open, honest and regular dialogue with the workforce will tell you all you need to know about what is working and not working and why. This ongoing conversation will also give you the foresight for what benefits employees will seek next and allow you time to consider them. Use the EVP, employee survey, listening events, employee resource groups and even 'benefits drop-in' hours to get feedback. If you are considering changes, do it using change management disciplines, testing the change, providing the opportunity to feed into it, testing the final proposal, getting early buy in, building allies, and then launching it. Listen to all the voices in the feedback – people of different ages, genders, cultural backgrounds and those in under-represented populations have different needs. While it's important to get scale where needed or mandate benefits where needed, it's also important to have an offering that is beneficial to everyone.

Traditional benefits programme offerings

There are several benefits that are typically offered by most organisations, no matter what size they are, as they are required by law or need to be offered to hire key skills into the company. The list below provides for those elements of a benefits package that are more typically offered. After that, we will consider the newer offerings being sought by employees, much of which fall under the umbrella of 'wellbeing benefits'. For now, the more traditional package may include:

- **Pension:** an occupational pension scheme is a long-term savings plan into which employees contribute, often in a tax-efficient manner through their employers, to provide a regular income on retirement. Many organisations have traditionally offered a pension scheme to employees, provided they have a certain minimum number of employees in a jurisdiction to make it viable, or where required by law. A defined benefit (DB) scheme is one in which a fixed income will be provided to the employee on retirement. These schemes have been, for the most part, phased out, although many tenured employees will still have one, as will many ex-employees. Defined contribution (DC) schemes are much more prevalent. In these schemes employees and employers pay specifically agreed amounts into a retirement fund. The income paid on retirement from a DC scheme will depend on the contributions paid in, the length of time the payments are in the fund, and the fund performance.[159] The advantage of DC schemes is that they can be customised to some degree by what the employee wishes to pay into their pension fund.

  In the UK, organisations are obliged to automatically enrol their employees in a workplace pension scheme[160]. In 2024 in Ireland, a new law on occupational pension schemes is expected to come into force, requiring employees not in an existing occupational scheme to be automatically enrolled in the proposed government run pension scheme by their employer. Employees will have a minimum of 1.5% of gross earnings deducted, which increases to a minimum of 6% over the first 10 years of the new legislation. Organisations must match the pension contributions saved by their employees, and the state will provide an additional top up. Employers will not need to establish their own pension scheme, and the contributions made by them will be deductible against corporate tax.

Pension auto-enrolment has been in place since 2012, albeit on a gradual level initially, in the UK and has also been implemented successfully in Australia. Pension contributions are generally tax deductible for employees. All DC pension schemes will allow employees contribute additional amounts, called additional voluntary contributions (AVCs) to increase retirement income or to facilitate employees starting retirement earlier than the statutory retirement age. AVCs often attract preferable tax treatment, up to a limit.

Due to a concept called 'vested rights' an employer can typically claim a refund on employer contributions to a pension if an employee leaves within two years of starting employment[161]. Similarly, an employee can also claim a refund of their own employee contributions if they leave within the two-year vested rights period. If an employee claims a refund of their contributions, they pay income tax on the amounts refunded at and the employer contributions are returned to their former employer.

- **Paid time off:** as we saw in chapters 11 and 12, paid time off – including annual holiday leave, maternity / paternity parental leave, jury leave and sick leave – is mandatory for employees in the UK and Ireland under a number of situations. Many organisations, in particular larger, more mature and profitable companies, will offer employees paid leave above what is required by law. These benefits may have the additional attraction of supporting people strategies in parallel. For example, offering the non-birth parent, who is often male, the same length of paid leave when they have a baby provides increased internal mobility opportunities for other employees to step into their positions for the duration of the leave, ultimately resulting in increasing their potential to move into new and more senior roles rapidly and more permanently.

This also supports reducing the gender pay gap in an organisation, while increasing the visibility of under-represented populations, levelling the playing field by elevating opportunities for career growth. Extending sick leave encourages employees to stay at home until they are well enough to return to work, thereby reducing the risk of infecting others if their illness is contagious, or indeed reducing the risk of multiple sick leaves due to returning to work too soon. Other benefits that can be offered under this heading include bereavement / compassionate leave, carer leave, sabbatical, career break or marriage leave, all of which may be paid, unpaid or partially paid.

- **Healthcare benefits:** examples of these benefits include employee assistance programmes (EAPs), life assurance, death in service insurance (part of some pension schemes), vaccinations, access to private medical and dental cover, personal accident insurance, critical illness insurance or permanent health insurance cover. All these benefits support the welfare and productivity of employees. If a company does not offer an actual group scheme, it may offer an amount of money in lieu of the employee joining their own healthcare scheme. It is prudent for the organisation to consider investing in these schemes; a cost-benefit analysis that shows the cost savings from reducing sick leave, long-term absence, temporary backfill costs and other disruption costs to the workforce, can often outweigh the cost of the scheme itself.

- **Salary sacrifice benefits:** voluntary benefits are sometimes offered as part of a flexible benefits scheme which ultimately result in the employee getting something at a reduced price, in a tax-efficient way. Voluntary benefits must be provided by and administered by the company and taken directly out of salary. An example of this type of benefit is when employees give up some of their pay for a travel pass at reduced price. These benefits are often subject to benefit in kind tax.

- **Other benefits:**
  - Some organisations offer a company car or car allowance to employees, in particular when there is a job need or where it's associated with reaching a certain level in the organisation.
  - Another financial benefit offered is where the organisation provides access to a financial advisor. This benefit may be offered in a personalised 1:1 setting for specific employees, or with more general advice in a group setting to all employees.
  - Snacks and abundant food and drinks may be offered as a free or discounted benefit and have been a popular feature of recent years.
  - Corporate Social Responsibility (CSR) activities have traditionally included time away from work to do something to benefit the community.
- **Benefit in kind:** it's important to note that there are some tax implications for certain benefits offered to employees. Benefit in kind (BIK) is the tax that an employee has to pay in respect of a non-cash benefit which has a monetary value. It usually occurs where an employee is given access to a product or service at a reduced rate, when purchased via the employer. Given the employee is making a gain by having access to a product or service at reduced cost, these benefits are deemed to be taxable income and a BIK tax will be applied to the amount saved by the employee. The amount of tax to be paid by the employee will be a certain percent of the reduced price. BIK is paid directly out of the employees' salary, and the amount of BIK tax paid will appear on the employee's payslip. An example of this may be a company car or car allowance being subject to BIK.

Benefits need be adaptable as employee expectations of them change over time. The current hyperfocus on financial benefits will change cyclically in line with inflation and cost of living concerns.

Different generations of the workforce will want different benefits to support where they are in their lives. The change in how, where and when we work will make some current offerings redundant imminently. And we don't even know what the Gen Z population will need or ask for (who, by the way will represent more than 30% of the workforce by 2030) because they don't even know yet.

<u>Workplace wellbeing programme</u>

The new employer-employee contract includes expectations from the employee that the organisation will support their wellbeing. Pre-pandemic, many organisations had some benefits offerings that supported physical wellbeing – gym membership, display screen equipment checks and eye tests, bike-to-work schemes and even access to resources for healthy eating. Some forward-thinking organisations embraced mental wellbeing years ago too, providing access to an Employee Assistance Programme (EAP), mental health training for managers or similar support offerings.

Fast forward to 2023. Due to a global pandemic, an ever-evolving workforce, and a world in which purpose and kindness are increasingly important, a comprehensive workplace wellbeing programme is just as much part of the proposition as pay and traditional benefits.

The biggest wellbeing challenge from the People function perspective is where to place the boundaries around the programme. The employer has a duty of care to its employees in providing a safe and healthy place to work, a workload that is manageable and achievable, as well as offering growth and stretch career opportunities. The challenge is where the duty of care around the provision of wellbeing support ends for the employer. This is especially keenly felt now, at a time in our evolution when there is an employee expectation that that same duty of care has expanded extensively, topped off with an appetite for personalisation. While wellbeing offerings can support the employee to be the best version of themselves, ultimate accountability with achieving that wellbeing actually lies with the employee.

As we saw earlier, a benefits programme is something that keeps the organisation compliant and mitigates the risk of not meeting business goals. Work-related burnout is an employer issue. It can be caused by a number of things that are the responsibility of the employer, including work design, role clarity, workload or a mismatch of competencies to the job at hand. For that reason, employee burnout can result in a breach of employment law. Legislation protects workers, obliging employers to put in minimum standards of wellbeing support – for example, the Equality Act 2010, the Health and Safety at Work Regulations 1999; and the Mental Health (Discrimination) Act 2013 in the UK – and there is similar EU legislation and comparable laws in the US. But don't set the standard at the level of not breaking the law – that won't attract or retain anyone. The gold standard is when employees thrive and flourish in the organisation. They will be highly motivated, resilient and will bring enjoyment, fulfilment and fun to the working day if allowed. The key, as with all people-related programmes, wellbeing included, is to be authentic – don't just tick the box – and set clear programme boundaries.

Take a holistic approach to all elements of your employee's wellbeing: create a wellbeing policy and put in place a number of programmes that support wellbeing throughout the employee journey and, like the overall benefits programme, have it customisable where possible. There are plenty of publicly shared frameworks to help you measure up how you are doing. Many frameworks, such as Deloitte's, centre around four key areas, *"the employee's physical condition, emotional resilience, social connections and financial health."*[162]

Another useful model to help you start or improve your position is the extensive Mental Health First Aid Line Manager resource which frames wellbeing support around the employee journey:[163]

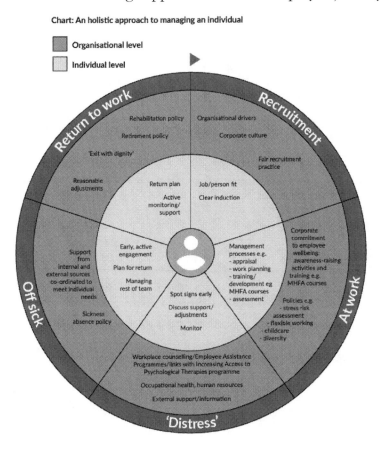

Figure 15.1: Sample mental health support resource for managers

Whatever wellbeing strategy you decide to put in place, take the same systematic approach to it as you do to the broader benefits programme: define a framework, philosophy, policy governance, measurement and communication standards.

As with all benefits, the guiding principle around wellbeing should not only focus on minimising the negative impact work can have on your employees but rather should focus on creating a workplace and work that supports them being able to be their best selves, insofar as your organisation can afford it. Therefore, it does not only include the hygiene and safety factors of wellbeing, rather it should embrace belonging and growth, and it should be aligned to your company values, your DEI strategy and your ESG / CSR purpose. Create a unique programme for your organisation, with your Executive team and with your employees. Create something you know will work.

Blending together the more traditional elements of a benefits programme, with the newer expectations of wellbeing-specific options (which are highlighted in the shaded boxes), the following is a non-exhaustive list of potential programme offerings under the four headings of physical, financial, emotional, social benefits. Not unexpectedly, the more traditional offerings are found in the physical and financial wellbeing categories. The newer categories of emotional and social wellbeing are likely to be where organisations can focus building out their offerings, with the emotional wellbeing category requiring the most development to meet the employer obligations of dealing with burnout:

Physical wellbeing		Financial wellbeing	Emotional wellbeing	Social wellbeing
Paid time off (e.g. Family or sick leave)	Medical check ups	Salary sacrifice (e.g. Car, travel pass)	Employee assistance programme	Employee town halls / conferences
Gym or other sports membership	Bike to work scheme	Retirement planning (pension)	Bereavement support	CSR volunteering days
Flu and other vaccinations	Personal Accident	Financial advice	Mental health apps	Jury leave
Medical and Dental Healthcare	Eye test and VDU checks	Discounted banking package	DEI training and networks	Sabbatical / career break
Life assurance	Permanent health insurance	Free or discounted breakfast, lunch and beverages	Mental health training and network	Employee discounts & perks
Death-in-Service	Critical Illness cover	Training on payslips and local tax laws	Resilience training	Cultural celebration events
Ergonomic checks	Fertility and surrogacy support	Increasing periods of paid leave / ability to buy holiday	Quiet time-away room	DEI employee resource groups
Breastfeeding and menopause support	Gender re-assignment support	Debt counselling or hardship loans	Domestic abuse support	

Table 15.1: Contemporary benefits and wellbeing programme

As always, managers have an additional responsibility to provide wellbeing support to their team members. According to a study published in *Forbes* in 2023, almost 70% of people said their managers had the greatest impact on their mental health, which was more than their doctor or therapist did.[164] That's enough to add another layer of personal stress to any people manager in itself, much less investing in their *own* personal wellbeing. Upskill your people managers on how to spot early signs of employee distress, provide them with the basic skills to triage the concerns with their employees and equip them with an accessible list of experts to contact immediately to get help on next steps. Encourage your managers to check in with their employee regularly, to be empathic and patient, and to seek support from the people team at any point. This will help put key information at the fingertips of managers, with the aim of equipping the employee with options for them to take away and sign up to as they see fit for their own personal situation and stressors.

Finally, ensure that your HRBPs are supporting managers who are helping an employee through a difficult patch, to ensure the manager themself is coping and supported.

Benefits and wellbeing metrics

Putting measures around the benefits programme can be a challenge. The following is a useful list of metrics to measure all your benefits offerings – wellbeing and traditional. Where you are able, categorise each data point further into workforce groups with your DEI information to ensure the programme is equally successful across the whole workforce:

- Employee engagement and satisfaction (engagement, happiness, work-life balance, job satisfaction, workload, intention to stay, recommend the company to a friend);
- Absence data (number of days, types of absence, trends, splits by employee type, wellbeing programme costs, healthcare costs);
- Occupational health data (usage, areas of concern, trends, costs);

- Retention data (new hire turnover, number of roles per person, number of promotions per person, progress through the talent planning boxes, regretted attrition);
- Leave data (use of leave programmes, by whom, trends, splits by employee type);
- Working hours data (breaches of total hours worked, not taking at least one day off in seven, not having an overnight break of 11 hours, trends, splits by employee type, overtime costs);
- Productivity data (workforce costs, revenue per employee, meeting hours, customer data like NPS or SLA metrics);
- External employee review data (Glassdoor, Indeed, other job websites);
- Turnover data (who is leaving, at what stage in their employee journey, voluntary vs. involuntary leavers, qualitative exit interview data);
- Wellbeing programme communication and updates (sign ups by programme, costs per sign up, knowledge of programmes); and
- Training programme updates (sign ups, attendance vs. non-attendance, splits by course type (mandatory vs. elective) and employee type, costs).

A 2023 Harvard Business School study found that that medical costs fall by $3.27 for every dollar spent on wellbeing programmes, and absentee costs fall by $2.73 for every dollar spent.[165] This, and other similar 'cost / benefit' data, should be used liberally in your benefits programmes business case submissions to your CFO.

While the benefits programme should meet the needs of your entire workforce where possible, the biggest – and likely most vocal – critics of the programme will be those newest to the workforce, the millennial and Gen Z populations. We already know that personalisation is one of the things they want most with their benefits – for example, not having to wait for the annual window to make changes or being able to find their own wellbeing solution. In addition, nobody knows what the next version of desired benefits will be, or which ones will no longer be relevant. The key is to have a system and build processes around it that facilitate change – it's the one thing we can be certain of. In the meantime, consider involving your newest workforce members in the creation and ongoing review of your whole benefits programme. They will become your biggest advocates, inside and outside the organisation, when the programme is right.

Aim to have a great benefits and wellbeing programme. When you do, share it regularly internally and sell it as a competitive advantage externally. In the UK, 'Britain's Healthiest Workplace', a scheme run by health insurance provider Vitality, seeks to *"track the health and productivity of employees and identify the best employers in the private and public sectors"*.[166] In Ireland, IBEC's KeepWell Mark[167] is an accreditation for companies reaching a quality standard of employee wellbeing across a number of categories. Join global forums like the World Wellbeing Movement[168] to show your organisation is serious about it. Link it to purpose. According to LaFawn Davis, Senior VP of ESG at Indeed:

> *"As employees experience well-being in the workplace, they actually keep a company's purpose in mind and the outcomes that a company wants to have. They're able to problem-solve better, be more innovative, and work for you longer because they're actually there."*[169]

Questions for a new CPO

- When was the last time you reviewed your benefits and wellbeing programme?
- What has been the governance around additions to and removals from the programme?
- What percentage of employees take up each element of self-selected options?

- What is the return on investment for each element of your programme? What can be retired?
- Have you considered a different mix of fixed and flexible benefits?
- How much time is the management of the programme taking your People team?
- How much of the process is automated on a platform that is self-service?
- What do your employees say about the benefits and wellbeing programme?
- What do candidates say about how enticing the programme is?
- What do the metrics say about how successful the programme is?

Summary

Pay, benefits and wellbeing – if employees are not talking about them, then they're being done right. However, even when the workforce is not talking about it, stay close to it, measure it often, check it is fit-for-purpose for your current and next cohort of employees, in order to get early sight of when and what needs to be adapted next. These are the most fundamental elements of the employee contract, and employee needs, that must be met. Trust will be lost quickly when they are not. On the plus side, employees don't want to be talking about pay and benefits – they prefer to concentrate on doing great work, reaching their potential and satisfying the higher echelons of the needs hierarchy.

Be very clear that while you, as the employer, will create the ecosystem for flourishing to take place, the employee has ultimate responsibility for it actually happening. Once you have good working practices in place, that offer employees a great EVP and challenging work, you are permitted to create a boundary where your duty of care as the employer stops. A robust, generous benefits programme which can be personalised where appropriate, offered over a self-service platform should meet employee expectations in that regard. In the wise words of Neil O'Brien, executive business coach and strategic advisor,

> *"... wellbeing version 2.0 isn't about increasing this [wellbeing] list to 1,000 things, it's about doing one thing, like making work more enjoyable, well. Call it an advanced wellbeing strategy and an advanced strategy is always a reduction. Less is more."*[170]

In support of human wellbeing, O'Brien adds that people should *"just spend more time with good people"*. Doing satisfying work with great people around you, has its own intrinsic reward too.

Chapter 16

Diversity, Equity and Inclusion

Introduction

It started as diversity (a fact) and inclusion (a process), in which diversity is the representation of people with different attributes in the organisation and inclusion is the framework set up to ensure those in under-represented group are elevated and proactively involved in it.

Verna Myer's, a well-known American activist, phrase *"diversity is being invited to the party; inclusion is being asked to dance"*[171], became an important message elevating these two different but related concepts in 2017. Since then, the Diversity, Equity and Inclusion (DEI) movement has evolved to include equity, accessibility, belonging, equality and justice to deepen our understanding of the importance of having every voice at the table in our organisations.

Notwithstanding this being the right thing to do, it's proven extensively that organisations with full representation in their workforce perform better, as a 2020 McKinsey report entitled *Diversity wins: How inclusion matters* attests: *"Our latest report shows not only that the business case remains robust but also that the relationship between diversity on executive teams and the likelihood of financial outperformance has strengthened over time."* [172]

Most organisations are on a journey to achieving diverse representation. As a loyal colleague said to Anne a number of years ago when she showed her vulnerability in this area and expressed concern about getting the terminology right for her organisation's Trans Celebration Week, *"it's ok to get it wrong, Anne, so long as you try"*.

It is crucial for organisations to keep trying until they get their strategy in this area right.

What are we solving for?

According to HR software company TechTarget: *"Diversity, Equity and Inclusion is a term used to describe the set of policies and programmes that promote the representation and participation of different groups of individuals, including people of different ages, races and ethnicities, abilities and disabilities, genders, religions, cultures and sexual orientations. This also covers people with diverse backgrounds, experiences, skills and expertise."* [173]

Masses of people across the globe have not had the same access to opportunities to reach their potential in life. In the world of business, this has resulted in organisations traditionally being run by one dominant group – white, heterosexual, able-bodied men. However, everyone has some form of privilege, and it is important for organisations to have open, healthy conversations about what privilege is, in order to achieve full employee representation in the workplace. The article by Inclusive Employers describes the challenge well and why we need to proactively tackle it:

"The concept of privilege now helps us to understand the way wider society has developed through time to give advantage to certain groups over others. Privilege is essentially the unearned *advantages we have because of different aspects of our identity. It's about whether or not the world has been designed with us in mind. Therefore, privilege is power."* [174]

Employers are encouraged in their efforts to address underrepresentation by a significant increase in legislation, some of which we described in chapter 11, however these rules only meet the lowest bar. Organisations need to create and prioritise DEI in their People strategies until ultimately every employee is represented, treated with respect and dignity and is given the same opportunity to succeed as everyone else.

Let's consider some of the ways that can be achieved, starting with some working definitions around what we are seeking to achieve:

- **Diversity:** according to the University of Washington: *"Diversity is the presence of differences that enrich our workplace. Some examples of diversity may include race, gender, religion, sexual orientation, ethnicity, nationality, socioeconomic status, language (dis)ability, age, religious commitment, or political perspective."*[175]
- **Accessibility**: according to ACAS: *"Accessibility at work is about removing barriers to make sure nobody is excluded from taking an active part in working life."*[176] An example could be a person with hearing difficulty able to engage fully in a virtual meeting.
- **Equality:** Human Rights Careers explains that *"...equality in the workplace runs deeper than simply the absence of discrimination. Businesses must also provide opportunities to all employees equally, so everyone has the chance to improve their skills".*[177]
- For example, everyone gets access to equal pay, to all relevant internal jobs, to learning and development, mentoring, sponsorship and interesting work opportunities.

- **Equity:** "*Equity is ensuring that access, resources, and opportunities are provided for all to succeed and grow, especially for those who are under-represented and have been historically disadvantaged,*"[178] according to the University of Washington. For example, a Latinx colleague gets specific access to language training in order to increase their job remit.

- **Inclusion:** defining inclusion, the University of Washington states: "*Inclusion is a workplace culture that is welcoming to all people regardless of race, ethnicity, sex, gender identity, age, abilities, and religion and everyone is valued, respected and able to reach their full potential.*"[179]

  Policies and procedures are insufficient for inclusion – the organisation and culture must intentionally, transparently and consistently live and breathe the policies and procedures, creating a space where everyone is provided with the opportunity to get fully involved.

- **Organisational Justice:** HR publication *HR Zone* reports that organisational justice is "*an employee's perception of their organisation's behaviours, decisions and actions and how these influence the employees' own attitudes and behaviours at work*".[180] Therefore processes and procedures need to not only *be* fair and just, they need to be *perceived* as fair and just. Only when employees feel that the playing field is fully level, available and accessed will it be celebrated as such by all.

What does success look like?

<u>DEI strategy</u>

First and foremost, the DEI strategy needs to be created, communicated and celebrated. It needs to be sponsored by the Executive team, owned by the business and driven by HR. An Executive team that discusses, embraces and gets involved in driving its success is crucial – they are the people who can make the space, finances and resources available to make it happen. Those companies that do it well will create a people and a business competitive advantage, as we will see later in our case study on Twitter.

Let's discuss establishing the DEI framework first, before we focus on how to execute on it. From the outset, you need a DEI strategy, DEI expertise on the People team and DEI data. Start with the top team. Create your DEI philosophy and framework with your Executive team, and from there, create your DEI strategy which will sit within your People strategy, and be inextricably linked to business goals. For example, if you are creating and selling a specific car insurance product to women, make sure you have women involved in development internally and market research externally at all stages of product development and go-to-market planning for that product. If you are expanding sales of your CRM tool into Latin America, make sure your DEI strategy highlights elevating Latinx employees and candidates to sell and provide customer support. Translate your DEI strategy into relevant workstreams, establish stretch targets to challenge the organisation, and set up a dashboard of metrics to track progress. If you are not sure what to focus on, carry out a diagnostic to see where the company is with existing goals, plans, resources and appetite to successfully execute on your agenda. Don't try to do everything at once and recognise that your work will never be 'done' in this space. Depending on where your company is on this journey, what you focus on will be different. Be selective, get the most fundamental policies, processes and behaviours in place first and work from there.

Now think about the resources you need to execute on your strategy. Ideally you should have a DEI specialist on your People team. If you don't have the headcount, spend money buying in that specialist knowledge temporarily to set up the programme, while you find the space to permanently invest. If you have the luxury, set up a DEI team, made up of business partners (who work with all stakeholders, business and HR alike) whose work is supported by a team of DEI specialists on communications, finance or event management. The team should be steered by an inspirational, passionate leader who can influence, negotiate and stand up for the importance of the function to the entire organisation. Spend time creating a brand for this team and their work and use it internally and externally to remind everyone that this work is ongoing, it's important work, and it permeates every part of the organisation. There is likely to be a lot of work to be done, but this work more than most needs to be widely and regularly celebrated, inside and outside the workplace.

Think about gathering systematically as much DEI data as you can. This starts as early as possible in the hiring process when candidates turn up to recruitment events and / or submit their job applications. Providing the data must be voluntary and have no impact on an application for a role; however, you should explain clearly why you are asking for this sensitive information – that your company is serious about intentionally hiring for diverse backgrounds and / or under-represented populations – and that such requests for personal information will facilitate this.

When onboarding, seek to gather as much information on personal characteristics including ability, age, education, ethnicity / race, gender, language, religion, sexual orientation and socio-economic status as possible. It's important to remain commensurately aware of how invasive it can feel to employees if they are asked for this information, in particular so early in their tenure into a new organisation about which they know little. Share early and often how important this information is in supporting you as an organisation to provide all the opportunities to all employees. Build trust with your employees by being open and transparent about how this confidential information will be used, including the very limited group of people who will have access to it.

When capturing DEI data, ideally via a secure form that feeds directly to the HR system, use dropdown options to standardise data as much as possible but seek feedback from employees to ensure you continue to add appropriate dropdown options that may be missing. Also, be considerate of the fact that some countries do not allow this type of candidate or employee data to be captured legally.

Finally, when using this information, be hugely respectful of it. This rich bank of data should be used throughout your employees' journeys with the organisation and to inform all your HR policies and processes. However, it is highly sensitive and personal. Never ever abuse it and wrap the highest security access measures around it: anonymise the data as often as possible, minimise the number of roles and people in the organisation who can access and use it, and put rules around when it can be used (e.g. only cohorts with X number of replies can be used for Y process) to ensure the highest level of confidentiality is maintained.

The real power in your DEI data is using it in tandem with all the other HR data available to you including, for example: recruitment stats at every point of the pipeline (who fell out of the process when); hiring stats (who was chosen ahead of who); training stats (who attended, who didn't, what channel was used, what was the feedback); promotion data (what is the profile of the people we promote, what employees get the most roles while in the company, who gets the manager roles); as well as talent and succession data (who is in the different talent planning boxes and how long are they in each one, who do we put on the bench as successors and why, what does our skills matrix tell us about the type of people who have the competencies we need most for business success). The use cases are endless – surface the ones that you need most at a given moment in time, depending on what business strategy is most pressing.

Once you have your strategy, resources and data, it's time to execute your DEI plan. It is likely your strategy will impact existing HR policies and processes, as well as create new opportunities for you to set up. Here are a few ideas to get you started:

<u>DEI policies</u>

At the most basic level, you need to ensure you are meeting your DEI requirements under the relevant legislation in the locations you operate in. All jurisdictions will have its own equality legislation to adhere to in order to prevent discrimination against any specific worker population, including for example; the Employment Equality Acts (1998-2011) in Ireland, the Equality Act (2010) in the UK, and the Title VII of the Civil Rights Act (1964) in the US. As always, it is advised to partner with local employment legal counsel to ensure you are meeting the requirements of the location you are operating in.

As well as being compliant with legislation, you should consider putting in place a DEI policy that raises the bar in terms of how discrimination and under-representation will be managed. A clear, well communicated DEI policy is a statement of intent.

The policy will show the world that your organisation celebrates a vibrant, transparent DEI culture where what you say you will do, is done and 'lived' by all employees. For example, if you want to provide equal leave benefits to both a birth parent and non-birth parent, then provide it in your leave policy. If you want to offer reasonable accommodations for employees experiencing mental health challenges, put it in your absence policy. If you will not tolerate micro-aggression to colleagues, call it out in your code of conduct policy. Breaches of your company DEI Policy, whether minimum standards provided under legislation or a higher, bespoke standard of how you celebrate difference and underrepresentation, will be corrected by the company via the grievance and disciplinary policy. What management chooses to ignore, is perceived as tolerance.

DEI processes through the employee life cycle

- **Talent acquisition:** use a mix of training, quantitative targets and bespoke resources with your TA teams to help them get this right from the start of the employee journey. Share your DEI culture in your Employer Value Proposition – show you are serious about this from the outset. Scrutinise job descriptions and working conditions (e.g. hours, location) to ensure they are equitable and inviting. Stipulate a specific gender and ethnicity mix on hiring panels to ensure all candidates are represented and assessed equally. Put specific diversity metrics in place for every step of the hiring process, and build it into your systems so the systems do the work for you. There is strong research that suggests the final panel for every hiring process should have a 50:50 split of men and women.[181] Only a gender-equal final slate will provide a statistically equal chance of any candidate getting hired. Sponsor, host or speak at events that pinpoints targeted candidate pools. For example, share senior leadership roles intentionally with female networks such as the 30% Club,[182] or attend the Black Girls in Tech Fest as part of your recruitment campaign.[183]

  Meeting diverse slates in hiring processes is not easy, but trading a little extra time for a quality final candidate panel is one of the best ways to hire for diversity. And I hear you asking, "But we want to hire the best person for the role – we can't do that if we have to have a fixed ratio of candidates?" The answer is that "you are correct, and this quality assurance check will mean you do get the best candidates in front of you, not simply the ones that have the loudest voices or those who look and sound like you."

A further word on DEI and the interview process for hiring leaders in particular, given leaders are hugely influential to the success of your DEI strategy. Questions such as: 'Can you tell me how you as a leader ensure you are creating equal opportunities for people in the business?' or 'How many people from under-represented populations did you hire / promote on your team in your previous position?' will help to truly understand their commitment to your organisational DEI culture.

- **Induction and onboarding:** share your organisational DEI culture from day one, making sure that new hires know the expectations of their behaviours and showing how these behaviours are not just expected but celebrated. Share resources on how people processes are checked for representation and direct your new hires to where they can read more. Get a sponsor or a DEI team member to speak at your new hire sessions to show how genuine and positively intentioned your company is about this. Share links to where and how your newest employees can get involved in the process.

- **Retention:** all HR processes – in particular those related to internal job marketplace, promotion, talent planning, talent development and succession planning – are at risk of being unconsciously biased. Largely, with no mal intent, those making decisions in these processes do not naturally lead with representation in mind. Therefore, your processes must intentionally put in checks and balances. That's not easy. Asking a manager to rate the performance of an employee they see in the office a couple of times a week, compared to one that they haven't met since induction or the last all hands meeting, through the same unbiased lens, is hard on them. Training and timely reminders at the moment they are making these decisions will help, as will auditing the decisions before they are finalised. For example, make sure your promotion decision-making panels represent all those being considered; make sure all those that should be considered are being considered, based on objective measures such as performance, achievement of the right outcomes, and displaying the right behaviours. For succession planning, audit trends over time and check if any employees remain in particular 'boxes' longer than expected.

For internal hiring, share roles with Employee Resource Groups purposefully and even before the hiring process formally opens, to elevate roles with those who may shy away the most from applying. When submitting year-end ratings, remind managers of recency effect, 'halo and horns' bias, and other checks before they commit them, and then audit the submissions for those on leave and those in particular under-represented populations for bias. For all processes, seek feedback from those involved to learn and do better continuously. If employees from under-represented populations are not involved in any of these processes, make sure to seek feedback from them too – there may be a good reason why or, crucially, there may be a bias that has left them out of the process that needs addressing. Use the feedback to tweak processes or to create learning opportunities for those who are not as successful as others in the organisation or to highlight lack of progress on your strategy to the Executive sponsors.

- **Pay and benefits:** One of the benefits of employment law regulation is that it demands fairness and equity, and DEI legislation is no different. The current requirement for gender pay gap reporting across the world is leading to organisations acknowledging and fixing legacy issues, and ensuring they don't resurface by, for example, putting salary ranges into job ads. It is also highlighting systemic differences between cohorts of workers that we as a global workforce can work on – for example, to help applications from women, many ads are now publicly stating that applicants don't need to have experience in all the job responsibilities listed in order to apply. Have an 'internal first' hiring process that places current employees into vacant roles based on potential, rather than going external first and hiring based on actual experience. Another initiative is highlighting that language and other training is available to help applicants who otherwise have the right experience to apply, encouraging a wider pool of applicants.

Benefits should be under scrutiny for being equitable and relevant for the full workforce. Benefits are so nuanced by employee cohorts or even individual employees, more and more companies are providing a fixed benefit allowance per employee based on role level, to be spent as they see fit. Consider offering customisable benefits via a flexible benefits programme (see chapter 15), where a benefit value is given to employees to spend on the benefits that work for them specifically. For example, an option to pay a higher pension amount is more important to older employees; flexible leave can be a blessing to those with parental or carer responsibilities; gym membership will only ever benefit a certain cohort of workers and will just result in the rest of us feeling guilty when we don't use it. Let each person decide what they need to spend their well-earned benefits on.

Business operating model ('ways of working')

- **Where will we work?** Office, home or both? Working at home has benefited traditionally under-represented populations more than those in the majority worker groups: women have had an outsized benefit due to the additional responsibilities that still seem to fall to them in the home; home working has helped employees with physical disabilities overcome the logistical challenges of getting to / from as well as navigating the office; neuro-divergent workers have been able to set up their home workstation up as they need e.g. quiet, lower lighting, no strong smells and neutral colours; and employees from under-represented populations in general avoid micro-aggressions due to spending less face time with colleagues in the office. Organisations need to be careful however that those working from home are not forgotten – intentionally creating opportunities for dialogue, training and networking, as well as rules around people processes that level the playing field, will ensure that does not happen.

- **How will we work?** Asynchronously on our own or together in a meeting? What about hosting an event: in-person, virtual or both? Whether you are hosting a big event or just leading a project or team meeting, make sure everyone who needs to can fully access and get involved in the activity. Consider introducing the following: if you have some meeting attendees remote and some in the office, have those in the office gather in a meeting room, use the meeting room audio, but sign into and turn down the volume on their own laptops – this results in a more equitable experience for all.

  Consider tools such as closed captioning, Communication Access Realtime Translation (CART) or interpreting for those with hearing impairments. Send the meeting materials out in advance, and / or have a screen reader for those with vision impairments. Don't forget your best practice meeting etiquette in general: be clear who attends, why they are invited, what they are expected to input on, expected pre-reads for meeting efficiency, go on mute when not speaking, and use hand up or chat offerings to give everyone a voice. Send out confirmation of actions, decisions and next steps when the meeting wraps. For events or big one-off subsidised meetings, request accommodations (i.e. encourage those that need extra support to request it) in the meeting invite.

- **When will we work?** Facilitate flexible working times so people can do different types of work at the best part of their day. For some employees, this flexibility may help them arrange their work around the other aspects of their life; for others it's more about doing work simply when they do their best work, which could be early morning or late evening. For meetings or events, try to avoid lunch times, prayer times or times that are outside the traditional working day. Be respectful of the world clock for organisations with a regional or global footprint. While some employees may like working early morning or late evening, it's likely the type of work they need to do is deep, individual work at those times, not dip into a meeting with colleagues on the other side of the world when their background is night-time. Give employees a clear licence to say no to meetings that are reasonably outside their working day, especially recurring meetings. Finally, use the meeting recording functionality more. Inform attendees that a meeting is being recorded at the outset, set the expectation that it is not to be shared outside the organisation, and share it to relevant stakeholders to listen to in their own time. While these considerations are important for all employees, they have an outsized benefit for our under-represented populations and will support them being fully involved in achieving business goals.

McKinsey proffers three well-researched principles to help ground this work:[184]

- **1. Work-life support:** demonstrating appreciation for employee's non-work demands, responsibilities, and interests.
- **2. Team building:** working to foster trust, collaboration, and healthy conflict among team members.
- **3. Mutual respect:** showing genuine concern for the well-being of all employees, and a commitment by employees to treat one another fairly and respectfully.

DEI learning and development initiatives

Start with upskilling everyone on the basics. Consider training for the entire organisation that creates a common language and shared understanding of what we mean by DEI and what are the expectations of everyone in the organisation within the DEI framework. The result is an open, transparent, consistent flow of conversation, documentation and healthy discussion about these matters. Potential training at this level could include understanding pronouns, disrupting bias and understanding privilege. It is absolutely necessary to create that baseline of common understanding before putting in place the next levels of DEI learning offerings.

Next you might consider bespoke training for different cohorts of employees to provide a level playing field based on a structural difference, such as those within a particular geography, with a common local language, or who need to meet a particular business need. For example, if you are setting up business in a new location, make sure that the team you place there, be they existing or new employees, understand the business culture they are going into, the rules around engaging a new cohort of external clients or potential employees, and how the government is likely to react to your new product or service. You should also consider a bespoke training curriculum for specific under-represented populations in your workforce. Many companies for example will have leadership training for women only, focusing on building networks, influencing and communication. But it does not just have to be classroom / in-person training – leverage your ERGs for coaching or to learn more about a particular type of employee group, offer places at relevant seminars and events, and share information about external forums where employees can learn about how to build their knowledge, competence and influence to reach their potential in the workplace. Consider this for all the under-represented populations in your workforce, beginning with the biggest so you make a big impact from the outset. Don't forget to make sure your offerings are accessible to every employee in each cohort.

There is, as always, a higher burden on our manager and leader populations to get this right. They should be upskilled in how to hire, onboard, performance manage, promote, mentor and coach in a way that creates this important level playing field. A programme of offerings around inclusive leadership will help to create a safe space for them to learn, ask questions, see what great looks like, and share experiences. This programme, again, must be made available and accessible to all leaders so that muscle is built through the entire network, ideally in as short a space as possible, and regularly reinforced so everyone experiences the learning, managers and employees alike, at the same time.

And remember, this is going to be challenging for your leaders to get right. Writing in *Harvard Business Review*, Juliet Bourke, Professor of Practice in the School of Management and Governance, University of New South Wales Business School, and Andrea Titus, Consultant at Deloitte, write: *"Leaders who are humble and empathetic will be open to criticism about their personal biases, and greater self-insight into personal limitations prompts greater humility, empathy and perspective-taking."*[185]

Those leaders who already have these traits will be more comfortable learning how to be a better inclusive leader. Those that don't will need some additional support.

As you will see in the next section, a vibrant empowered set of ERGs can and will elevate your DEI strategy above and beyond everyone's wildest dreams. Invest in these employees from a training perspective by creating time and space to upskill their committees on running an ERG, chairing their meetings, running events, and managing a (likely very tight) budget to do everything they wish for to create community around their group. It's likely you can leverage existing training programmes around managing, prioritising, decision-making to help them make their communities a success.

Employee resource groups

Employee resource groups (ERGs), or business resource groups (BRGs), are communities of employees that gather together around a common identity, interest or experience. Employees will join an ERG either as a full member, that is they personally associate with the focus of the group, or as an ally. Allyship is an important and powerful element of an ERG because, according to employee engagement consultancy Great Place to Work: *"Allies wield their influence to amplify the voices and elevate the employee experience of their under-represented co-workers."* [186]

An ERG is owned and run by employees themselves. Your role as CPO will be to create an ecosystem around them to allow them flourish. The most commonly found ERGs include those focused on women, race and ethnicity, LGBTQI+, Latinx, older workers, those with a disability, people with carer / parenting interests, those from a military background, those with a religious affiliation and those passionate about climate change and sustainability. Employees who are active in ERGs can be an important source of insight for the CPO too. Their specialist knowledge may be invaluable in helping solve the most complex challenges in the workplace.

A word on psychological safety here, which is *"the belief that employees will not be punished or humiliated for speaking up with ideas, questions, concerns or mistakes."*[187] We saw the importance of creating psychological safety in general in your organisation in chapter 3. Creating psychological safety for those in under-represented populations is crucial – without it, real change will not come. While DEI initiatives are necessary, they are not sufficient. A report from business consultancy August, states:

> *"… new research suggests that a lack of psychological safety can drag a diverse team's performance down significantly, sometimes erasing its advantage altogether. Conversely, high psychological safety can be the key to unlocking a diverse team's full potential."*[188]

The report's authors go on to emphasise that creating the policies, programmes, training and data is necessary but not sufficient to generate psychological safety; the organisation must ensure these behaviours are being lived visibly and embraced by all. Only then will the organisation be a place where this rich ecosystem flourishes.

Case study: Twitter

At Twitter, one of the key DEI goals was, *"building a culture where every Tweep* [Twitter employee] *can bring their full, authentic self to work"*.

Twitter first formed an Inclusion and Diversity team. In 2021, this team was merged with practitioners from the Centre of Excellence for Accessibility and External Partnerships team to become the Inclusion, Diversity, Equity and Accessibility (IDEA) team and was set the goal of becoming the world's most inclusive, diverse, equitable and accessible tech company.

Twitter's DEI hashtag, #UntilWeAllBelong, appeared everywhere – whether it was celebrating inclusion, highlighting diversity imbalances or elevating the Employee Value Proposition. Everyone inside the organisation – and thanks to the power of the Twitter platform, many of those *outside* the organisation – knew exactly what the company stood for in this important area of work. Courageously, Twitter shared its DEI journey on a publicly available blog between 2019-2022. Search for 'Twitter inclusion diversity equity accessibility report', to read about the journey for yourself; the highs the lows, the plans and targets, the disappointments and the joyous wins.

Twitter did more than just tick the box. Twitter went above and beyond to authentically elevate every single voice. The business case for a robust DEI framework was straightforward and to the point: inclusion is foundational to Twitter's purpose of servicing the public conversation. To achieve it, the organisation built a best-in-class framework that embraced accessibility, equality, accessibility and inclusion. Let's look at how Twitter differentiated itself from the rest:

- Including a 'no wrongful discrimination' policy in the company handbook, which listed protected characteristics, provided reasonable accommodations, and ensured accessibility for, for example, neurodiverse candidates and employees.
- Linking the DEI strategy to the global objective of diversification of the workforce and aiming high with stretch targets. In its public *March 2020 Diversity & Inclusion report*, the social media giant stated that, by 2025 at least half of its global workforce should be women (a figure which stood at 42.5% at that time), with further targets

around the representation of women across technical roles (42%) and leadership positions (41%) too. Within five years, Twitter had also pledged to ensure that at least one quarter of the US workforce would be made up of under-represented populations, including Black and Latinx employees.

- The DEI team itself was significant. Led by a passionate and experienced strategist and supported by a talented global team, Twitter went about executing its strategy with knowledge, skills, passion and a drive that any business would be proud of.

- The BRG ecosystem flourished. The DEI team produced a quarterly newsletter providing updates on all upcoming ERG events, spotlighting new BRGs (there were 11 by mid 2022), and ensuring that every Tweep knew what was going on where, when and why. A playbook was available for those who wanted to find out more and to get involved. The team held a tentpole event for one BRG every month with an associated campaign # – for example September was Latinx Heritage month #PalFrente and October was Disability Awareness Month #DisabledAndAble .

- Those giving up their time to run a BRG were supported transparently by Twitter and were compensated for sharing their specialist knowledge and skills with the organisation. Nothing speaks more to the authenticity of DEI at Twitter than the *HR Drive* article which headlined 'Twitter to pay resource group leaders saying the work shouldn't be a 'voluntary activity'.[189] Talk about putting your money where your mouth is.

- Company-wide training was provided to ensure everyone was provided with the basics from the outset, ensuring there were shared definitions, clear understanding, and practical tools to support open, honest and vulnerable conversations around DEI.

- Executive sponsorship was visible – each member of the top team sponsored a BRG, consistently and authentically, to help elevate their voices. Donald Hicks, the then Global Lead for the Customer Experience team, got to the heart of the matter, describing how Twitter and other social platforms are built to understand a particular language such as African-American Vernacular English (AAVE) , adding that: *"Black and Brown voices are literally being silenced; voices that could otherwise be sharing important information, breaking news, or simply promoting a new project"*.[190] Leaders like this understand the power of DEI.

- In moments of difficulty in the world, the relevant BRG hosted a safe space for those impacted by a significant event to turn up and talk. Tweeps were gently and ably led through confidential conversations that ultimately worked through pain, sadness, raw emotion, support, shared stories and hope for the future.

- In 2021, right in the middle of the global pandemic, Twitter celebrated its DEI journey with a spectacular global #TwitterTogether 24-hour summit, repeating the success the following year. The epitome of one team in unison voice over one day around the world:

Olivia McEvoy
@Olivia_McEvoy

All the Friday Feels for the epic #OneTeam @Twitter @TwitterTogether effort to realise the inaugural, 24 hour, around the sun #UntilWeAllBelong summit this week.

6:54 PM · Sep 17, 2021

2 Retweets   **2** Quote Tweets   **31** Likes

Figure 16.1: @TwitterTogether global DEI summit

Questions for a new CPO

- Does your leadership and board truly embrace the purpose, goal and need for DEI? Do you have sponsors at the highest levels?
- Do you have a fit-for-purpose DEI Strategy and implementation plan, to which the Executive team is committed and is sponsoring, and which has plans and stretch targets against it?
- Have you gathered as much DEI data as you can? Are there the highest levels of access and data security around this information?
- Do you have sufficient financial and human resources to execute your DEI strategy successfully?
- Do you have policies, processes, tooling and training in place that embeds your DEI culture, and which will result in every single employee reaching their career potential?
- Where, when and how do you celebrate your DEI successes?
- Have you secured buy-in from the top to create a vibrant ecosystem around your employee resource groups and which will truly support all employees bringing and being the best version of themselves in the workplace?

Summary

Diversity, equity, inclusion, equality, belonging, accessibility, justice – there is a lot to do. Don't get overwhelmed with the amount that you can – or feel you need to – achieve. Create your strategy, commit your sponsors to it and build up your resources, human and financial. Collect the data, everywhere and as often as possible, and use it in tandem with your other HR data. Once you have those in place, identify the key gaps that risk your strategy being executed successfully, close them, then re-evaluate and focus on the next set of actions with the most impact.

Don't expect it to happen by magic – you will need to work at levelling the playing field intentionally and consistently in every aspect of people in your organisation. Buy in the expertise if you don't have it. Make sure your sponsors are authentic and intentional about the company DEI framework – don't just do it to tick the box, your employees will see right through you; do it because it will bring business success, because it will excite your employees, because it will make you more attractive to new employees, and because it will elevate purpose into the fabric of your organisation.

Do it, above all else, because it's the right thing to do.

Chapter 17

Information systems for people management

Introduction

The core objective of people systems is to enable the completion of people processes – to input necessary people data into the system, and action that information to complete people-related tasks.

This can include everything from checking the work authorisation of new hires to capturing qualitative information in an exit interview, and everything in between. People technology has improved continuously in recent years, facilitating significant change in how people processes are accomplished. These systems can now facilitate manager and employee self-service (should the organisation choose to go that route), they have changed how information is collated and analysed, creating richer information that helps the organisation meet its legislative requirements and supports employees reaching their full potential, and they can offer the all-important customisation that is increasingly expected by employees.

Automation, new technologies and business intelligence systems are all reducing the amount of time and effort spent on people-related activities across the entire employee experience. Some organisations will have a single system that captures core people data and runs the fundamental people-related business of the organisation; others may have several systems for different processes, including recruitment, learning or benefits; others again may have one significant Human Capital Management (HCM) system along with a small number of additional systems which support specific people processes. There are pros and cons to all the different architectures, as we will see later.

Whatever is in place in your organisation, it's very likely that more can be done to elevate the people processes to a better place using people systems, and now is a good time to consider that.

What are we solving for?

There are strategic choices to be made in how the people technology architecture is set up in any organisation. Those choices are often a function of the size, shape, age, budget and geographical footprint of the company. As noted in the introduction, there are pros and cons to all set ups. There are advantages and disadvantages to having a single HCM system that captures all the relevant people data, processes, activities and analytics in one place versus having a number of best-in-class systems in place.

A single system will be able to offer more actions covering more HR programmes but to a lesser quality (akin to a buffet meal) whereas a smaller bespoke system can offer speciality programmes very well (akin to a great Italian restaurant).

The other strategic choice to make in regard to the people system architecture is whether to build your own system or buy one in.

The advantages to building in-house is that it can be created solely for the people needs of the organisation, whereas off-the-shelf may only be customisable to a point. The advantage to buying a system is that it is likely to be less expensive from a cost and a maintenance perspective.

The ultimate objective must be that the employee experience is be seamless; the technology should be easy to access, simple to navigate, intuitive and rule-based where appropriate, and efficient to use. Every decision made around a new system, or system upgrade, should have a great employee experience as its ultimate outcome.

The choice of building vs. buying, and the choice of what to buy if you elect to go that route, will be strongly influenced by the Chief Technology Officer (CTO). A strong, collaborative relationship with them should be cultivated for that very reason. Whatever strategic decisions are made in the end, what the organisation does need to do is to capture relevant, timely and a significant amount of data, in order to automate processes and produce evidence-based solutions to people issues. Such technology will allow managers and employees to focus on the day job – the reason we hired them in the first place – and it will facilitate the People team spending time doing impactful work elevating people, maximising their potential and delivering on business outcomes.

In thinking about those outcomes that you want from the people technology, Josh Bersin advises to *"build a long-term architecture and make sure every tech decision you make focuses on ease of use and improvement of employee productivity with HR functionality and data capabilities as secondary"*. [191]

In the following section we look in more detail at the different categories of technology that can be considered for the people system architecture. Firstly however, it's useful to call out a number of principles that should be applied to every decision regarding technology:

- **Customer first:** this principle takes the *organisation's* customer into consideration when planning the people architecture. How will the technology facilitate the company meeting its external client's needs? Will system users (i.e. employees and managers) be on the road meeting those clients, and need to access systems over mobile technology? Is the business strategy to set up in new locations, thereby requiring people platforms to be expanded to meet the geographical footprint? Will the company grow by acquisition, requiring functionality to customise for legacy contractual obligations from the acquired company?

- **User experience (UX):** The user experience, whether manager, employee or People team, should be a very high priority for all system decisions. In considering a new system, how seamless will access to it be from existing systems? What rules can be built in to allow the user validating or approving information rather than inputting and checking it? Through what channels can the user access the various platforms, and can single-sign-on between them be facilitated? How customisable is the system to facilitate employee self-service at a time and on a device that suits them?

- **System outputs:** the data analytics and reporting capability of the technology is also a high priority consideration. It's important to get the balance right between user experience, collecting pertinent data, and not collecting data that will either not be used or which breaches data privacy legislation. Putting the right people systems in place will facilitate the creation of predictive and prescriptive analytics, rather than simply raw data points and trends. More on this in the next chapter on data and analytics.

- **System outcomes:** people systems will facilitate intelligent automation, which is the automation of business processes using AI and related technologies. However great systems will not bring the benefits promised without broader change. Standardisation of people processes is the key to unlocking automation with more and better technology. All technology change projects must include the time and resources needed to update, close down or amend the processes that are affected by the change, including capturing the benefits that come from it.

What does success look like?

We need to transform people processes digitally – and urgently. Digital transformation of the People function is way behind where it needs to be. What could fully automated people processes look like?

Employees would have quick, easy and customisable access to manage their own data, change their pensions, select their wellbeing offerings, update their skills and apply for interesting roles to further their career. Managers would be able to spend much more real time with their employees, listening, talking, creating, teaching, mentoring and celebrating rather than stuck in spreadsheets and lengthy, unfocused calibration meetings. And the People team would be able to have more impactful onboarding conversations with new hires, increased time collaborating on process improvement projects together, and better-informed performance and career conversations with managers.

Additionally, the entire organisation would be better aligned due to a smart feedback system which audits qualitative performance data; it would be higher performing due to a recognition programme that prompts, nudges and links great behaviours to all types of rewards; and more inclusive than ever, due to DEI data permeating every system, programme and process the organisation possess.

What's not to like?

Automation and intelligent systems come at a cost, so you want to get your investment right. In considering new technology, or additions to your existing technology, there are a couple of key questions to ask. Adapted from a paper on talent mobility systems, the following questions resonate for all people systems considerations[192]:

- What's your overall business, people and talent strategy? What are you trying to solve?
- How configurable is the technology? Whether you buy an off-the-shelf best practice system or create your own, it's likely that any single system will need to talk to other technologies at a minimum. If you know you want specific customisation, be sure to ask the question up front.
- How comprehensive is the solution? Seek to find solutions that offer the broadest end-to-end user experience, and are capable of interacting with other systems, such as payroll, user access and broader enterprise resource planning (ERP) offerings, and organisational systems including accounting, supply chain and risk management.
- What capabilities do you need today, and into the future? The system needs to be configurable for future organisational capability as well as current.
- How useful and accessible is the technology? It should be accessible on multiple devices, at all times, and customisable for and by the user where appropriate. The

user experience should be intuitive, without requiring hours of training.

- How easy is it to connect the platform with other technologies? Vendors need to have an open application programming interface (API) strategy, which means that the platform can integrate with others already in place, to support everything the organisation needs to do for its various people workflows.
- How will success be measured? A dashboard of time, effort and other success metrics should be created around the people system architecture to ensure the benefits that everyone should be getting from automation and better intelligence are being experienced.
- Can the technology provider consult on best practices? Getting the people system architecture right is complex – ask for advice and learnings along the way.
- What has worked for others? Talk through the experience of your CPO network to learn from mistakes and leverage best practice.

Additional considerations include:

- What is the outlay cost of the platform as well as the annual and other costs, i.e. the total cost of ownership?
- Does the application produce the reporting functionality that you need?
- What support and training does the provider offer?
- Is the platform cloud-hosted, reducing the requirement for in-house maintenance, and future-proofing it?
- Will the system capture and integrate business metrics that can be collated into useful dashboards for users?
- Is the user interface intuitive and does it provide seamless access to different technologies that may be part of the people and other functional architectures?

- Is the technology regularly updated to take account of changing regulation?
- Does the technology meet the strictest data security and data privacy requirements needed for a people system?

Let's have a look at 11 potential categories of people technology in more detail. It's important to note that the technologies listed are a small selection of vendors in each category, and that those listed often have functionality across a number of categories.

The Human Resources Information System (HRIS)

Human Capital Management (HCM), Human Resource Management System (HRMS), and Human Resource Information Systems (HRIS) are the employee system of record. There are small differences between each of these three technologies but they all share broad functionality that captures the requisite people data and carries out the basic activities needed to run the organisation's people processes. Given the similarities, we will focus on HRIS, to cover all three systems. Any HRIS may include any or all of the following functionality:

- Employee personal data;
- Position management;
- Recognition and feedback;
- Recruitment and onboarding;
- Compensation and benefits;
- Training and development;
- Performance management;
- Talent and succession planning; and
- Offboarding and exit information.

As with all people technology platforms, there are a proliferation of different systems available on the market to suit the size, shape and requirements of every organisation. Examples of HRIS include

Paycor, Workday, SAP Success Factors, Personio, Peoplesoft, BambooHR and Oracle Human Capital Management.[193]

Recruitment platform

Often called the applicant tracking system (ATS), this is the system that will capture the talent acquisition workflow, from sourcing initial candidates through to onboarding successful new employees. The ATS may be supplemented with a Candidate Relationship Management tool (CRM): the ATS focuses on workflow whereas the CRM focuses on managing the relationships with candidates, offering the facility for example to add notes for organisation fit or future roles.

There is a selection of applications to consider out on the market, and the questions captured in the previous section will help select the right one for your organisation. There are some specific considerations to give in selecting the right ATS and CRM platforms for the organisation, including what you want for the candidate experience, the ability to build specific rules to elevate organisation capabilities, social networking capabilities, and the ability to insert DEI rules and checks throughout the whole process. Ideally, they will both also facilitate the organisation's Internal Talent Marketplace requirements (see next category), where the ATS will cross-post roles and required skills to the internal job board, the CRM can house information on current employees as well as candidates, and both systems will have the capability to send data to the analytics system. Both systems must facilitate the talent acquisition team spending more quality time with candidates, really maximising face-to-face time to find and engage the best candidates the organisation deserves, rather than spending time pushing information through a candidate pipeline funnel. Some of systems that are best known for their ATS and CRM functionality include BambooHR, Workable, Bullhorn, Greenhouse and SmartRecruiters.[194]

Internal talent marketplace platform

An internal talent marketplace platform will be a single system that pulls together the required data from other people systems to match current employees proactively and intentionally to their next potential role or project. The objective of the internal talent marketplace platform is retention, and the system will work by pre-empting the next suitable role or project that keeps employees in the organisation. An internal talent marketplace platform is more than the traditional 'internal jobs board' that many organisations already have in place. This platform should match current employee career aspirations dynamically with internal open roles (new and backfill positions) to facilitate employees building bespoke and self-directed careers. Such a system requires multiple data points:

- **Organisation-wide information:** workforce planning (the full company's organisation design), current and future vacant roles, an advertising capability, talent planning data, succession planning data, learning and development offerings linked to specific skills.
- **Employee specific information:** employee's current role, time in current role, total tenure with the organisation, most recent performance ratings, recognition information, individual skills, and career preference information.
- **Matching capability:** this is the core functionality required from this technology. The system will require skill matching capability (skills required in the job ads being matched to skills of current employees), appropriate rules to identify employees with the highest potential to fill the roles (e.g. there may be a rule that the employee must be one year in their current role, and / or have a certain performance history to be identified by the system), elevate and nudge those with the potential skills in filled roles to apply for the open roles, and learning and development

information to help potential candidates fill any skills gaps. This is complex and requires a consistently updated job catalogue, with skills / competence by proficiency, to work. It needs to capture employee expectations about their next position or the next skill they wish to develop. It also needs to match positions and employees in a way that will lead to business goals being met.

The system should facilitate not only permanent and temporary positions but also be set up to advertise project roles. Employees can submit applications for part-time projects in addition to their current roles, or request to be temporarily assigned to the projects for a period – an internal gig workplace if you like - in the knowledge that they can return to their core position afterwards. Setting up the workflows around these processes is complex but as important as the technology itself – strong governance over a system like this is core to building trust in it.

There are technology solutions on the market with this functionality, including Hitch, Fuel50, Gloat, Ceridian, Worksome, Talentguard, Degreed and Eightfold.ai.[195] In addition, project management software or team-creation software such as GanttPro, Teamwork or Zoho Projects[196] may be somewhat helpful, in particular for capturing temporary project teams. We saw the positive outcomes that a vibrant internal talent marketplace will have on engagement, loyalty, motivation, tenure and retention, in chapter 8. Putting some form of technology behind this process to support it will be more than worth the time and effort.

The learning platform

Learning and development (L&D) in organisations needs to meet a number of objectives. L&D needs to be customisable to meet individual employee expectations, engaging for mandatory training (perhaps using gamification), intelligent for efficiency purposes, and impactful so it meets business goals.

There are a significant number of learning platforms available on the market. Again, the questions outlined above will help structure any consideration given to getting a new platform or upgrading a current one. In addition, and specific to the learning platform, Deloitte outline a helpful taxonomy of different systems[197]:

- **Learning management system (LMS):** core learning administration system, tracking and scheduling all programmes. Examples of LMS's include Workday, SAP SuccessFactors, Docebo, Oracle, MatrixLMS, TalentLMS, Absorb, Saba and Cornerstone.
- **Learning experience platform (LXP):** some organisations are choosing to replace an LMS with an LXP, which is a platform that also retains organisational skills information, while also proactively recommend learning courses. Typically the internal talent marketplace or CRM can push through recommendations based on current position in the organisation, and future career aspirations. Percipio, Valamis, Edcast and Fuse Universal are examples of this technology.
- **Learning content providers:** specialist learning companies that create and sell programmes for broad audiences, such as for compliance, leadership and diversity. Providers of this technology include Pluralsight, Udemy, Skillsoft and Coursera.
- **Learning in the flow of work platform:** platforms that help employees access learning on systems they already use in their daily work. Examples here include Axonify, Stream and Area9.
- **Learning creator tools and platforms:** providing the opportunity to crowdsource learning, these platforms offer employees the ability to create their own customised

learning content. For example, a member of the finance team can create and upload expense approval training for the organisation. The risk associated with this type of application is that someone needs to approve content and assure quality. Examples include 360Learning, Articulate and Inkling.

By making smart investments in the latest learning systems, the Talent Development team can turn their attentions to impactful work such as ensuring the right content is available at the right time to meet business requirements and elevate employee potential, as well as ensuring the system creates all the rich information needed to guard against current and future skills shortages.

Case management system

For confidentiality purposes, many organisations house sensitive case management information and other related compliance data in a separate system. This system may take individual employee information from the HRIS, and capture additional grievance, bullying, disciplinary and related case information in a completely separate system. An example of such a system is I-sight.

Benefits and wellbeing platform

While the HRIS may capture compensation and benefits information, consideration could be given to a bespoke benefits and wellbeing platform. We saw in chapter 14 the importance of creating a flexible benefits and wellbeing programme offering that allows employees to be self-sufficient in creating a personalised portfolio. Examples of these applications include Remote, Oyster, Benefex and onPay.[198]

Recognition platform

Chapter 5 discusses the importance of creating a recognition culture through the organisation. There are a number of recognition platforms that can meet this need. The platform should be much more than 'coffee and cake' vouchers and needs to offer public 'shout out' capability, which drives pride and motivates employees, as well as potentially proactive matching of employees to mentors or sponsors, given research suggests that it is a *"short walk from recognition to mentorship"*.[199] Examples of these technologies include Slack, Workvivo and Beqom.

Employee survey platform

There is a wide selection of platforms available from which to run employee annual and pulse surveys. Ideally these platforms will take current organisation design information from the HRIS and use the data and organisation structure to extend bespoke surveys that ask nuanced questions to the workforce. The system should support the entire survey process end-to-end. That can include auto-prompting employees to respond to the survey during the open window and providing 'league tables' of response rates to managers and leaders to maximise the response rates through the organisation.

The reporting capability should include historical trend information, splits by level / function / location / DEI categories and should propose actions to the Executive team, functional leads and team leads based on the employee responses. The system should allow rules to be built into it based on organisational requirements, including the ability to only produce reports when a certain minimum number of responses per cohort has been received. This preserves anonymity which helps builds trust in the survey process. Examples include Glint, Officevibe and Mentimeter.

Analytics platform

An analytics platform is a business intelligence tool that will have the facility to retrieve, collate, mine and model data, with a view to presenting the insights in visual diagrams and presentations. An analytics platform is not the same as reporting - each people technology will have its own reporting functionality. The objective of the analytics platform is to tell a story with the data that leads to better decisions being made in the business. The people team may have their own analytics platform, however it's more likely that they will use an organisation-wide ERP system that captures analytics from across the company. As with all people-related data, this information is highly confidential and often sensitive, and should therefore be subject to rigorous rules around data protection, data privacy and bespoke access rules. Examples of analytics applications include Tableau, Microsoft Power BI Desktop, Qlik and SAS Visual Analytics.[200]

External platforms

There are likely to be external platforms that the organisation can use to supplement internal people systems. These include labour statistics, industry-specific reports and peer company information. There are further exciting platforms that can be considered, particularly in relation to emerging challenges organisations are facing such as remote / hybrid working, corporate responsibility and creating links to purpose via ESG policies. One such example is the Abadoo platform, backed by the European Commission, which is *"an interactive talent map for each village containing key information and insights need to attract remote workers, create jobs and support rural regeneration"* across Europe[201].

Other external platforms to consider using include the previously mentioned applications that professional gig workers are signing up to, to supplement your internal employee workforce.

Employee experience platform

Employee expectations of HR technologies have increased, and the People function needs to keep up. Starting with the basic, functioning system of record like a HCM or HRIS, many organisations opt for a proliferation of tools, applications, platforms and systems that sit around that core system, each with its own system of record, and each of which the employee may need to access separately in order to carry out one single action. Most of them are listed above. The employee experience (EX) platform seeks to make engagement with all the different people platforms in the organisation a single, consistent experience. Described by Josh Bersin as the layer that sits on top of all the other systems of record, an EX platform is designed to *"mask the complexity of the back-office systems and create a service-oriented interface that employees find easy to use…. and it needs to be included in every organization's technology plan."*[202]

Spanning not only HR, but also IT, facilities, finance and other functions, these platforms focus on a single place where the employee can complete end-to-end activities from one platform. Like the rest of the HR technology market, there are a number of vendors providing this technology too, including ServiceNow, Willis Towers Watson, Deloitte (ConnectMe), PeopleDoc, Ti-People, PeopleSpheres, GuideSpark, Spencer.co and IBM.

Bersin also argues that *"intelligent chatbot companies like Mya, Leena, Workgrid and new chat tools being embedded into core HCM platforms are also part of this market."*[203]

It would be remiss to write about people systems without a word on how artificial intelligence (AI), machine learning, deep learning and related technologies will impact the People function. All business functions will be impacted by these technologies – supply chains will get shorter, finance and accounting will get faster, marketing outcomes will provide better insights, and people management will probably have the benefits of all the above: shorter time to hire, faster and better people analytics, and more nuanced career options for employees. It is beyond the scope of this handbook to discuss this area in great depth. Suffice to say, and for example, ChatGPT or something akin to it will eventually become the primary contact with employees to answer tactical HR questions, and that some other AI-powered system will all but cleverly-automate the recruitment process end-to-end.

Remain open to learning about the emerging types of technology. Be careful at what point you implement them – recent studies are showing how crude technology can be, in terms of reading human information accurately. They will get the point where they can do it successfully – from a risk management perspective, make sure you wade in carefully, and at the right time for your organisation.

Questions for a new CPO

- Do you have digital transformation of people processes on your People strategy, for now and for the next number of years?
- What size budget do you have for digitally transforming HR, and do you have access to the people resources and skills to make the necessary changes?
- When have you surveyed your users most recently (employees and managers) to ask what can be improved in the current people systems?
- How strong is your relationship with the CTO / Head of IT and Head of Security, as two key relationships that can greatly facilitate or otherwise hinder your ability to put a best-in-class people system in place?
- New systems always require changes to existing policies and processes - how well equipped are you to change your processes to support the implementation of a new system?

Summary

According to the CIPD: *"HR is still among the departments that are less involved in decisions to introduce intelligent automation or in its implementation",* falling at the bottom of the list behind finance, procurement, marketing and sales.[204]

Employees should be able to create, adjust and pursue their careers using people-related systems. Managers should have the expectation that people-related actions will be automated, have rules built into them, and will nudge them to either validate a data set (e.g. like performance ratings), complete an important action (e.g. confirm the transfer of an employee to an exciting new position), or consider team workload (e.g. if work-life balance scores drop). The People team should be doing all the impactful work involved in interacting with the other humans across the organisation and not be pushing documents around different workflows.

Invest in people systems as a priority – where appropriate – and make sure they talk to each other with smart workflows. For example, try to avoid a benefits platform that cannot take relevant employee information from the HRIS – there should be system compatibility. Take the time to streamline the processes built on and around the technology and elevate everyone's work on the back of it. The People team routinely supports other system automation and implementation projects, sometimes at the expense of their own efficiency. It's time to prioritise the people systems. Investment in people technology will be the tide that will lift all boats.

It's important to remember that machines will never take the place of human interaction. Technology will challenge and change the current HR service delivery model fundamentally, allowing for elevated, effective, value-added work to be carried out by the People team. People team members will never be out of a job – our jobs will simply get more interesting, impactful and rewarding with smarter technology.

Chapter 18

People data and analytics

Introduction

The objective of people analytics, as with all data and analytics, is to inform management and drive the organisation to use data to inform its decisions, resulting in better outcomes and bigger impact. People data is one of the most powerful tools for making an impact on business success when it results in the business user doing something different, something better.

The discipline of people analytics, also called HR analytics, talent analytics, human capital analytics or workforce analytics, can be defined as *"a number of processes, enabled by technology, that use descriptive, visual and statistical methods to interpret people data and HR processes."*[205]

Many People teams have a data analytics specialist or, where the headcount is not available, secure resources in a COO analytics team assigned to people work. Similar to people systems in the previous chapter, a lot more needs to be done to bring this discipline to the required level in the organisation, that is, to upskill the People team to the level required to successfully tell the story of why investment in people is crucial to organisational impact and business success, and to optimise the performance of the people they have. The whole People team must learn to leverage analytics by becoming data literate. People analytics is not a stand-alone action that we should make time for – rather it's about embedding it into existing processes and ways of working.

What are we solving for?

The people analytics strategy will, like everything, start with the business strategy. It is crucial to lead with a business question. This could be something surfaced anecdotally in a business meeting or via a direct request from the business to the analytics team. It could also be something the analytics team has observed and wants to investigate. When people analytics is embedded in the organisation successfully, there will be a healthy mix of 'pull' requests from the business as well as 'push' requests from HR. The ultimate users of this information are: business leaders, who should be keen to use this information to solve an issue within their function; employees, to allow them to be self-sufficient in completing their HR actions and personalising their benefits packages; and the People team, to provide evidence-based proposals for improving people programmes and making investments (e.g. creating business cases for keeping, changing, sunsetting people programmes). People analytics should also be used in business wide OKRs to measure the success of the business and people strategies and their related goals.

A skilled people analytics team will take data from a number of internal and external sources, using it to create and communicate the necessary evidence-based stories around people investment across the organisation. Robust people data is one of the most valuable ways the CPO can optimise the performance of people in the organisation. The more data you have, the more stories can be created, and impact can be made.

As well as having data specialists, the CPO needs to ensure they have robust data to work with. Using storytelling techniques with HR data can help the People function to drive and exceed business performance. Some questions that can be asked that drive business success include:[206]

- **Predicting retention:** which employees are likely to stay or leave the organisation?
- **Recruitment:** what makes certain teams with certain capabilities more or less successful? What are the gaps in low performing teams, what is common with high performing teams?
- **Revenue generation:** how can knowledge sharing and capability development impact sales and customer retention?

Internal sources of relevant data will include the HRIS, talent acquisition database, compensation database, benefits platform, employee engagement database and any other internal tool that captures people-related information. They may well also extract data from non-people functions, such as expense information from finance and compliance information from the legal systems. They may also use revenue-generation information from the sales systems.

The types of data captured from the people system will include: personal data, job information, compensation, diversity information, performance information, learning and development achievements – many of which have been listed in the previous chapter on people systems. Much of the organisation's employee data will be sensitive, and therefore needs to be aggregated and protected. Data privacy and confidentiality must be of the highest standard for people data – enlist the help of the Data Protection team to ensure the processes around using people data are watertight.

External information, required for creating broader stories, will include labour market information, competitor and industry reports. The data analyst work will ideally be carried out on a single technology platform, often called the Business Intelligence (BI) system, that pulls all the information together from multiple sources, facilitates flexibly and creatively collating the data using multiple rules, and allows for powerful reporting functionality. As mentioned in the previous chapter, the BI platform may be enterprise-wide and used by data analysts across the entire organisation.

The people analytics team, like all analytics teams, should not be 'order-takers' but strong partners, in particular to HRBPs and business leaders. Assuming the analytics team is aware of the business strategy and their role in it, data scientists and other analytics specialists should have a good sense of what information should be produced and why, and they should be allowed to drive the analytics agenda. They are the experts in creating evidence-based outcomes that drive action, that drive improvement. The team should be creating 'data products' with real insights and sharing it to the right business leaders at the right time to make better decisions, to better inform themselves about an issue, or to put in a solution to something.

In addition, there should be a process that allows business leaders request dashboards to be created for them to peruse. This balanced two-way partnership between the business and the People Analytics team is important; leaders will know what data will help them achieve business success, while the people analytics team expertise will provide additional specialist insights to help the business reach its potential in ways leaders hadn't even thought about. While ad hoc requests may be needed from time to time, governance over this type of process should be set very high, when a bespoke request is made of the people analytics team.

What does success look like?

There is hugely positive impact to be had from democratising data – in the right way – given the nature of this highly sensitive information. Each relevant chapter of this book has referenced key people metrics to collect in relation to the topic under discussion, and they are only a starter list. The data analytics specialist should be able to articulate what data need to be captured, from what systems, in order to review the most important historical trends and create future potential direction for people investment in the organisation.

Raw data generally comes in two forms. Quantitative data is information that can be quantified simply in numbers. Examples include turnover, absence days, employee survey response rates, number of employees signing up to a particular benefit or number of high performers leaving the organisation.

Qualitative data is non-numerical and can be defined as *"non-numeric information such as in-depth interview transcripts, diaries, anthropological field notes, answers to open-ended survey questions, audio-visual recordings and images"*[207]. Examples include new hire survey comments, performance rating commentary, employee survey comments, and exit interview information.

There are generally four levels of information that can be produced from people data[208]:

> **1. Descriptive analytics:** these comprise historical data, already available and which can be learned from. While

interesting, descriptive analytics is the least impactful type of analytics as it is a simple data point in the past. Example: employee turnover in Q1 was 10%. The real strength of this data is in baselining where the organisation is starting from. Descriptive analytics are great as a 'health check' into a particular area.

2. Diagnostic analytics: these metrics seek to determine the cause of a problem, to understand the reason behind data. Again this uses past data, where causation is attached to the data point. Example: Q1 employee turnover of 10% was higher than prior quarters, primarily due to low salary increases this year.

3. Predictive analytics: this is the forecasting of future events with historical patterns, the probability of something happening in the future. This type of analysis is obtained by statistical techniques like machine learning, artificial intelligence and data modelling, and produces helpful information, allowing business users do something different to affect a different outcome in the future. Example: if there is no explanation given for prior salary increases, and everything else stays the same, the prediction is that future employee turnover will rise to 12% by the end of this year.

4. Prescriptive analytics: these are the most mature form of analytics which propose future actions based on predictions made by predictive analysis. Created by statistical modelling and simulation to understand consequences of action, prescriptive analytics provide optional actions and solutions that can be taken to make the desired change. Example: a one-off bonus payment in Q3 to stem financial pressure; or an increase in the learning allowance; or better access to temporary sustainability projects, will stem the current increase in employee turnover.

As discussed in the previous chapter on people systems, people data is often housed in a number of different databases including, for example, the HRIS, applicant tracking system, learning system, employee engagement platform and benefits platform. Extracting consistent, trustworthy data from a number of sources can be complex. Therefore how the data analytics team defines and consistently uses the various data will engender trust in the outcomes as there will always therefore be one source of truth.

A simple example can be found in the employee survey, where terms such as 'executive', 'leader' and 'manager' must be clearly articulated at the start of the survey. For example: an executive is a person reporting to the CEO (often known collectively as the C-suite of the organisation); a leader is a manager of managers; a manager is the person to whom you directly report; team is the group of people who all report to your manager.

Similarly, the data analytics team will define the timeframe for each of their metrics consistently. For instance turnover may be the number of people who leave in a given a month divided by the average headcount during that month.

So how does the data analyst build great metrics from the BI system to churn out dashboards? Gartner provides the following steps:[209]

1. "Assess business requirements for HR.
2. Identify measurement areas.
3. Translate raw data.
4. Evaluate identified metrics."

The aim overall is to start with a business objective, translate that into raw data, build metrics around it (by, for example, creating a comparison, ratio or correlation to another figure) and create predictive metrics that tells you when a goal is in danger of not being achieved. One of the most important elements in producing great people data is to wrap a human storyline around it. The best data analysts will pre-empt the recipient asking, 'so what?' when they share their stories. There are a number of other recommendations for creating great people analytics:[210]

- Integrate people analytics and new perspectives on people risk and opportunity: the risk and opportunity perspective offers a unique way to understand value creation and value capture by organisations. Using people data can help to uncover how this works in practice.
- Build stronger cross-functional relationships to improve the impact of people analytics: non-HR functions require encouragement to increase the use of people data in their practices and for long-term decision-making. HR leaders and business partners should use this opportunity to build relationships using people data and focusing on delivering business value. Examples include: providing the facilities teams with information about who is using the office the most and why (e.g. data based on DEI categories, location, tenure etc); overlaying best sales offices or salespeople with people data to surface what drives the highest performers; and providing the finance team with retention insights, outlining how much longer employees stay based on wellbeing benefits or learning programmes.
- Build people analytics skills and confidence in the profession: an important story to emerge from this study is the impact of low skills and low confidence on the quality of outcomes from people analytics. HR leaders must invest in and develop the skills and confidence of HR professionals, and ensure they have the opportunities to undertake credible people analytics projects.

The following is a small sample of the types of people metrics that can be considered, categorised by organisational effectiveness, the employee journey, and the HR centres of excellence. These are but a drop in the ocean and by no means the full set the organisation should be considering. The metrics tracked will differ depending on what the priorities and strategy of the organisation are at a point in time:

Sample metrics by organisational effectiveness		
HRIS	**Position management**	**Engagement / culture**
Personal data	Vacant roles	Engagement:wellbeing score
Skills and competencies data	Vacant roles in succession plan	Burnout v employee location
Diversity raw data	% positions hybrid / remote / office	Recommend a friend statistics
Sample metrics by employee experience journey		
Talent management	**Talent acquisition**	**Talent assessment**
# Career frameworks	Diverse slate adherence	Top / bottom performers
Hybrid working splits	Hiring panel gender split	No. Single points of failure
Pay increase v perf. Rating	Offer:accept ratio	'Words' in perf reviews
Talent mobility	**Talent development**	**Talent offboarding**
Promotions by gender	Attendance / take up	Leave reasons
No. Roles by tenure	Skill / capability gaps	Attrition by level
Org. Capability / skills gaps	Revenue per salesperson	No. Of rehires
Sample metrics by HR centres of excellence		
DEI	**Total reward**	**Ticket / ER / cases**
# on leave of absence	Benefits programmes take-up	Numbers by function
Members of ERGs	Top / lowest earners	Numbers by manager
Leavers by diverse cohorts	Gender pay gap trend	Absenteeism costs

Table 18.1: Sample people metrics

Questions for a new CPO

- What are they key questions or challenges you're trying to solve with your HR analytics function?
- Do you have someone on your team managing data analytics?
- If not, do you have a resource in the data analytics team in the COO or other function?
- How well equipped is the People team to extract robust raw data from the people and other systems, in order to build impactful analytics?
- Are you confident that the people data is fully protected and only accessed by the appropriate people?
- Does the people team, and data analytics team specifically, have the right influencing and negotiation skills to say no when asked to create non-impactful metrics?
- Does the People team broadly think 'data first' in how it seeks to influence the business with evidence-based proposals?

Summary

Leading with data has been a mantra for the People team for many years, and yet many teams have yet to elevate this to the required level to be truly able to tell the story about how to optimise performance for business success. The CEB Corporate Leadership Council, now part of Gartner, said as far back as 2013: *"HRBPs who employ a 'leading with data' partnership style can increase their own strategic effectiveness by 22%."* [211]Systems and tooling has now made sharing that data with the business more efficient and effective in the stories it can tell.

The most insightful and impactful conversations the People team have with the business are those that are grounded in evidence – whether it's a conversation with the CFO about investment in a multi-year digital transformation of the People function, or a HRBP upskilling managers on improving how they calibrate performance, or a talent development associate creating a bespoke training programme to improve absence. Building business acumen and data literacy are two of the people team capabilities that should be prioritised for investment across the whole People team.

The value of people analytics does not stop there. As well as creating value for the People team, analytics create value for employees, giving them insights into their strengths and areas for development, supporting them in their career journeys, building wellbeing offerings, and providing access to great sustainability projects.

The biggest impact the people analytics team can have, is when it creates value for the entire organisation. Data 'products' should be created and shared with business leaders in the form of predictive and prescriptive solutions to people challenges that arise within their businesses, while leaders should be asking for people insights that they know will help them meet their goals. Always linked to business goals, data analytics will be one of the foremost ways to set up the organisation for continued success. Plucking figures from the air, especially when they are in an area that is already scoring well to start with, is ineffective. Make sure the metrics being tracked are focused on the right areas for business success and where they can drive the biggest impact.

One final word on analytics. Some things are best 'measured' with gut instinct. When a target value is put against them, they turn into something that simply must be measured until they reach that number. This can destroy any creativity or 'magic' that can materialise when people are acting freely. For example, learning, innovation and experimentation are best left unmeasured, for fear of stifling the creators or unduly focusing them on an endgame.

Engagement questions are answered with the heart, not the head – why have a target of 100 against that? Surely if we get a maximum score of 100/100 for engagement we don't stop there? Perhaps we should simply ensure the trajectory of certain people metrics is going in the right direction, so we don't overindulge ourselves in measurement at the mercy of simple enjoyment, creativity and even happiness. Progress over perfection.

SECTION FOUR - PULLING IT ALL TOGETHER

Chapter 19

Managing People risk

Introduction

Generally accepted risk management theory says that there are three lines of defence in managing risk in organisations.

1. The first line is the management of the organisation. They are the 'owners' of the business risk and primarily responsible for the management and mitigation of the risks in their function.

2. The second line is the risk function. They implement the risk framework and provide check and challenge to the first line.

3. The third line relates to independent assurance functions, such as internal and external audit. They perform periodic independent inspections to validate and provide assurance to stakeholders.

As CPO, you typically hold first line responsibility for the management of People risks in your organisation. This is an important and solemn function. Indeed, in the UK financial services sector, according to the Senior Managers and Certification Regime (SM&CR), the Head of HR could well be considered a regulated role, with all the attendant responsibilities and consequences. In its analysis of SM&CR, corporate law firm Shepherd and Wedderburn reports:[212]

> *"Many HR professionals, however, may feel that they didn't sign up for those obligations. They might also fear that they simply don't have the scope of influence, the experience and the support of the senior team to be able to assume such responsibilities personally.*

> *"Recent enforcement by the regulator is increasingly focused on conduct issues, poor governance and a failure to instil compliance-based cultures and accountability across organisations.*

> *"[Senior Management] need to take it very seriously indeed and they need to empower their HR function and invest it with the influence and respect required to achieve these challenges. That means higher salaries, better skills and generally the best people in the HR function rather than seeing it as a secondary, back-office function."*

In addition, if you work in the financial services sector, you and your team will play a pivotal role in identifying senior management roles, working with Compliance to ensure all the correct submissions are made, that people are advised and upskilled to be able to perform their roles, and that any changes, breaches or other issues are reported on a timely basis.[213]

Specific roles that may be relevant to the HR function are:

- SMF6 – Head of Key Business Area
- SMF14 – Chair of Remuneration Committee

What this means, in summary, is that the management of People risk is a critical function, one that you must master in your CPO role.

Defining and prioritising People risk

So, what do we mean when we talk about People risk? The Institute of Operational Risk defines people risk as: *"The risk that people do not follow the organization's procedures, practices and / or rules, thus deviating from expected behaviour in a way that could damage the business's performance and reputation."* [214]

The sister publication to this handbook, *How to be a Chief Risk Officer* [215] defines people risk as:

> *"Risks relating to people, incorporating the areas of diversity, conduct, culture, incentives, productivity, health and wellness, employee data privacy and reputation. Another angle to people risk is the risk of not being able to attract, hire or retain the right people for your organisation at the right cost."*

A number of recent publications are highlighting how people risk is racing up the list of highest priority risks for organisations to manage, if not already at the top. The recent *Risk in Focus 2023* report [216] places 'Human capital, diversity and talent management' in second place as one of the top five risks its surveyed audience is facing, with cybersecurity and data security in the top spot.

Interestingly the report predicts this risk will still hold that spot in three years' time. Almost all of the 15 risks that are being given highest priority by the study's participants have some element of people risk in them, among them:

- Changes in laws and regulation;
- Digital disruption, new technology and AI;
- Climate change and environmental sustainability;
- Business continuity, crisis management and disaster response;
- Organisational culture; and
- Fraud, bribery and the criminal exploitation of disruption.

In a global survey of board members and C-suite executives conducted by global consulting firm Protiviti and the NC State University ERM Initiative[217], the top 10 risks identified for 2023 include no less than eight relating to people. The study also projects the risk outlook forward to 2032 – here, the number of risks directly attributable to HR reduces, however the people impact of every risk on the list is noteworthy:

Top risks for 2023	
1.	Organization's succession challenges and ability to attract and retain top talent in a tightening talent market may limit ability to achieve operational targets.
2.	Economic conditions in markets we currently serve may significantly restrict growth opportunities.
3.	Anticipated increases in labor costs may affect ability to meet profitability targets.
4.	Resistance to change may restrict the organization from making necessary adjustments to the business model and core operations.
5.	Uncertainty surrounding core supply chain ecosystem.
6.	Changes in the overall work environment may lead to challenges in sustaining culture and the conduct of the business.
7.	Adoption of digital technologies may require new skills in short supply, requiring significant efforts to reskill / upskill employees.
8.	Organization's culture may not sufficiently encourage the timely identification and escalation of risk issues.
9.	Approach to managing demands on or expectations of a significant portion of workforce to work remotely or as part of a hybrid work environment.
10.	Organization may not be sufficiently resilient and / or agile to manage an unexpected crisis.

Figure 19.1: People risks within the top 10 company risk lists

Indeed, the Deloitte *2023 Human Capital Trends Report*[218] has a section dedicated to this matter, encouraging organisations to not only look at internal people risks but to consider the human risks associated with financial and operational risks.

Current thinking on People risk

PwC[219] identifies an over-arching set of people-related risks, starting with business risks. A resilient organisation needs a number of elements to work well, and the role of the CPO is to support the following:

- Creating an organisation that is agile and adaptable to change;
- Dealing with uncertainty in the political and / or economic environment;
- Attracting, mobilising and retaining the right talent and skills;
- Identifying a strong succession and leadership pipeline;
- Embedding a diverse and inclusive workforce;
- Leveraging your culture to drive desired conduct and behaviours; and
- Enhancing workforce wellbeing and resilience.

In addition, PwC identifies that the HR function itself, in performing its own core tasks, needs a robust set of controls to manage risk around:

- Collecting, understanding and organising people data, while maintaining confidentiality.
- Enabling regulation through enhancing HR systems, capabilities and processes – to be able to evidence that you are meeting all current regulation.
- Evolving and upskilling the HR function; equipping them with the right skills and knowledge to perform their roles competently.
- Aligning HR and the business; so that goals are aligned, and the teams are working together, rather than against each other.
- Compliance with increasing regulatory and legal requirements.
- Protecting organisation and employee data.
- Ensuring fair and transparent pay, promotion and performance management.
- Minimising the volume and complexity of people policies and processes, so the organisation can be efficient and effective in the pursuit of its mission.

Identifying People Risks

The first step in the management of any set of risks is to identify the potential events that could derail the achievement of your goals, whether business-wide or relating to people. To help with this, we leveraged a number of frameworks and compiled the following, non-exhaustive, list of people risks to consider.

People Risks			
Attrition	Employer liability	Key Person	Retention
Conduct	Engagement	Leadership	Safety
Cybersecurity	Financial (people)	Legal (people)	Skills obsolescence
Data Privacy (people)	Health	Mental Health	Strategic (people)
Diversity & Inclusion	Hiring	Pensions	Succession
Employee Relations	Incentives	Resilience	Technology (people)
Environmental issues: - Changing nature of work - Social unrest - Environment / Sustainability			

Fig 19.2 List of potential people risks

The list above provides a useful starting point and catalogue of risks for you to tailor to your own situation. It can be useful to hold working sessions to brainstorm these with your Executive team, your People team, and cohorts of staff around the organisation.

Assessing People Risks

Not all risks are created equal. Once you have a list of risks that you believe to be as comprehensive as possible, it's time to rank them in terms of both *impact* if they occurred, and *likelihood* of them occurring. Your Risk team should be prepared to support you in this exercise with a framework, or there are plenty that are publicly available.

Again, brainstorming these risks with colleagues at all levels is a good and obvious start. This can be supplemented by data sources, such as the following:

- Employee survey scores e.g. using anonymous survey platforms such as Officevibe;
- Employee and former employee reviews from platforms such as Glassdoor;
- Absenteeism;
- Number of unfilled vacancies and time to fill vacancies;
- Productivity measures;
- Staff turnover; and
- Qualitative and quantitative feedback from exit interviews.

External horizon scanning and looking across to other industries is also an important element of identifying impact and likelihood.

Managing People Risks

Once you have assessed and prioritised your risks, you then have to do something about them. There are multiple ways in which you can deal with risks. You can:

- Avoid the risk altogether by not undertaking the activity, e.g. choose not to launch in a certain market;
- Reduce the likelihood of the risk by putting controls in place (more about controls below);
- Transfer or outsource the risk, for example via insurance;
- Mitigate or reduce the impact of the risk; or
- Accept the risk as part of doing business.

As CPO, you have primary responsibility for putting in place the controls that will manage people risks. Your CRO and risk team will help and advise you, but the responsibility rests with you.

The following sample sets of controls will help you to discharge your responsibility to mitigate risk in the people space.

You want to create a people risk framework to house all things people risk related. Going back to the author's *How to be a CRO* handbook, Jennifer outlines the following core elements of the HR control strategy, that is those controls associated with specifically with the HR systems, tools and processes:

Over-arching People controls:

- Strategic resource and talent planning;
- Succession planning;
- A well-defined recruitment strategy;
- A motivating onboarding and induction journey;
- Encouraging staff engagement;
- Clear performance management processes;
- Staff development and talent management;
- Fair reward frameworks;
- Management of appealing employee benefits;
- Support for smooth termination, resignation and redundancy processes;
- Professional legal advice;
- Proactive handling of employee-employer relations; and
- Grievances, disciplinary and capability processes.

Conduct risk is a particular element of People risk that was borne out of actions in the financial services sector. It is broadly defined as any action of a financial institution or individual that leads to customer detriment, or has an adverse effect on market stability or effective competition.

Controls to counter conduct risk include:

- A customer-centric culture
- Robust supervision and oversight
- An ethical business structure, including governance, incentives and information barriers.
- Transparency to customers;
- Suitability of products for customers;
- Whistleblowing mechanism;
- Complaints monitoring;
- Personal account dealing and transaction monitoring; and
- Communications monitoring.

Detailed processes:

- Recruitment

    o Governance around identification of role requirements

    o Internal marketplace – giving existing employees a 'fair crack' at the role

    o Advertising compliance, equal opportunities

- Onboarding
  - Background checks; applied consistently and fairly
  - Capture of correct employee data (personal, tax etc.)
  - Pension administration (employee joining the correct scheme, being correctly informed, tax implications etc.)
  - Role-based access granted to correct systems
  - Training for the role
  - Capture of mandatory compliance content
- Payroll
  - Capture of correct information
  - Application of correct tax treatment, monitoring of residence
  - Changes to bank account data
- Privacy
  - Data governance around employee data– Information classification, role of least privilege, roles-based systems access, periodic audits, destruction of data post the legitimate holding period
- Performance management
  - Discipline, capability and grievance procedures performed legally and equitably
  - Movers process for people moving role (e.g. changing systems access)
  - Whistleblowing hotline

- o Employee support helpline
- o Health and benefits scheme
- o Office safety processes (e.g. fire safety, employee training, first aid, office hygiene)
- o Mental health support programme
- Off-boarding

  - o Capturing organisational property; passes, equipment, intellectual property
  - o Revoking systems access
  - o Terminating payroll
  - o Maintaining confidentiality
  - o Responding to reference requests

Like all things in managing risk, the level of appetite for accepting some degree of risk in how we do business is key. Having a zero-risk appetite could limit innovation, which will hinder the organisation reaching its potential and miss out on grasping key opportunities. Having too liberal an appetite will result in issues arising which can negatively affect the reputation, finances and operations of the business.

There is an art vs. science in judging the proportionality of the controls you put in place. You want to put the right amount of control in place, as expected by industry practice, and to bring risks to within tolerance. You will have zero tolerance for some risks, e.g. data privacy. However, good risk management is not about stifling activity. Well-designed controls should help the People team and the organisation do what is needed, in a safe, efficient way, but without putting a brake on necessary work.

The main formal tool for the identification and mitigation of risks is the Risk and Control Self-Assessment (RCSA). This is where, assisted by your risk function, you and your team will identify the key people risks facing the organisation, how well-controlled they are, how serious they would be if they materialised, and what further actions you can take to manage the risk.

What are we solving for? Culture above all else

All of the good practices throughout this book serve to strengthen your people risk environment. However, at its core, you want to embed a strong risk culture. Culture is how we really do things around here (yes, you've heard it before). Having a risk-aware culture is ensuring that there is a robust, visibly, monitored risk framework in place and that framework is lived and breathed by its people. People risks permeate the entire organisation. You need every single one of your people thinking about risk and acting as guardians of the organisation.

What does success look like? Value-adding advice and opportunity

As CPO you will be tasked with considering the risks to be captured within the HR team, which are the risks and opportunities associated with HR tools and processes. You will own these risks and capture, monitor and action them as appropriate within the HR team, with the support of the central risk team if required.

In addition to the specific risks associated with running the HR function, a robust people risk culture means seeing every risk through the lens of employees. Therefore it could be incumbent on the CPO to review key strategic risks from all the other functions around the C-suite table and support them in capturing additional risks for their function related to the people impact of their risks. The Deloitte *2023 Human Capital Trends Report*[220] goes into this in detail, noting:

"When it comes to human-related risks, organizations and their most senior leaders focus on a narrow set of workforce risks – the potential risks that human workers pose to the business... Yet all risks have a significant human element. Some have an outsized effect on humans. Others are affected and driven to some degree by humans. As such, we refer to these as human risks because they affect humans' professional and personal lives in palpable ways, in addition to the impact they have on your organization's short-term performance, long-term viability, and reputation and brand."

Going back to the *Risk in Focus 2023* report cited earlier in this chapter, the authors call out the most important human capital, diversity and talent management risks as:

- Adapting to hybrid working;
- Defining normal work practices;
- Building social purpose; and
- Environmental and Social Governance (ESG) sustainability goals

When we add in the people impact of the other strategic risks outside of HR (i.e. financial and credit risk, operational risk, technological risk, economic risk, political risk, environmental risk, social risk), it's clear that the CPO can and should use their knowledge and expertise across the entire organisational risk register. This is a strategic CPO input that is as yet undervalued by most organisations.

Questions for a new CPO

1. Is there a clearly-defined risk register capturing people risks in the organisation?
2. Does it align with what you, and others, view as the key people risks and opportunities?

3. Does the organisation review data regularly and horizon scan for emerging people risks and opportunities?
4. How risk-aware is the culture of the organisation? What more can be done to foster the thinking that everyone is responsible for managing risk?
5. What are the new and emerging people risks and is the organisation positioned to respond to them?

Summary

Creating a people risk framework within the HR team, as well as influencing and challenging other functions to review their risks through a people lens, is a critical strategic function of the CPO.

Good risk management starts and ends with culture. A strong people risk culture is created when everyone in HR knows about, understands and is aligned on what the risks are that relate to HR systems, processes and tools, and behaves in a way that actively monitors and actions controls to mitigate people risks and elevate people opportunities. On top of that, the CPO should be playing an active part in supporting their C-suite colleagues to understand people-related risks based on the human impact of their business risks.

It's been said before: people are the organisation's greatest asset. Protecting and elevating that asset via managing risks and opportunities is a crucial factor in business success.

Chapter 20

Your People team

Introduction

The People function has evolved over the past 20 years to having a leading seat at the C-suite table of top executives. With that has come a huge increase in expectations of the department and the CPO. As *Irish Times* US Business Editor Andrew Edgecliffe-Johnson bluntly says in his 2022 article 'Why personnel departments need to return to basics'[221], with hybrid working, a global pandemic, inflation, talent supply-demand issues, skills shortages, the great resignation, a new employer-employee contract based on mutual collaboration, burnout, union recognition, better wellbeing offerings and – oh yes – quiet quitting: *"There are few current management preoccupations that do not end up becoming the human resources team's problem."*

There is nothing tougher and more rewarding than having a day job of elevating fellow colleagues to be the best they can be. However, as Edgecliffe-Johnson goes on to attest in the article above, it is imperative that HR as a function focuses on actions that add the most value.

As we have seen throughout this book, employees demand equitable pay, relevant benefits, growth opportunities, purpose and a say in how their company operates. In return, they will provide skills, opinions and ingenuity, create innovative products and services, and do it with energy, happiness and loyalty. The HR function is at the heart of making this happen and as CPO, you need the right team around you to make it happen.

What are we solving for?

Traditionally human capital has viewed the employee as a cost and an expendable asset. Even now, when we are beginning to more fully appreciate that in fact people really are the most valuable differentiator for an organisation, the initial go-to option for cost savings is still to reduce headcount – often beginning with the HR team itself.

There have been swathes of lay-off cycles over the past 20 years – the 'dot com' bubble bursting in 2000, the financial crisis in 2008, the crypto crash in 2017, and the current culling of roles in the tech sector which is in the order of 150,000+ to date.[222]

This does not even begin to account for the automation of manufacturing and the decimation of administration roles due to technology. However, the glass is more than half full. As Sinéad McSweeney, former Managing Director of Twitter Dublin, says: *"I could not have named or imagined any one of the jobs that I went on to do when I was 15 years old. Most of them didn't even exist."* [223]

The tricky exam question that is being posed to HR is 'how will you future proof your organisation?' for employees, leaders, investors and the global good in general. A worthy challenge that the HR team will be happy to take up.

What does success look like?

The HR team needs to set itself up in a way to deliver everything that we have discussed in this book successfully. There are a number of ways it can do that. The traditional 'Ulrich model' organised the delivery of the HR function in an operating model of three broad groups as follows, which will be prevalent in some form in most organisations today:

1. **HR Business Partners:** generalists who know a little about a lot of things. Often coming from HR administrator, HR operations or HR generalist roles, they are the primary business-facing team for HR, and build the closest, strongest relationships with managers, leaders and executives.

2. **HR shared services:** generalists who offer operational HR services to managers and employees. Powered by HR administrators, who may have some specialist knowledge or training about employee relations, legal policy and process or payroll for example, this service is often offered by way of a ticketing system and solved electronically. Rich HR data emerges from the service and support that this team provide.

3. **HR centres of excellence:** HR professionals with deep specialist knowledge in a particular area of HR. These may include talent acquisition, remuneration and benefits, Diversity Equity and Inclusion, industrial relations, employee relations, learning and development, communications, data analytics or data systems. Increasingly the workplace facilities team and / or the health and safety teams are becoming part of the HR team, particularly with the emerging world of work

encompassing not only when and how we work, but where we work.

CSR and even elements of the ESG agendas may also fall into the remit of HR, in particular sustainability, requiring the People team to build skills and knowledge in these developing areas.

Also increasingly, the People team has a project or PMO team: not only are there cyclical programmes of work to be carried out (e.g. performance management, talent planning, succession planning, salary changes and benefits renewal) but increasingly change and improvement programmes are required constantly and need to be delivered consistently using project management disciplines. While PMO support can be secured from a central PMO team, it can be challenging to get to the top of their workstack, so having your own in your team will improve your ability to control delivery as well as save time building business cases for resources.

Since Dave Ulrich developed this initial model for the People team, the programme of work for the People team has increased significantly. Conceivably the following is a comprehensive list of the current jobs to be done by the People team:

Team name and leader	Programme of work
People team *Chief People Officer*	People strategy and annual people goals Work design (organisation design, organisation development) Workforce planning Culture and engagement C-suite relationships Board reporting and relationships
People programmes and experience *Head of People Experience*	<u>TALENT MANAGEMENT PROGRAMME OF WORK:</u> Career Framework Employee Value Proposition Talent acquisition (source, attract, select, hire, induct, onboard) Talent assessment (performance, talent planning, succession planning) Talent mobility (promotion, internal talent marketplace) Talent development (L&D curriculum, leadership training, organisational capability) Talent offboarding <u>OTHER PROGRAMMES OF WORK:</u> Business operating model (how, when and where we work) Feedback culture Recognition culture Employee surveys Internal comms HR continuous improvement programme
People policies and legal *Head of People Policies and Legal*	Employee legal documentation People risk management Policies and procedures Employee relations and industrial relations

Remuneration, benefits and wellbeing *Head of Rewards*	Remuneration Benefits programme Wellbeing programme Environment Social Governance (ESG) and Corporate Social Responsibility (CSR)
Diversity, equity and inclusion *Head of Diversity Equity and Inclusion*	Diversity Equity Accessibility Inclusion
People systems and analytics *Head of People Systems and Analytics*	People systems Data and analytics

Table 20.1: Sample People team structure and programmes of work

There is emerging research, from organisations such as McKinsey, that indicates that the HR team should rethink how it sets itself up, following the seismic global shifts across the globe in the past 20 years. McKinsey captures eight innovation shifts that drive a new way of thinking about the HR operating model:[224]

1. Adopt agile principles, for swift reallocation of resources to enable faster rate of change in the business. This includes standing up temporary teams from across the People Team to focus on a significant programme of work (e.g. opening an office in a new jurisdiction) as well as expanding the remit of People team members beyond their traditional deliverables (e.g. talent acquisition partner leading onboarding or learning and development partner hosting career conversations with employees)

2. Excel along the employee experience journey, to win the race for talent. Enable employee health and resilience throughout their time with the organisation and not just when things go wrong. This includes designing interesting work, empowering employees to make good choices

around where, when and how they work, and measuring work around outcomes, not time or effort.

3. Re-empower frontline leaders in the business, to reduce complexity and put decisions back where they belong. This means reducing the people administration actions from them and building in more automation: for example, building rules into performance management ratings and requesting they only need to authorise critical decisions.

4. Offer individualised HR services, to meet expectations of personalisation. An example of this in action is offering a flexible benefits and wellbeing programme, where employees self-select how they wish to spend their benefits fund.

5. 'Productise' HR services, to build fit-for-purpose offerings based around the needs of the business. Enable end-to-end responsibility for those services through cross-functional product owner teams in HR. For example, create a 'performance management' product which is designed specifically around relevant business goals, and which is owned by a member of the PMO or HRBP or even Talent Development team. We already saw in chapter 17 that the analytics team should be the driver of what analytics are created and why.

6. Integrate design and delivery with end-to-end accountability, to address strategic HR priorities and reduce back-and-forth. Assigning ultimate accountability to a single HR leader will drive better cross-functional collaboration and focus on delivery. For example, if a key goal on the People strategy is to rebuild the wellbeing offering, give accountability to deliver it to the Total reward lead; they should build a project team that includes

representation from the benefits, DEI team, CSR / EST, analytics and systems team at a minimum.

7. Move from process excellence to data excellence, enabling broader decision making through better data, leveraging artificial intelligence and machine learning where applicable. Chapter 17 on people analytics captured some examples of where business intelligence and new technologies will elevate the role of the people on the People team engaged in more impactful activities.

8. Automate HR solutions, to capitalise on the power of digitalisation of HR. Chapter 16 highlighted how an excellent people systems architecture will provide seamless sharing of people data as well as the opportunity to build rules and assumptions into them, reducing the amount of time employees, managers and the People team themselves need to spend on operational and administrative matters.

The People team you design and build will ultimately be a function of the age, size and shape of the organisation, the industry it operates in, its complexity, geographical footprint, and the level of investment available. Notwithstanding the HR operating model to which you align your team, the skills required by the team to deliver the people agenda broadly include the following. As CPO, you need to be cognisant of your own skills and strengths, and where the gaps exist, in order to build a complementary team.

- **Relationship management:** the HR team needs to be focused on the 'employee and stakeholder' experience; including the Board, the C-suite, leaders, managers and individual contributors. We cannot help the organisation without seeing the world through their lens, as they experience all people-related matters, from how the workforce is hired, onboarded, managed, led, rewarded, recognised and inspired. Develop a selection of skills that can be used in all situations with all stakeholders; coach, mentor, sounding board, critique, ally, negotiator, challenger, consultant, dealmaker, and – if needed – deal breaker. At all times your team needs to be open, consistent, humane and empathic. We only ever know a tiny part of what a colleague is experiencing at a point in time in their lives.

- **Business acumen:** a key differentiator in a HR professional, especially as they get further into their career, is understanding their organisation's business. What is the mission? How does it make money? Where, when and how does it offer its products and services? How does it differentiate itself? What are its customer success scores? How does it market itself? What are the organisation's key risks? A fully rounded HR practitioner – whether interacting directly with the business or not – will be a stronger, more impactful and ultimately more successful professional when they can articulate the business goals and can link what they specifically do in HR to achieve them. Consider how to build this muscle in your HR team, by bringing in guest speakers at HR team meetings, having mentoring across the business, internal / external training programmes or even secondments to other roles across the business.

- **Data literacy:** consultancy AIHR describes the four key skills under this competency as: comprehend and establish metrics and KPIs;[225] read and interpret reports; produce data visualisations (e.g. dashboards) for storytelling; and understand where people data and business acumen meet. Everyone on the People team needs to have a fundamental level of ability in all four areas and, depending on role, advanced competency in some of them. For example; a HRBP needs to be able to tell a story with data, that resonates with the business they are supporting; a talent acquisition partner must be able to articulate how well, or otherwise, their hiring campaign is going at every stage of the process; even the newest people operations team member must be able to interpret the HR ticket dashboard to identify where the hot spots are and where there are opportunities for improvement.

- **Critical evaluation:** contrary to what some employees and stakeholders may believe, HR is not an order-taker service. Writing in *Harvard Business Review*, Eric Garton, Partner at Bain & Co., outlines how the function is in charge of delivering value for money for the company's greatest asset, that is, in how the organisation uses employee time, talent and energy[226]. Be selective about what services are offered, what projects are undertaken, and how highly digital transformation is prioritised. Place the right people into the right jobs at the right time for the organisation – not for the person who shouts loudest or has the loftiest title. Use data to create business cases, to back up decisions, to share successes, and – in the words of Garton in his article cited above – to *"eradicate the factors that steal time from employees"*.[227]

  Your stakeholders, investors, prospective employees and indeed current colleagues will enjoy the fruits of your independent thinking and expertise on what needs to be done and when in terms of people investment.

- **Ethical practice:** ethical behaviour is the responsibility of every single employee. However, there are cohorts within the organisation that have a greater responsibility to cultivate a culture of principled behaviour: the board, leaders and managers, and those in the HR function. We are one of the guardians of ethical behaviour, not least due to the fact that HR has responsibility for the process of investigating and disciplining unethical behaviour. HR also has privileged access to some of the most sensitive information about its organisation's people, from pay, to health issues, to personal problems that individuals may be facing. This must be handled with the greatest sensitivity and discretion. HR team behaviours, processes and systems must be of the highest standard to help protect the organisation from poor behaviours.

- **Technical HR knowledge:** As with any function, there are set of core HR fundamentals that all HR professionals should know at least a little about. They may know a little about a lot of the employee journey (e.g. HR Business Partners) or a lot about a part of that journey (e.g. centres of excellence). Either way, having a growth mindset and seeking to stay informed about the future of HR is key to having outsized impact.

  A suggestion to those early in their HR career – seek out opportunities to get direct experience of as many HR specialisms as possible. Even if you end up in an area of HR that focuses on gaining deep specialist knowledge, understanding how it fits into the building bricks that makes up the full HR offering, and being able to speak the relevant language will be widely appreciated by employees, stakeholders and HR colleagues alike.

- **Communications:** internal communication with employees as well as external communication of the employer brand are the channels by which the HR function articulates its service to its stakeholders. Listening to our employees and stakeholders, like any successful product or service team, is crucial for the success of our offerings. Transparency of HR processes, programmes and decisions is becoming more and more important as employees and external stakeholders demand a more collaborative relationship with the organisation. Having excellent two-way communications channels will be rewarded with employee loyalty.

Interestingly five of the above seven skills could conceivably be on the organisation's capability list discussed earlier in chapter 9 – this bodes well for the People function's standing in the company, as well as the opportunity for those working in the people team to grow their careers in other areas of the business should they wish to do so. Gartner provides what it sees as a contemporary structure for the People team, embodying the above while calling out that there is:

"no singular 'perfect' model… the HR operating model of the future provides a set of guiding principles that can help every HR leader – independent of functional size, geography or maturity – upgrade their structural model and achieve their functional goals." [228]

The HR Operating Model of the Future

Head of HR	
Strategic Talent Leaders	**HR COO**
	HR Operations and Service Delivery Team
	Shared Services
HR Problem-Solver Pool	People Relations Managers
	Human Capital Intelligence
Next-Generation COEs	HR Technology Team

Figure 20.1: Gartner's HR operating model for the future

While the organisational design of the HR team and the key competencies expected within it are relatively clearly defined, it is worth thinking differently about how the different HR teams and team members can work together.

As the McKinsey report *HR's new operating* model, cited at the beginning of this chapter[229] states, you can embrace agile working by creating temporary cross-functional teams who work on a specific assignment together for a fixed period of time. While the reporting lines based on the traditional structure of the People team defined above should remain intact so that every employee has a direct line manager to guide them, agile teams offer a new way to get HR work done.

Putting together temporary teams to deliver a defined piece of work can result in any given member of the HR team temporarily reporting to a project or other HR (or business) leader during the performance year. For example, if the business is expanding to a new geographical region, set up a team with representatives from the talent acquisition, operations, remuneration, benefits and payroll teams to focus on delivering on this plan for a fixed quarter or half-year. Similarly, a project to re-invent the performance management process could be delivered by a team represented by onboarding, operations, systems, talent development, systems, analytics and business partnering functions, led by a project manager.

The other way to think differently about how HR gets its work done is to consider how traditional HR roles could be combined, or how work can be redesigned to make traditional HR roles bigger, requiring broader skillsets. There are a number of new roles emerging from the research[230] and indeed in reality, which mirrors the earlier discussion on creating broad positions that evolve over time, rather than narrow career ladders. For example, rather than having a number of specific roles in the Talent Development team, such as administrator, training facilitator, or instructional designer, is there merit in creating a Talent Development Officer position that moves fluidly across everything that the team delivers?

The vibrant internal talent marketplace discussed in chapter 8 needs focused resources to ensure that current employees are ready for and given the opportunity to step into new roles as they arise – a team of Internal talent marketplace officers, who have TA skills, relationship skills and a keen interest in career management, could deliver that work. Could a talent acquisition team extend their remit into onboarding so there is a single point of contact up to when the new hire is 3 months into the company rather than doing a handover of HR contacts on day 1? Could a member of the Talent Development team take up a career officer position as a partner to employees for all things career related, showing the organisation is thinking about every employee's next role before even they do?

The options are endless, and the outcome should be an invigorated People team who are excited to work on cross-functional roles within and outside of HR, building skills and knowledge consistently towards their broader career. All good food for thought.

Summary

This chapter started by heralding the HR function coming into its own and having its time in the spotlight – and it is. Investors, shareholders, CEOs and the Executive team are finally truly realising the importance of this function and how its success permeates every function, team and person in the organisation. We will see in the next chapter, on emerging topics, that there is more to do to truly realise the power of people in organisations. In all matters, whether building strong foundations or looking around the corner for what's next, build a best-in-class People team who are confident, brave, undaunted and proud to ensure that the organisation sees the power of investing in its people, ultimately playing its crucial part in setting up the organisation for success.

Given the demands placed on them, People teams are frequently exhausted. Don't forget to spend time listening to how they are doing too. Look closely at the team's employee survey results and make time for whatever it is they need – they deserve it – and that must include time and space to have fun too. Invest in them – they do the best kind of work possible, elevating other people to achieve their potential. Let's make sure they reach theirs too.

Chapter 21

Linking the People function to ESG, CSR and sustainability

Introduction

These days there are three things employees really want: career, community, cause[231]. We in the People function have focused on building career frameworks for a long time. In terms of community, many of us have facilitated a 'company day out' to build something or raise money for the community. Cause is a newer phenomenon and links to the bigger purpose that employees and candidates expect organisations to have.

The bigger picture that organisations – and therefore People functions – have to consider can be captured under the following three topics: ESG, CSR and sustainability. How should the People function be thinking about these? What do these terms even mean? And how can the CPO plan to meet this much bigger purpose for both its employees and for all the organisations stakeholders, internal and external alike?

ESG, CSR and sustainability

ESG stands for environment, social and governance. While environment and climate are the topics that are usually at the top of most minds currently, the fuller scope of ESG includes topics such as the following:[232]

- Environmental: greenhouse gases, carbon emissions, supply chain, operational emissions, financed emissions, waste management;
- Social: diversity, equity and inclusion, staff relations, community involvement; and
- Governance: the composition of the board, involvement of wider stakeholder groups.

An ESG framework is used when a company considers its long-term business survival through the lens of 'profit, purpose and survival', further defined as:[233]

- Environmental criteria: all the energy and resources a company uses and waste it discharges;
- Social criteria: all stakeholders, or relationships, impacted by the organisation including customers, suppliers, shareholders, communities and employees; and
- Governance: all internal systems and processes used to govern the organisation.

We view Corporate Social Responsibility (CSR) as a subset of ESG, generally falling into the social category. Defined as *"the idea that a company should play a positive role in the community and consider the environmental and social impact of business decisions"*,[234] CSR activities are focused on giving back to the community, they are usually associated with a 'feelgood' factor for employees, and centre around four areas:

- Environment (e.g. reduce pollution, increase renewable energy);
- Ethical (fair treatment of all);
- Philanthropic (donations to charities); and
- Economic (contributing to community programs).

Most of us have had the opportunity in work to take a day away from the office to build a sensory garden for a children's school, give out food at a homeless shelter, or take part in collecting money for a nominated charity on the company annual fundraising day – all great CSR activities. However, these initiatives are no longer enough to engage the current workforce, especially those making up the millennial and Gen Z workforces – purpose is much bigger and more important than that.

What does success look like?

Alignment with a greater purpose dramatically increases employee engagement and loyalty and makes a company more attractive to new hires (make sure you incorporate purpose in the company EVP). While a company can run activities under both ESG and CSR frameworks concurrently, there are differences between them. CSR activities are primarily focused on giving back to and improving society at large, which can lead to attracting more candidates, elevating purpose in existing employees, improving engagement, and improved relationships with investors. ESG initiatives are measurable, more likely to materially affect the company bottom line, and most importantly, required by legislation, primarily the EU Corporate Sustainability Report. Tangible benefits include:[235]

- Lower cost of capital
- Improved financial performance
- Enhanced brand and competitive advantage
- Customer loyalty

- Improved risk management
- Fostering innovation
- Attracting, engaging and retaining employees

Tim Koller and Robin Nuttall of McKinsey, along with Witold Henisz, a professor at the Wharton School of the University of Pennsylvania, capture the bottom-line value from a strong ESG proposition as follows:[236]

1. Top-line growth: opening up more opportunities.

2. Cost reductions: in energy and resources.

3. Regulatory interventions: subsidies and government support.

4. Productivity uplift: increased motivation.

5. Optimising investments: allocating capital based on sustainable resources.

So where can and should the CPO focus their attention in order to have an outsized impact on ESG and CSR? Some forward-thinking CPOs are embracing the broader concept of sustainability. Sustainability can be defined as *"Meeting the needs of the present without compromising the ability of future generations to meet their own needs"*.[237] Let's see where that impact can really be made.

Good to great – a focus on sustainability

Beyond complying with regulation, to really embrace the purpose that your people crave, we believe you have to look deeper at what it takes to become a truly sustainable operation. Below are listed some of the tenets of a truly strong sustainability risk framework. It is based on Patagonia's blueprint, from its 40 years of operating as one of the most admired and sustainable organisations in the world.[238] While not every organisation will attain the levels below, they set a bar to which others can aspire.

- The very mission of the organisation should speak to doing some degree of good in the world. In his book *Net Positive*[239], Paul Polman refers to this as "*finding the organisation's soul*".
- The organisation should fundamentally believe in treating its employees well. This means a People framework comprised (mostly) of permanent roles with pensions, benefits and maternity leave. Childcare, shared parental leave, flexible, hybrid working and a trust-based approach are even better.
- The organisation should foster a culture of trust, wellbeing, transparency and open dialogue. It should not cover up dissent.
- The organisation should have visibility up and down its supply chain and continuously monitor it to ensure its sources are ethical, based on fair trade, a working wage and non-exploitation. From a people standpoint, having checks in place, a transparent culture and the ability to raise issues and 'whistle blow' are important safeguards.
- The organisation should do all it can to source materials which are sustainable. It should work with its suppliers to constantly improve and should swap out better materials whenever they can, even when this costs more.
- The organisation should have a waste management strategy, reducing waste as far as possible, and favouring recyclable and recycled materials.
- The organisation should push back against one-dimensional expectations of ever-increasing quarter-on-quarter financial performance in favour of shared growth, product innovation and sustainability. Think this

is unrealistic? Read *Net Positive* to see what was done at Unilever to address the culture of short-termism.

- The organisation should report on its sustainability efforts, avoiding superficial 'greenwashing' and taking care to be just as transparent about areas in which it can do better as about its successes.
- The organisation's physical spaces (offices, factories, etc.) should be designed or upgraded to be energy-efficient, sustainable and human-friendly places.[240]

Your People strategy probably already has many of the above principles embedded in it: elevating DEI initiatives, providing mental health and wellbeing offerings, having a paperless contract offer and accept process, and offering company days to do community work. Make sure you make the link between what you are doing in your People strategy on ESG, CSR and sustainability to the organisation-wide strategies. Success will come from having top-town executive visibility and commitment, as well as bottom-up employee engagement in what, where and how they want to effect meaningful change.

In an exclusive interview, Sinéad Kilkelly, Executive Director of People and Organisational Development, talks about the great work that ESB, Ireland's leading energy provider, is doing in this space:

"ESB has always had a proud tradition of making a difference in the communities we serve – right back to its origins in the electrification of rural Ireland in the 1920s and the building of the Ardnacrusha hydro-electric power station. The current business strategy 'Driven to make a difference – Net Zero by 2040'[241] sets possibly the biggest ambition of all and has sustainability at its very core, with a lead taken from the 17 UN Sustainable Development Goals (SDGs).

"As a People Director how you choose to define sustainability and the leadership role you play can make the difference between a purpose state-

ment that sits with the strategy function or is in fact embedded in every aspect of the people proposition and organisation capability. Growing your knowledge base of the topic of sustainability is important to be able to lead effectively, but also is really an imperative for any HR professional or senior manager today given the progress needed on the SDG goals – there are plenty of good executive level programs available.

"At ESB we reserve the term ESG for the financial sector (typically the lens through which investments are viewed) and use the broader term sustainability across all aspects of our business. One of ESB's four foundational capabilities is 'Sustainable and Socially responsible' with a need to 'step forward' in this area.

"We have threaded the business purpose, strategy and culture throughout the people strategy giving it an incredible platform from which to really derive the ability for each of our people to make a difference. We know this is important, because we asked our people – and yes we know it's particularly important for early career people or those new to the workforce, but it's also important to those in more established careers. Sustainability is all about people, our people today and particularly those of tomorrow.

"With ownership for the centre of expertise for sustainability within the People organisation at ESB, a program was established to determine what that 'stepping forward in being sustainable and socially responsible' meant, in very real terms. We collaborated with many people across the organisation as well as gathered inputs from experts and stakeholders. They challenged traditional thinking and encouraged us to step forward further and faster, consistent with our values of being courageous, caring, driven and trusted. That culminated in late 2022 with the Chief Executive setting out an ESB Sustainability Leadership Statement (see figure below). It places equal weight on environment and people."

> **Driven to make a difference through electricity as an enabler for regeneration.**
>
> ESB's purpose is founded in the consistent belief in electricity as an enabler of social regeneration.
>
> We commit to:
>
> - Playing a full role in building a resilient electricity system of the future, where renewable electricity will displace carbon emissions in electricity, in buildings and in transport
>
> - Enhancing nature wherever we operate, and supporting our host community to develop and grow stronger.
>
> - Empowering our people in a healthy workplace to act sustainably, supporting our customers to reach net zero and working to protect the rights of all people in our value chain
>
> By listening, learning and collaborating we will create a brighter future where everyone can thrive.

Figure 21.4: ESB Sustainability Leadership Statement

"Introducing the term regeneration as our leadership intent is significant; it is expressed most easily as care *— for all humans we encounter, for the environment and for future generations — and sits squarely with our values. We are setting out key commitments and a plan for delivery, building on important work already underway. The People organisation is the catalyst for the sustainability ambition, but these commitments and plans are owned across the executive leadership with everyone playing their part. The People strategy 'to enable the culture and capability required for a sustained performance, where everyone can make a difference to achieve net zero by 2040' is how we lead on commitments in areas like inclusion and diversity, sustainable leadership, communications, systems and decision making.*

"One of ESB Board's subcommittees — the Safety, Sustainability & Culture Committee, is the means through which the Board oversees and governs the sustainability strategy, linking it clearly with culture.

Making progress on the UN SDGs[242] *and achieving our ambition of electricity as an enabler for regeneration really does require the courage, care, trust and drive of all our people. It also provides an exceptional opportunity for HR to lead at a strategic level and one we should embrace — operating at the intersection between people and sustainability, culture and purpose."*

ESB is a great example of how the People and sustainability agendas can be intertwined. When Unilever published its *Unilever Sustainable Living Plan*, aimed at re-orienting the organisation towards purpose, albeit still with profit, they also took steps to ensure that the people framework was aligned. This included re-working the HR systems, tying job descriptions to the USLP, allocating their best people not to the 'biggest' jobs, but the ones most critical for future success and creating a USLP-aligned executive education programme to ensure the new goals permeated the organisation.[243]

"We can shift from faceless and robotic organizations and economies and recognise each other's humanity."

Paul Polman

Putting your ESG plans into action

In addition, for ESG to happen, the human capability framework described by Dave Ulrich informs choices and helps with decisions.[244]

Talent:

- What skills are required for ESG to happen?
- How can the organization acquire or develop those skills?
- How can commitment to ESG improve employee commitment and engagement?

Leadership:

- Who is the leader of the ESG effort?
- What can executives say and do that will lead the way and sustain the ESG agenda?

Organization:

- Where does ESG fit in the organization structure?
- How does ESG fit with strategic purpose, customer promises, and investor disclosures?
- How can ESG move forward quickly through a disciplined change and accountability process?
- What are the metrics for ESG and how can they be tracked and be part of performance accountability?

Human resource function:

- How can HR practices (performance management, development, communication) be designed to foster ESG progress?
- How can HR professionals partner with ESG professionals to make progress?"

Questions for a new CPO

- What is the CEO and C-suite committing to from a sustainability perspective?
- Where are the People-related elements of the sustainability plan? Are they goals that will stretch the organisation to be better, and will give employees added purpose and drive to achieve them?
- Does each member of the Executive team sponsor a particular pillar of the plan?
- Have employees been engaged in co-creating the sustainability agenda with the Executive team?
- Have employees committed to actively engaging in the achievement of the sustainability plans, and given the time and related resources to be successful?
- Have you shared the organisation's purpose and sustainability vision externally, in particular with

prospective and prior employees via the Employee Value Proposition and other online channels?

Summary

"Young people - they care. They know that this is the world that they're going to grow up in, that they're going to spend the rest of their lives in. But I think it's more idealistic than that. They actually believe that humanity, human species, has no right to destroy and despoil regardless." [245]

Sir David Attenborough

If there is one thing that will attract and keep our current and future workforces engaged, it's going to be our organisational commitment to making the world a better place. Whether you are in an organisation that is more naturally part of climate change and sustainability challenges, or one which is well placed to accelerate the solutions, do something to have an impact, capture it in your sustainability strategy, tell your employees about it, and then give them the space and time to make a difference.

Trust us, they will.

Chapter 22

Emerging topics – what's around the corner?

Introduction

Helping your organisation see around the corner is one of the areas of biggest impact for you as CPO. Try and make space for ongoing reading and networking to get ahead of the next 'black swan' (a negative event that's impossible to predict) or the next glorious opportunity to differentiate your organisation from the rest. While you may never be prepared completely for all eventualities, as we saw in the managing people risk chapter, many key people risks that have emerged as issues are well flagged on global risk registers.

Monitoring global business and HR trends should give you as much foresight as you can be expected to have, short of bringing your crystal ball along to all your hybrid work locations. Combining that with agility and empowerment should stand you in good stead to react quickly and appropriately to whatever comes your way.

At the time of writing, in early 2023, here are some of the emerging people topics that you might consider.

Ways of working v2.0 – a new business operating model

In 2013, Dave Coplin, then Chief Envisioning Officer at Microsoft UK, wrote a book called *Business Re-imagined* [246] in which he predicted a move away from commuting into a central office every day. It took a global pandemic and seven more years for this vision to come to pass.

Post-Covid, we've really only just started figuring out new ways of working. Most companies have or will imminently have new policies around where we work (hybrid working), when we work (quiet quitting, legislation on right to disconnect), how we work (asynchronous working, team agreements) and even why we work (empowered employees).

These policies are only version 1.0 of the real step change the world is making to create the workplace of the future. We now know this way of working is here to stay and these policies which provide optionality for employees will be necessary but still insufficient for business success. The next version of the business operating model will need to use the data and feedback from our current initial policies to truly figure out how to measure the ultimate next way of working. Author and people analytics expert David Green[247] calls it *"Solving the 'Productivity Paradox' of hybrid"*, and highlights that HR and analytics have the opportunity to *"lead the design of the organisation of the future, one that is fully adaptive to hybrid work, workplace and workforce, and also has purpose, value and culture at its heart"*.

Productivity and purpose create wellbeing and engagement – as we've said, employees want to have impact, they want to work on projects that are meaningful, and they feel great when they do. Adaptable teams (redeploying employees, fluid internal talent marketplace, temporary teams), truly empowered employees (selecting projects, owning deliverables), digitisation of people matters (to free up space to collaborate on meaningful goals) and elevating team performance over hierarchical organisation design will be the next landing zone for the future of how we do work. You never know – truly reorganising work may result in being able to do more impactful, meaningful work within a shorter working week. And on that note……

The four-day working week

Somewhat linked to the next business operating model, but worthy of its own section, if for no other reason than it strikes fear into the heart of many people leaders and executives! Linked predominantly to wellbeing, the core principle to achieving a shorter working week is not just working fewer hours for the sake of it; rather it is founded in re-thinking how jobs are currently done in order to produce the same, if not more, outputs more efficiently over a shorter amount of time – and crucially, not backfilling those extra hours with, you guessed it, more work. However, creating a case to trial a four-day week based on improving wellbeing is not going to be enough to get buy in from your C-suite peers or your board – you must link it to business success. There are a number of well-publicised trials ongoing, in the UK, Ireland, Iceland and New Zealand to name a few, that you can consider if you are thinking about doing this in your organisation.

The Adam Grant *Re:Thinking* podcast on this matter, entitled 'The four-day working week: luxury or necessity'[248] brings together four eminent and different leaders who advocate for it, summarising their discussion saying that *"employees should be evaluated on the contribution they make, not on the time they put in"*. It's an excellent listen.

If the time is right to consider this in your organisation: get your fiercest C-suite challengers onside or at least open to discussing the concept: make sure you have financial as well as HR data on potential outcomes, both cost-saving outcomes, such as reduction in absence, as well as productivity outcomes including improved customer service. Find some forward-thinking executives who will be willing to trial it for you; and link success to Environment Social Governance (ESG) or Corporate Social Responsibility (CSR) wins that your organisation can market if the trial turns out a success. Read widely around where it has been successfully trialled and get support from expert organisations like the Centre for Work Time Reduction (www.worktimereduction.com).

At all times, and as always, keep your employees informed on why this is a strategy that you are willing to consider or not consider at this time – don't put your head in the sand. Grant's podcast predicts that this question is coming to employers whether employers like it or not. Have your answer ready.

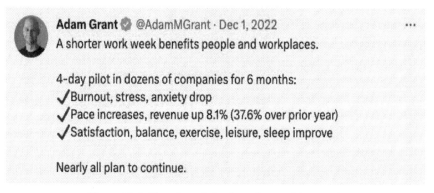

Figure 21.1: Benefits of the four-day working week

Lifting the burden off managers: HR digital transformation and work re-design

This book has been sprinkled with the theme of manager burden. Re-thinking the manager persona is an important consideration if we are to truly reconfigure how work gets done. Managers should be spending more time with their teams, teaching, listening, influencing, learning, elevating, and developing them together or individually for their next project or position. They should *not* be writing goals, pouring over spreadsheets of rating options, researching what learning options are available, or approving expenses.

The digital transformation of people activities is already on many executive to-do lists, and if it's not on yours, then either strongly consider putting it on there - or write a book on how you successfully achieved it and share your knowledge widely with the rest of us! There is an ever-growing selection of people systems, tools and apps that automate everything from employee self-service benefit sign up to recognition awards to capability management.

Where there must be manager intervention, build rules into HR programmes that anticipate the majority of people doing the right thing most of the time (e.g. 70% of our employees will meet performance expectations every year; the other 30% are either over or under achieving) and focus on the outliers. Put in robust audit actions to test if these rules are working and create manager actions solely around auditing these exceptions. Imagine the delight on the face of the manager who only needs to spend 30 minutes confirming the list of 'exceptions' and only needing meetings with that small group to discuss their performance at the year end.

Let's re-design the role of managers, allowing them to spend their time doing what they love – that's why they are in the job in the first place. There are interesting approaches out there that may expand your thinking on this topic. As Claire Doody, Work in Motion Founder, attests:

"The role of the manager is becoming unsustainable. In addition to being a domain expert, a people leader ad holding a considerable amount of organisational overhead, today's leaders are expected to redesign work for hybrid teams, adopt a coaching style, and operate effectively in a more fluid organisational context.

"Perhaps it's time to rethink the scope of the role. McKinsey offers the Helix Model where the role is split into a Capabilities Manager (career and performance focus) and a Value Creation Manager (sets priorities and is responsible for business objectives). Others like Bosch and Zappos are experimenting with less hierarchical models. Frederic LaLoux, in his book Reinventing Organisations, *studies various self-managing organisations illustrated with case studies from Buurtzorg, Patagonia, Morning Star and others."*

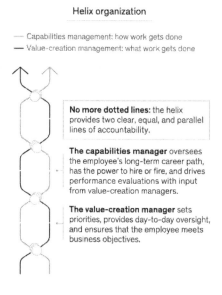

Helix organization

---- Capabilities management: how work gets done
—— Value-creation management: what work gets done

No more dotted lines: the helix provides two clear, equal, and parallel lines of accountability.

The capabilities manager oversees the employee's long-term career path, has the power to hire or fire, and drives performance evaluations with input from value-creation managers.

The value-creation manager sets priorities, provides day-to-day oversight, and ensures that the employee meets business objectives.

Figure 21.2 Contemporary manager roles[249]

There is plenty of well-researched support available for reimagining how, where and when our managers spend their time. In his book *Making the Matrix Work,*[250] Kevan Hall, CEO of training provider Global Integration, captures the key elements required for managers working in agile teams under a matrix reporting structure, some of which will come naturally to some, but not to all, of our managers:

- Demystify the matrix for their people;
- Build clarity and organisational alignment;
- Streamline co-operation;
- Create and support accountability without control;
- Communicate effectively to diverse groups and through technology;
- Exercise power and influence without authority;
- Lead others toward empowerment and freedom;
- Find the right balance of trust and control; and
- Build a culture that supports matrix working.

None of this will happen overnight, without executive support, or without significant financial, human and time resources. But it needs to happen, and soon, or we may run out of a talent pipeline for people manager positions. The Josh Bersin book, *Irresistible*[251], is a must read when considering how to redefine this work. As a starter, however, think about splitting the role of manager into technical leader, who leads the work, and people leader, who leads the people. High street retail banks got it wrong for years – the only career path from bank official to higher levels was to become an assistant manager and then manager from early in your career. If you didn't want it, you had to leave.

Accenture, like other professional services companies, has done it right for years by having career coaches in place for employees – a leader who receives the feedback from all the employees and stakeholders they worked with through the year, who rates their work based on this feedback for performance and reward purposes, and who provides ongoing career advice throughout their tenure. Let's use the natural human strengths that employees have rather than exploit their weaknesses: let those who are good at it and want to do it, lead people. For those who don't, let's use their talents differently.

Placing tangible value on human capital investment

The People function traditionally has a lot of interested stakeholders. These stakeholders, both internal and external, are increasingly focused on the strategic impact of the People function, in particular where it brings value to the organisation. We know the People function is absolutely coming into its right place from a strategic importance perspective – what does the CPO need to do to convince the world that people are the beating heart of the organisation and that without people, the company may simply shut up shop?

The answer, according to Dave Ulrich, lies in articulating the value of people from the 'outside in', that is, seeing the business of HR as being the business of the organisation:[252]

> *"The essential premise of HR from the outside in is that the business of HR should be the business – the external conditions that shape the business and the stakeholders who are invested in its success. HR professionals must take those considerations and incorporate them into everything they do, tailoring their practices to serve the needs of the business as a whole and not just their own department. When HR professionals start and ground their work with the business in mind, they are thinking and behaving from the outside-in."*

The short-term approach to people costs, where layoffs are viewed as cost-effective ways of retaining short term shareholder value, has been an easy fix for shareholders to make a saving for years. Why is it still one of the first go-to strategies when organisations need to re-balance the P&L, when everyone knows by now, in theory at least, that people make the organisation?

Alarmingly, many articles describe the current swathe of layoffs in the tech sector across the globe as being based on contagion and expectation management, rather than to cut costs or increase revenue margins – you have to be seen to do it because everyone else is, because boards and shareholders are asking 'why are we not doing it when everyone else is?'.

In her article for *RTE Brainstorm*, Jean Cushen, Deputy Head of School (Accreditation) and Associate Professor at Maynooth University School of Business notes: *"In earlier decades, layoffs were associated with business failure and closure. Today, layoffs are often framed as a positive sign of strong leadership, and even rewarded with a short-term boost to an organisation's share price."*[253]

Research indicates that that expending people to make profit does not work, nor is it ethical: that layoffs based on contagion can not only lead to increase in risk of suicide of those let go, that this indiscriminate method of saving money don't always even meet that required goal of improved company performance[254]. Taking this thinking even further, perhaps organisations can exist without measuring human effort in terms of cost, that is, can companies exist other than to provide a return to their shareholders? A case in point beautifully articulated by the Greyston Bakery in the US, which has the philosophy: *"We don't hire people to bake brownies, we bake brownies to hire people."*[255]

So how do we solve the paradox whereby we know human capability has material value to the organisation, but people are still seen as a cost, and one that is readily reduced through layoffs? The CPO should place themselves at the heart of discussions with the Executive team, the Board and other key stakeholders about the importance of people, corporate knowledge and culture to the bottom line. A 2016 report from the Financial Reporting Council advises that, *"the way companies create and sustain value is directly linked to the debate about the role of business in society"* and says that the company, and therefore the CPO, needs to build trust with key stakeholders including employees, suppliers, regulators and shareholders, to name a few.[256]

Throughout this book we have reflected on several core areas for success for the CPO, including in particular people (talent), leadership, culture and the HR function. Dave Ulrich and G3 team describe how stakeholder value is created under all four pillars collectively, called Human Capability, and is not solely about the 'people'. All the organisations' stakeholders care about the People function creating value, and the G3 team's research includes six practical steps for business leaders and CPOs to take to create more value from HR[257]:

Why do stakeholders care about human capability?

Figure 21.5: Key stakeholders concerned with investment in human capability

The Maturity Institute wants to prove that mature organisations can create shareholder value as well as general well-being and social good for all stakeholders and wider society concurrently – they are not mutually exclusive:[258]

"Financial resources are used to pay people (in many cases the largest portion of expenditures) but people create value which drives business

success and therefore should be thought of less as a 'cost' and more as an 'investment'. The competitive advantage of many organizations … will be their ability to optimize the creativity and innovation of its workforce."

Its freely available OMINDEX® Workforce tool[259] helps companies rate their organisational health, a measure that investors are increasingly using to quantify ESG impact in organisations. Its Ten Pillar framework focuses on ensuring that *"human capital is fully vested in the delivery of its purpose of maximising societal value"*, and its 'Reconciling Responsibility and Performance: 32 Questions a Mature CEO Asks' helps CEOs and the C-suite ask the right questions to help deliver and articulate that human capital value to investors.

What else is within the gift of the CPO to control in terms of investment in people? At its most fundamental, the CPO can drive prudent hiring, using all the workforce planning in the HR toolkit (i.e. permanent FTE, temporary FTE, insourced or outsourced managed services, agency workers, internships, fellowships, apprenticeships, gig workers (i.e. professionals who are choosing to work with corporates on their own terms, often via global platforms), and consultants). This will help ensure deep-rooted hiring success, where the permanent workforce is hired for the broad skillsets and culture fit that are needed for current and future requirements; bringing in fixed-term or temporary talent only when and as needed.

Do everything possible to retain, retrain, upskill and reskill your great employees before opening up the talent acquisition purse. Calculate the cost reductions achieved from this deliberate strategy and use tenure and other engagement metrics to show how the People strategy is producing savings and investment in other ways by not simply hiring more people. Quantify all the above into monetary value where possible.

We saw the metric previously, in which absence costs are reduced by more than the investment in well-being programmes; capture the return on investment that you are getting from your training programmes; calculate the talent acquisition savings from internally filling new roles rather than external hires (60%+ of the salary saved every time as a starter), which is on top of the savings achieved by either redeploying TA headcount into value-added work on managing careers or by having a smaller TA headcount altogether.

The organisation's stakeholders and employees will thank you for building a company with a strong reputation for leading with people first, rather than engaging in unnecessary hiring and firing. The financial rewards will happily find their way to your balance sheet too.

Summary

Your work as a CPO will never, ever be dull. No one day will be like the next. Most days you will go home, or leave your home office, walking half an inch taller because you have made a positive difference to someone's life that day. You will have the opportunity to influence the working lives of hundreds or thousands of people throughout your career, from the day you start your HR career to the day you wrap up, helping them achieve potential that they never thought possible. Your ability to pre-empt, plan for and execute change proactively rather than reactively will rubber stamp your impact visibly at the top table, financially in the bottom line and culturally in how your organisation proves its resilience to change and its ability to differentiate itself from the rest.

Keep doing what you are doing, whether it's taking 10 minutes to listen to a concerned colleague or looking for the next opportunity to make your company stand out from the crowd. Don't forget to share what you and your People team achieve and put the financial data against those achievements. Publicly celebrate with your workforce regularly — we can certainly do a lot more of that in the workplace.

As the celebrated writer Maya Angelou famously stated:

> *"People will forget what you said, people will forget what you did, but people will never forget how you made them feel."*

As CPO, never forget your outsized impact on the human race for one single minute. It's a truly wonderful gift with which to be presented — grasp it with both hands.

Acknowledgements

Our thanks to the technical reviewers and experts who gave generously of their time to provide input and feedback, including the following: Dave Ulrich, Supriya Panje Iyer, Amy Weidner, Joan Morgan, Orla Stafford, Claire Doody, Amy Randall, Sinéad McSweeney, Melanie Crowley, Olivia McEvoy, John McNicholas, Neil O'Brien, Ger Mitchell, Stuart Wollard and Chris Lee.

Particular thanks to Paul Cutler and Sinéad Kilkelly for providing the case studies in the book.

Thank you to our wonderful editor, David Woods-Hale whose expertise and thorough but light touch made the process very enjoyable.

Thank you to Brett Hilker and the Self-Publishing school team for their support through the publishing process.

Thank you to the following wonderful authors for contributing such strong content and for allowing us to reference their material where permission was required. Every effort has been made to trace the owners of copyright material. If there are any omissions, please contact Jennifer at jennifer@coo-author.com.

Reading list

Alan Gibson, *Agile Workforce Planning: How to align people with organizational strategy for improved performance* (London: Kogan Page, 2021).

Brené Brown, *Dare to Lead: Brave Work. Tough Conversations. Whole Hearts.* (London: Vermilion, 2018).

David Attenborough, *A Life on Our Planet: My Witness Statement and a Vision for the Future* (London: Ebury Press, 2020).

Dolly Chugh, *The Person You Mean to Be: How Good People Fight Bias* (New York, NY: Harper Business, 2018).

Josh Bersin, *Irresistible: The Seven Secrets of the World's Most Enduring, Employee-Focused Organizations* (Oakton, VA: IdeaPress Publishing, 2022).

Kevan Hall, *Making the Matrix Work: How Matrix Managers Engage People and Cut Through Complexity* (London: Nicholas Brealey Publishing, John Murray Press, 2013).

Max McKeown, *The Strategy Book: How to Think and Act Strategically to Deliver Outstanding Results*, (London: FT International Publishing, 3rd ed, 2019).

Niamh O'Keeffe, *Your First 100 Days: Make Maximum Impact In Your New Role.* (London: Financial Times/Prentice Hall; 2nd Ed., 2019).

Paul Polman and Andrew Winston, *Net Positive: How Courageous Companies Thrive by Giving More than they Take* (Brighton, MA: HBR Press, 2021).

Richard Rumelt, *Good Strategy/Bad Strategy: The Difference and Why it Matters* (London: Profile Books, 2011).

Sheila Heen and Douglas Stone, *Thanks for the Feedback: The Science and Art of Receiving Feedback Well* (London: Penguin Random House UK, 2014).

Wayne Brockbank, Dave Ulrich, Mike Ulrich and Jon Younger, *HR from the Outside In: Six Competencies for the Future of Human Resources* (Amacom, 2012).

Yvon Chouinard and Vincent Stanley, *The Responsible Company: What We've Learned from Patagonia's First 40 Years* (Ventura, CA: Patagonia, 2016).

Thank you to the following organisations for their highly relevant content:

- Advisory, Conciliation and Arbitration Service (ACAS), UK
- CIPD
- Deloitte
- Forbes
- Gartner Group
- Harvard Business Review
- The Josh Bersin Company
- LinkedIn
- Strategic HRM
- Workplace Relations Commission (WRC), Ireland

References

1 'First-time chief people officers: A guide from current to future chief people officers' Heidrich & Struggles, accessed 4 April 2023,

https://www.heidrick.com/en/insights/human-resources-officers/first_time_ chief_people_officers_a_guide.

2 Sigrid Artho, Heiko Mijnarends, Simone Siebeke, Deborah Warburton, Bastian J Wilhelm, 'CHRO 2025. How leaders are preparing for change (updated edition, 2020)', Spencer Stuart, accessed 4 April 2023,

https://www.spencerstuart.com/research-and-insight/chro-2025.

3 Gartner for HR Leaders. Introducing the Model of a World-Class CHRO: Chapter 2, Gartner Inc., accessed 4 April 2023,

https://www.gartner.com/en/webinar/426750/998209.

4 Paul DeNicola, 'A deeper dive into talent management: the new board imperative', The Harvard Law School Forum on Corporate Governance (2021), accessed 4 April 2023,

https://corpgov.law.harvard.edu/2021/08/12/a-deeper-dive-into-talent-management-the-new-board-imperative/.

5 Ibid.

6 Niamh O'Keeffe, Your First 100 Days: Make Maximum Impact In Your New Role. (London: Financial Times/Prentice Hall; 2nd Ed., 2019).

7 William (Bill) McNabb, 'The Character of the Corporation', Directors and Boards, accessed 14 April 2023,

https://directorsandboards.com/articles/singlecharacter-corporation.

8   'The role of the Chief People Officer in today's 'new normal'', Ernst & Young LLP, 2020, accessed 4 April 2023,

https://assets.ey.com/content/dam/ey-sites/ey-com/en_gl/topics/workforce/workforce-resources/ey-role-of-cpo-in-todays-new-normal.pdf?download.

9   Edgar Schein and Peter A Schein, Organizational Culture and Leadership (San Francisco, CA: Jossey-Bass; 5th Ed., 2016).

10   Melissa Daimler, 'Why Great Employees Leave "Great Cultures"', Harvard Business Review, 11 May 2018,

https://hbr.org/2018/05/why-great-employees-leave-great-cultures.

11   Dave Ulrich, 'HR's Ever-Evolving Contribution', The RBL Group, 18 January 2021, accessed 4 April 2023,

https://www.rbl.net/insights/articles/hrs-ever-evolving-contribution.

12   Amy Edmondson, 'Psychological Safety and Learning Behavior in Work Teams', Administrative Science Quarterly, Vol. 44, No. 2 (Jun 1999): 350-383.

13   Amy Edmondson, 'What is Psychological Safety', accessed 14 April 2023,

https://psychsafety.co.uk/about-psychological-safety/.

14   PS202: Building a Culture of Safety. Quizlet Inc., accessed 4 April 2023,

https://quizlet.com/318290443/ps-202-building-a-culture-of-safety-flash-cards/.

15   Rachel Burnham, 'Developing Psychological Safety in the Workplace', Sketchnote, 2022,

https://rachelburnham.blogspot.com/2022/11/why-do-visuals-work.html.

16   Paul J Zak, 'The Neuroscience of Trust', Harvard Business Review, January-February 2017, accessed 4 April 2023,

https://hbr.org/2017/01/the-neuroscience-of-trust.

17   Dieter Veldsman, 'Employee Feedback Strategy: 5 Approaches to Consider', AIHR, accessed 4 April 2023,

https://www.aihr.com/blog/employee-feedback/.

18   Greg Satell and Cathy Windschitl, 'High-Performing Teams Start with a Culture of Shared Values', Harvard Business Review, 11 May 2021, accessed 5 April 2023,

https://hbr.org/2021/05/high-performing-teams-start-with-a-culture-of-shared-values.

19   'First-time chief people officers: A guide from current to future chief people officers' Heidrich & Struggles, accessed 4 April 2023,

https://www.heidrick.com/en/insights/human-resources-officers/first_time_chief_people_officers_a_guide.

20   Stephanie Jones and Martin Tynan, 7 Entrepreneurial Leadership Workouts (London: Anthem Press, 2022).

21   Paul Polman and Andrew Winston, Net Positive (Brighton, MA: HBR Press, 2021).

22   Podcast with Seedcamp, David Singleton, 'This much I know', accessed 4 April 2023

https://podcasts.apple.com/ro/podcast/stripes-david-singleton-on-technology-innovation-putting/id962121995?i=1000569774533.

23   Jennifer Geary, How to be a Chief Risk Officer, A Handbook for the Modern CRO (Kindle Direct Publishing, 2022).

24   Human Resources Strategic Planning, Gartner, accessed 4 April 2023,

https://www.gartner.com/en/human-resources/trends/strategic-planning-for-hr-cpc?utm_ .

25   Adam Gibson, Agile Workforce Planning. How to Align People With Organizational Strategy for Improved Performance (London: Kogan Page, 2021).

26   Organisation Design', CIPD, 25 November 2020, accessed 4 April 2023,

https://www.cipd.co.uk/knowledge/strategy/organisational-development/design-factsheet#gref.

27   Erik Devaney, 'The 6 Building Blocks of Organizational Structure [Diagrams]', hubspot.com, 3 June 2020, accessed 4 May 2023,

https://blog.hubspot.com/marketing/organizational-structure-building-blocks.

28   Cat Symonds, 'What is Organizational Design? HR Guide', Factorialhr.com, 18 November 2022, accessed 4 April 2023,

https://factorialhr.com/blog/organizational-design/.

29   Ibid.

30   Kevan Hall, *Making the Matrix Work: How Matrix Managers Engage People and Cut Through Complexity* (London: Nicholas Brealey Publishing, John Murray Press, 2013).

31   Santiago Comelia-Dorda, Christopher Handscomb and Ahmad Zaidi, 'Agility to action: Operationalizing a value-driven agile blueprint', McKinsey & Company, 16 June 2020, accessed 4 April 2023,

https://www.mckinsey.com/capabilities/people-and-organizational-performance/our-insights/agility-to-action-operationalizing-a-value-driven-agile-blueprint.

32   'Organisation Development', CIPD, 25 November 2020, accessed 4 April 2023,

https://www.cipd.co.uk/knowledge/strategy/organisational-development/design-factsheet#gref.

33   Natalie Sheils, 'Optimising your operating models for the future', CIPD, 17 March 2023, accessed 4 April 2023,

https://www.cipd.co.uk/knowledge/work/trends/future-work-insights/operating-models#gref.

34   Mark LaScola and Peter Turgoose, 'The Difference Between Organization Development and Organization Design', On The Mark , accessed 4 April 2023,

https://on-the-mark.com/the-difference-between-organization-development-and-organization-design/.

35   Jennifer Geary, *How to be a Chief Risk Officer, A Handbook for the Modern CRO* (Kindle Direct Publishing, 2022).

36 'Gartner for HR. How to Identify, Fix and Prevent Change Fatigue', Webinar.gartner.com 21 March 2023, accessed 4 April 2023,

https://www.gartner.com/en/webinar/462138/1090629.

37 Dave Ulrich, 'What Makes an Effective HR Function? An HR Value Logic', LinkedIn.com, 16 March 2023, accessed 4 May 2023,

https://www.linkedin.com/pulse/what-makes-effective-hr-function-value-logic-dave-ulrich-1c/.

38 'Gartner for HR. Top 5 Priorities for HR Leaders in 2023' Gartner, accessed 4 April 2023,

https://www.gartner.co.uk/en/human-resources/trends/top-priorities-for-hr-leaders.

39 Yves Van Durme and Erica Volini, *Organization Transformation. Enabling Organizational Performance,* Deloitte, accessed 4 April 2023, chrome-extension:

//efaidnbmnnnibpcajpcglclefindmkaj/https://www2.deloitte.com/content/dam/Deloitte/ca/Documents/consulting/ca-en-Organization-Transformation-EN-Final_AODA.pdf.

40 Gyöngyvér Martin, 'The CFO and the HR Director: Opposites Attract' HR Lead, 2 September 2020, accessed 4 April 2023,

https://hrlead.at/2020/09/02/the-cfo-and-the-hr-manager-opposites-attract/.

41 '2023 HR Budget and Efficiency Benchmarks', Gartner, accessed 14 April 2023,

https://gartner.com/en/human-resources/trends/benchmarking-hr-budgets-and-staffing.

42 'What does an employee relations specialist do?', CIPD.ie, accessed 14 April 2023,

https://www.cipd.ie/careers/career-options/employee-relations-roles#gref.

43 'Checklist for Updating HR Strategy', Gartner, accessed 14 April 2023,

https://www.gartner.com/en/human-resources/trends/updating-hr-strategy-checklist

44 'The Trust Equation: A Simple Summary', World of Work Project, accessed 4 April 2023,

https://worldofwork.io/2019/07/the-trust-equation/#:~:text=The%20 trust%20equation%20says%20an,addressing%20these%20underlying%20 trust%20factors.

45 'Talent Management and Strategic Workforce Planning', Ringo, accessed 4 April 2023,

https://www.goringo.com/blog/talent-management-and-strategic-workforce-planning.

46 Dinora Fitzgerald Dobru, Ruth Imose and Gunnar Schrah, 'Building a talent-first organization begins with addressing these 3 biases', McKinsey and Company, 26 May 2020.

47 'Competence and competency Frameworks', CIPD, 23 November 2020, accessed 4 April 2023,

https://www.cipd.ie/news-resources/practical-guidance/factsheets/ competency.

48 'Integrated Talent Management Framework for Organization', SlideTeam. net, accessed 11 April 2023,

slideteam.net/integrated-talent-management-framework-for-organization.html

49 Brooke Green and Hannah Kenney, 'Using Job Architecture to Enable Digital Transformation', Aon, March 2019, accessed 4 April 2023,

https://humancapital.aon.com/insights/articles/2019/using-job-architecture-to-enable-digital-transformation.

50 *Sales Leadership Competency Framework*, Canadian Professional Sales Association, October 2019, accessed 4 April 2023,

chrome-extension://efaidnbmnnnibpcajpcglclefindmkaj/https://www.cpsa. com/docs/default-source/pd-templates/sales-leadership-final.pdf?sfvrsn=2.

51 *Competency Framework*, OECD, 28 November 2014, accessed 4 April 2023,

chrome-extension://efaidnbmnnnibpcajpcglclefindmkaj/https://www.oecd. org/careers/competency_framework_en.pdf.

52   'Job Design', CIPD, 15 June 2021,

https://www.cipd.co.uk/knowledge/strategy/organisational-development/job-design-factsheet#gref.

53   Sue Cantrall, Kraig Eaton, Michael Griffiths and Karen Weisz, 'Navigating the end of jobs. Skills replace jobs as the focal point for matching workers with work', *Deloitte Human Capital Trends Report 2023*, Deloitte, 9 January 2023, accessed 4 April 2023,

https://www2.deloitte.com/us/en/insights/focus/human-capital-trends/2023/skills-based-model-end-of-jobs.html.

54   David Green, '12 HR Trends for 2023: Humanising (the Future of) Work', LinkedIn.com, 8 December 2022, accessed 4 April 2023,

https://www.linkedin.com/pulse/12-hr-trends-2023-humanising-future-work-david-green-/.

55   'Employee Value Proposition', Gartner Glossary, accessed 14 April 2023,

https://www.gartner.com/en/human-resources/glossary/employee-value-proposition#:~:text=The%20employee%20value%20proposition%20is,through%20employment%20with%20the%20organization.

56   Amy Edmondson and Mark Mortensen, 'Rethink Your Employee Value Proposition', *Harvard Business Review*, January-February 2023.

57   Matt Tenney, 'What is a Feedback-Rich Culture?' *Business Leadership Today* , accessed 4 April 2023,

https://businessleadershiptoday.com/what-is-a-feedback-rich-culture/.

58   '4 Companies Winning with Feedback in the Workplace' Culture.io. , accessed 4 April 2023,

https://culture.io/resources/companies-that-understand-importance-of-feedback-in-the-workplace/.

59   'What Is a Feedback Model? Benefits and Common Types', Indeed.com, 25 June 2022, accessed 4 April 2023,

https://www.indeed.com/career-advice/career-development/feedback-model.

60   Michelle Bostian, 'What's your Philosophy of Feedback?' LinkedIn.com, 22 July 2021, accessed 4 April 2023,

https://www.linkedin.com/pulse/whats-your-philosophy-feedback-michelle-bostian/.

61   Sheila Heen and Douglas Stone, *Thanks for the Feedback: The Science and Art of Receiving Feedback Well* (London: Penguin Random House UK, 2014).

62   Claire Hastwell, 'Creating a Culture of Recognition', Great Place to Work, 2 March 2023, accessed 4 April 2023,

https://www.greatplacetowork.com/resources/blog/creating-a-culture-of-recognition.

63   Adam Grant (@AdamMGrant), 'Being appreciated doesn't make you feel good...', 28 November 2020, accessed 4 April 2023,

https://twitter.com/AdamMGrant/status/1597280836801687552.

64   Melody Beattie, 'Gratitude – Day 6', Melodybeattie.com, 13 November 2020, accessed 14 April 2023,

https://melodybeattie.com/?s=gratitude+turns+what+we+have+into+e-nough.

65   Ron Gutman, 'Did you know: One smile can generate the same level of brain stimulation as up to 2,000 bars of chocolate?!', LinkedIn.com, accessed 4 April 2023,

https://www.linkedin.com/posts/ted-conferences_did-you-know-one-smile-can-generate-the-activity-6997960397672570880-qdGs/?utm_source=share&utm_medium=member_desktop.

66   Ashira Prossack, 'Why Recognition Matters in the Workplace', *Forbes*, 30 August 2021.

67   Valerie Daunt and Vicky Menzies, 'Recognition programmes, Are they important?', Deloitte.com, 2023, accessed 4 April 2023,

https://www2.deloitte.com/ie/en/pages/deloitte-private/articles/recognition-programmes.html.

68   Paul J Zak, 'The Neuroscience of Trust', *Harvard Business Review*, January-February 2017, accessed 4 April 2023,

https://hbr.org/2017/01/the-neuroscience-of-trust.

69   'How to Improve the Employee Experience', Gallup.com, 2023, accessed 4 April 2023,

https://www.gallup.com/workplace/323573/employee-experience-and-workplace-culture.aspx.

70   Shayna Hodkin, ' What's the connection between onboarding and retention?' Hibob.com, 10 November 2020, accessed on 14 April 2023,

https://www.hibob.com/research/hibob-research-finds-64-of-new-hires-leave-a-job-after-a-bad-onboarding-process/

71   www.shrm.org.

72   Ibid.

73   Ryan Roslansky, 'You Need a Skills-Based Approach to Hiring and Developing Talent', *Harvard Business Review*, 8 June 2021, accessed 4 April 2023,

https://hbr.org/2021/06/you-need-a-skills-based-approach-to-hiring-and-developing-talent.

74   Minami Rojas, 'Dear female jobseeker: Apply for the job, ignore the 'qualifications'' Fastcompany.com, 3 August 2021, accessed 4 April 2023,

https://www.fastcompany.com/90661349/dear-female-jobseeker-apply-for-the-job-ignore-the-qualifications.

75   Jen Dewar, 'Recruiting Active vs Passive Candidates', LinkedIn Talent Blog, 20 Dec 2013, accessed 4 April 2023,

https://www.linkedin.com/business/talent/blog/talent-acquisition/recruiting-active-vs-passive-candidates.

76   Robert D Austin and Gary Pisano, 'Neurodiversity as a Competitive Advantage', *Harvard Business Review*, May-June 2017, accessed 4 April 2023,

https://hbr.org/2017/05/neurodiversity-as-a-competitive-advantage.

77   Cat Contillo, 'Neurodiverse Candidates Find Niche in Remote Cybersecurity Jobs', *Wall Street Journal*, 13 April 2022, accessed 4 April 2023,

https://www.wsj.com/articles/neurodiverse-candidates-find-niche-in-remote-cybersecurity-jobs-11649842380.

78 'Supporting neuro-diverse colleagues at work', Accenture, 3 December 2021, accessed 4 April 2023

https://www.accenture.com/in-en/about/inclusion-diversity/vaahini-supporting-your-neuro-diverse-colleagues.

79 'Accenture's Neurodivergent Internship Programme', Business In the Community Ireland, 6 May 2022, accessed 4 April 2023,

https://www.bitc.ie/newsroom/news/accenture-neurodivergent-internship/.

80 Gys Kappers and Sinazo Sibisi, 'Onboarding Can Make or Break a New Hire's Experience', *Harvard Business Review*, 5 April 2022, accessed 4 April 2023,

https://hbr.org/2022/04/onboarding-can-make-or-break-a-new-hires-experience.

81 Mary Driscoll and Michael D Watkins, 'Onboarding a New Leader – Remotely', *Harvard Business Review*, 18 May 2020, accessed 4 April 2023,

https://hbr.org/2020/05/onboarding-a-new-leader-remotely.

82 Josh Bersin, *The New World of Talent Mobility; Flexibility Rules*, joshbersin. com, April 2021, accessed 4 April 2023,

chrome-extension://efaidnbmnnnibpcajpcglclefindmkaj/https://joshbersin.com/wp-content/uploads/2021/04/2021_04_Bersin-Talent-Mobility.pdf.

83 'A New Way of Doing Performance Management – Real-Time Reviews', HR Locker, 5 December 2022, accessed 22 April 2023,

hrlocker.com/hr-software/time-management/performance-management-real-time-reviews/.

84 'Developing a Performance Management Strategy That Works', abcsignup. com, ADP.org Automatic Data Processing Inc., accessed 22 April 2023,

chrome-extension: https://admin.abcsignup.com/files/%7B0F916658-03DA-4619-ADD5-95B8FC087AA3%7D_6/28516/DevelopingAPerformanceMgmt StrategyThatWorks-St.Louis.pdf .

85   Peter Cappelli and Anna Tavis, 'The Performance Management Revolution', *Harvard Business Review*, October 2016.

86   'A New Way of Doing Performance Management – Real-Time Reviews', HR Locker, 5 December 2022, accessed 22 April 2023,

hrlocker.com/hr-software/time-management/performance-management-real-time-reviews/.

87   Josh Bersin, 'HR Predictions for 2023', The Josh Bersin Company, 2023,

https://joshbersin.com/josh-bersins-predictions-for-2023/ .

88   Jocelyn Stange, 'The Who, What, Why, and How of Performance Management', Quantum Workplace, 19 November 2020, accessed 13 April 2023,

quantumworkplace.com/future-of-work/performance-management.

89   Cat Symonds, '10 Types of Bias in Performance Reviews', Factorial, 31 March 2022, accessed 4 April 2023,

https://factorialhr.com/blog/bias-in-performance-reviews/.

90   Ibid.

91   *Performance Management that Delivers*, Gartner, 27 September 2019, accessed 4 April 2023,

https://www.gartner.com/en/documents/3969809.

92   Sakshi Jain, 'Netflix performance appraisal method explained: No more annual reviews', Grove HR, accessed 4 April 2023,

https://blog.grovehr.com/netflix-performance-appraisal.

93   Dave Ulrich, 'Knowing Which Organization Capabilities Make a Difference', LinkedIn, September 2020, accessed April 2023, https://www.linkedin.com/pulse/knowing-which-organization-capabilities-make-dave-ulrich/.

94   *Gartner Glossary*, Gartner, accessed 4 April 2023,

https://www.gartner.com/en/glossary/all-terms

95   Erik van Vulpen, 'The 9 Box Grid: A Practitioner's Guide', AIHR, December 2021, accessed 4 April 2023,

https://www.aihr.com/blog/9-box-grid/.

96   James Peters, 'Tell or Don't Tell? Talking talent with your employees', Korn Ferry, accessed 13 April 2023,

kornferry.com/insights/this-week-in-leadership/tell-or-dont-tell-talking talent-your-employees.

97   Mary Baker, '5 Succession Risks That Threaten Your Leadership Strategy', Gartner, 29 January 2020, accessed 4 April 2023,

https://www.gartner.com/smarterwithgartner/5-succession-risks-that-threaten-your-leadership-strategy.

98   'Engaging in Succession Planning', SHRM, accessed 4 April 2023,

https://www.shrm.org/resourcesandtools/tools-and-samples/toolkits/pages/engaginginsuccessionplanning.aspx.

99   'Ibec publishes findings of HR Update 2022 report', IBEC, 20 October 2022, accessed 4 April 2023,

https://www.ibec.ie/connect-and-learn/media/2022/10/19/ibec-publishes-findings-of-hr-update-2022-report.

100 Amy Weidner, *How to be an extraordinary candidate – a guide for those who dare to stand out* (Kindle Direct Publishing, 2021).

101 Josh Bersin, *The New World of Talent Mobility; Flexibility Rules*, joshbersin. com, April 2021, accessed 4 April 2023,

chrome-extension://efaidnbmnnnibpcajpcglclefindmkaj/https://joshbersin.com/wp-content/uploads/2021/04/2021_04_Bersin-Talent-Mobility.pdf.

102 Dave Ulrich, 'Human Capability and Company Performance', The Conference Board, 17 November 2022 , accessed 4 April 2023,

https://www.hrdconnect.com/events/the-conference-board-human-capability-company-performance-webinar/.

103 Tess Taylor, 'Talent Development: 8 Best Practices for Your Organisation', AIHR, accessed 4 April 2023,

https://www.aihr.com/blog/talent-development/.

104 Dan Hawkins, 'What are your Organization Capabilities?,' Summit Leadership Partners, 16 February 2016, accessed 4 April 2023,

https://www.summitleadership.com/what-are-your-organization-capabilities/.

105 'Talent Development: Strategies to Future Proof Your Workforce', Workhuman.com, 26 January 2023, accessed 14 April 2023,

https://www.workhuman.com/blog/talent-development/.

106 Association of Training and Development, ATD.org.

107 'Top 5 priorities for HR leaders in 2023', Gartner, accessed 4 April 2023,

https://www.gartner.com/en/webinar/423847/989926.

108 Norm Smallwood, Kate Sweetman and Dave Ulrich, *The Leadership Code: Five Rules to Lead by* (Brighton MA: Harvard Business Press, 2008).

109 Jack Zenger and Joseph Folkman, 'The 3 Elements of Trust', *Harvard Business Review*, 2 February 2019, accessed 4 April 2023,

https://hbr.org/2019/02/the-3-elements-of-trust.

110 Dan Cable, 'How Humble Leadership Really Works', *Harvard Business Review*, 23 April 2018, accessed 4 April 2023,

https://hbr.org/2018/04/how-humble-leadership-really-works.

111 Ibid.

112 Tony Schwartz, 'Create a Growth Culture Not a Performance-Obsessed One', *Harvard Business Review*, 7 March 2018, accessed 4 April 2023,

https://hbr.org/2018/03/create-a-growth-culture-not-a-performance-obsessed-one.

113 Timothy Gallwey, *The Inner Game of Tennis: The Classic Guide to the Mental Side of Peak Performance* (New York, NY: Random House; Revised ed., 1997).

114 The Coaches' Journal (@TheCoachJournal),

https://twitter.com/TheCoachJournal/status/1600672707968131072.

115 Catharine Broadnax, 'Managing a Global Workforce in the 'Work Anywhere" Era', LinkedIn, 18 November 2022, accessed 14 April 2023,

https://www.linkedin.com/pulse/managing-global-workforce-work-anywhere-era-catharine-broadnax/.

116 Liz Kislik, 'How to Retain and Engage your B Players', *Harvard Business Review*, 19 September 2018, accessed 4 April 2023,

https://hbr.org/2018/09/how-to-retain-and-engage-your-b-players.

117 Juliet Bourke and Bernadette Dillon, *Six Signature Traits of Inclusive Leadership Thriving in a Diverse New World* (New York, NY: Deloitte University Press, 2016).

118 Erica Keswin, 'To Retain Your Best Employees, Invest in Your Best Managers', *Harvard Business Review*, 1 December 2022, accessed 4 April 2023,

https://hbr.org/2022/12/to-retain-your-best-employees-invest-in-your-best-managers.

119 Josh Bersin, 'Building A Company Skills Strategy: Harder (and More Important) Than It Looks', joshbersin.com, 4 February 2022.

120 Norm Smallwood and Dave Ulrich, 'Capitalizing on Capabilities', *Harvard Business Review*, June 2004.

121 Ibid.

122 Peter Aykens and Emily Rose McRae, '9 Future of Work Trends for 2023', Gartner, 22 December 2022, accessed 4 April 2023,

 https://www.gartner.com/en/articles/9-future-of-work-trends-for-2023.

123 Alex Gruhin, 'Why Josh Bersin Recommends Uniting Around the Capability Academy', Association for Talent Development, 18 October 2022, accessed 4 April 2023,

https://www.td.org/atd-blog/why-josh-bersin-recommends-uniting-around-the-capability-academy.

124 'What is the Difference Between a Career Development Plan and an Employee Development Plan', getsmarter.com, 1 October 2019, accessed 14 April 2023,

https://www.getsmarter.com/blog/employee-development/what-is-the-difference-between-a-career-development-plan-and-an-employee-development-plan/.

125 Ann Hiatt, 'How to Figure Out What You Want Next in Your Career', *Harvard Business Review*, 23 December 2021.

126 Jacqueline Brassey, Lisa Christensen and Nick van Dam, 'The essential components of a successful L&D strategy', McKinsey, 13 February 2019, accessed 4 April 2023,

https://www.mckinsey.com/capabilities/people-and-organizational-performance/our-insights/the-essential-components-of-a-successful-l-and-d-strategy.

127 Ibid.

128 'The Psychological Contract', CIPD, 9 February 2022, accessed 4 April 2023,

https://www.cipd.co.uk/knowledge/fundamentals/relations/employees/psychological-factsheet#gref.

129 Patrick Collinson and John Collison, 'CEO Patrick Collison's email to Stripe employees', Stripe.com, 3 November 2022, accessed 14 April 2023,

https://stripe.com/ie/newsroom/news/ceo-patrick-collisons-email-to-stripe-employees.

130 https://www.acas.org.uk/

131 https://www.workplacerelations.ie/en/

132 'Terms of Employment', Workplace Relations Commission, 16 December2022, accessed 4 April 2023,

https://www.workplacerelations.ie/en/what_you_should_know/employer-obligations/terms-of-employment/.

133 https://www.hsa.ie/eng/.

134 https://www.hse.gov.uk/.

135 https://www.osha.gov/

136 Ibid.

137 Ibid.

138 integrityline.com.

139 'At-will Employment – Overview', National Conference of State Legislatures, 15 April 2018, accessed 4 April 2023,

https://www.ncsl.org/labor-and-employment/at-will-employment-overview.

140 'ACAS. modern slavery and human trafficking statement 2022 to 2023' , ACAS, accessed 4 April 2023,

https://www.acas.org.uk/acas-modern-slavery-and-human-trafficking-statement.

141 Naz Beheshti, 'Pet-Friendly Workplaces Are a Win-Win For Employee Wellbeing And For Business' 22 May 2019, accessed 4 April 2023,

https://www.forbes.com/sites/nazbeheshti/2019/05/22/pet-friendly-workplaces-are-a-win-win-for-employee-wellbeing-and-for-business/?sh=483cbb1c5dbc).

142 Catharine Broadnax, 'Managing the Global Workforce in the "Work Anywhere" Era', LinkedIn.com, 18 November 2022, accessed 4 April 2023,

https://www.linkedin.com/pulse/managing-global-workforce-work-anywhere-era-catharine-broadnax%3FtrackingId=nMwkl61ERQuubeBfMR3vwQ%253D%253D/?trackingId=nMwkl61ERQuubeBfMR3vwQ%3D%3D.

143 Judith Stein, 'Decision-making Models', MIT Human Resources, accessed 4 April 2023,

https://hr.mit.edu/learning-topics/teams/articles/models#:~:text=A%20decision%2Dmaking%20model%20describes,will%20team%20members%20be%20involved%3F.

144 Mark Batson Baril, ' Three Ways The Organizational Ombuds Can Guide You Through A Crisis', Forbes, 2 June 2020, accessed 4 April 2023,

https://www.forbes.com/sites/forbescoachescouncil/2020/06/02/three-ways-the-organizational-ombuds-can-guide-you-through-a-crisis/?sh=290f66d83116.

145 'Strategic reward and total reward', CIPD, 18 May 2022, accessed 4 April 2023,

https://www.cipd.co.uk/knowledge/strategy/reward/strategic-total-factsheet#gref.

146 'What are total rewards strategies? Can you give me some idea on how to develop a total rewards strategy?', SRHM, 2023, accessed 4 April 2023,

https://www.shrm.org/resourcesandtools/tools-and-samples/hr-qa/pages/totalrewardsstrategies.aspx.

147 Kathi Enderes, 'Solving the Complex, Important Pay Equity Problem', LinkedIn.com, 14 March 2023, accessed 4 April 2023,

https://www.linkedin.com/pulse/equal-pay-solving-equity-puzzle-kathi-enderes/.

148 Tara Chandler, 'Time to Get Real With Rewards', Workhuman, 26 April 2019, accessed 4 April 2023,

https://www.workhuman.com/blog/time-to-get-real-with-rewards/.

149 Monique Danao, 'What is A Compa Ratio & How Is It Used?', *Forbes*, 24 October 2022.

150 Ruadhán Mac Cormaic, '20 years of social partnership agreements, 1987-2007', *Irish Times*, 4 August 2008.

151 'Ireland Unemployment Rate', Tradingeconomics.com, February 2023, accessed 4 April 2023,

https://tradingeconomics.com/ireland/unemployment-rate#:~:text=Unemployment%20Rate%20in%20Ireland%20is,macro%20models%20and%20analysts%20expectations.

152 Momodou Musa Touray, '1.2m Baby Boomers left workforce during Covid', *Money Marketing*, 11 August 2022.

153 Tamra Chandler, 'Rethinking Recognition and Rewards: A Vital Element of Impactful and Modern Performance Programs', workhuman.com, 10 April 2023.

https://www.workhuman.com/blog/rethinking-recognition-and-rewards/ .

154 Josh Bersin, 'The Growing Role of Pay in employee Experience and Business Performance', Joshbersin.com, 2 November 2022, accessed 4 April 2023,

https://joshbersin.com/2022/10/the-growing-role-of-pay-in-employee-experience-and-business-performance/.

155 Josh Bersin, 'The Business Roundable Manifesto: What Should CEOs Do?', joshbersin,com, 26 August 2019, accessed 14 April 2023,

https://joshbersin.com/2019/08/the-business-roundtable-manifesto-what-should-ceos-do/.

156 'Employee benefits: an introduction', cipd.ie, 19 April 2021.

https://www.cipd.org/ie/knowledge/factsheets/benefits-factsheet/ .

157 Stacey Lowman, 'Employee benefits: how much should you spend and why?', Reward and Employee Benefits Association, 14 February 2023, accessed 4 April 2023,

https://reba.global/resource/how-to-work-out-how-much-to-spend-on-employee-benefits-budget-strategy.html.

158 Cynthia Meyer, 'How Much Are Your Benefits Really Worth?' *Forbes,* 24 September 2018.

159 Stephen Dooley, 'What Happens My Pension Benefits When I Leave Employment?', Independent-trustee.com, 16 November 2022, accessed 4 April 2023,

https://www.independent-trustee.com/blog/what-happens-my-pension-benefits-when-i-leave-employment.

160 https://www.gov.uk/workplace-pensions/joining-a-workplace-pension

161 https://assets.publishing.service.gov.uk/government/uploads/system/uploads/attachment_data/file/197272/725summ.pdf.

162 Jason Flynn and Melanie Langsett, 'Rewards to Relationships, Rewards and Wellbeing for the Workforce of the Future', Deloitte, accessed 4 April 2023,

https://www2.deloitte.com/us/en/pages/human-capital/solutions/employee-rewards-to-employee-relationships.html.

163 *MHFA Line Managers' Resource*, Mental Health First Aid, 2016, accessed 4 April 2023,

chrome-extension://efaidnbmnnnibpcajpcglclefindmkaj/https://cdn. mentalhealthatwork.org.uk/wp-content/uploads/2018/07/05111111/line_ managers_resource.pdf.

164 Tracy Brower, 'Managers Have Major Impact on Mental Health: How to Lead for Wellbeing', *Forbes*, 29 January 2023.

165 Jessica Perkins, '9 Employee Wellbeing Metrics to Track Right Now', AIHR, accessed 4 April 2023,

https://www.aihr.com/blog/employee-wellbeing-metrics/.

166 Zesha Saleem, Rafe Uddin and Abby Wallace, 'Pictures of health: the winners of Britain's Healthiest Workplace', *Financial Times*, 28 November 2022.

167 https://www.ibec.ie/employer-hub/corporate-wellness/the-keepwell-mark-public-page.

168 'Launch of the World Wellbeing Movement', University of Oxford, accessed 4 April 2023,

https://wellbeing.hmc.ox.ac.uk/world-wellbeing-movement.

169 Sinann Fetherston, 'LaFawn Davis on why we need more happiness in the workplace', RTE.ie, 25 January 2023, accessed 14 April 2023,

https://www.rte.ie/lifestyle/living/2023/0125/1351779-lafawn-davis-on-why-we-need-more-happiness-in-the-workplace/.

170 Olive Keogh, 'Corporate wellness concept needs a reality check', *Irish Times*, 3 February 2023.

171 Ripa Rashid and Laura Sherbin, 'Diversity Doesn't Stick Without Inclusion', vernamyers.com, 4 February 2017, accessed 13 April 2023,

vernamyers.com/2017/02/04/diversity-doesnt-stick-without-inclusion/.

172 Sundiatu Dixon-Fyle, Kevin Dolan, Dame Vivian Hunt and Sara Prince, 'Diversity wins: How inclusion matters' McKinsey, 19 May 2020, accessed 4 April 2023,

https://www.mckinsey.com/featured-insights/diversity-and-inclusion/diversity-wins-how-inclusion-matters.

173 Nick Barney and Linda Rosencrance, 'Diversity, Equity and Inclusion (DE&I)', TechTarget, accessed 4 April 2023,

https://www.techtarget.com/searchhrsoftware/definition/diversity-equity-and-inclusion-DEI.

174 Courtney Wright, 'What is privilege? How to navigate it at work', Inclusive Employers, accessed 4 April 2023,

https://www.inclusiveemployers.co.uk/blog/what-is-privilege-how-to-navigate/?cn-reloaded=1

175 'Diversity, Equity and Inclusion Definitions', University of Washington Research, accessed 4 April 2023,

https://www.washington.edu/research/or/office-of-research-diversity-equity-and-inclusion/dei-definitions/.

176 'Accessibility at work', ACAS, accessed 4 April 2023,

https://www.acas.org.uk/accessibility-at-work#:~:text=Accessibility%20at%20work%20%2D%20Acas&text=Accessibility%20at%20work%20is%20about,as%20many%20people%20as%20possible.

177 'Equality in the Workplace: What Does It Mean?', Human Rights Careers, accessed 4 April 2023,

https://www.humanrightscareers.com/issues/equality-in-the-workplace-what-does-it-mean/.

178 'Diversity, Equity and Inclusion Definitions', University of Washington Research, accessed 4 April 2023,

https://www.washington.edu/research/or/office-of-research-diversity-equity-and-inclusion/dei-definitions/.

179 Ibid.

180 'What is Organisational Justice?', *HRZone,* accessed 4 April 2023,

https://www.hrzone.com/hr-glossary/what-is-organizational-justice#:~:text=Organisational%20justice%2C%20first%20postulated%20by,attitudes%20and%20behaviours%20at%20work.

181 Elsa T Chan, David R Heckman and Stephanie K Johnson, 'If There's Only One Woman in Your Candidate Pool, There's Statistically No Chance She'll Be Hired' *Harvard Business Review*, 26 April 2016, accessed 4 April 2023,

https://hbr.org/2016/04/if-theres-only-one-woman-in-your-candidate-pool-theres-statistically-no-chance-shell-be-hired.

182 30percentclub.org.

183 Blackgirlsintech.org.

184 Bonnie Dowling, Drew Goldstein, Michael Park and Holly Price, 'Hybrid work: Making it fit with your diversity, equity and inclusion strategy', *McKinsey Quarterly*, April 2022.

185 Juliet Bourke and Andrea Titus, 'The Key to Inclusive Leadership', *Harvard Business Review*, 6 March 2020, accessed 4 April 2023,

https://hbr.org/2020/03/the-key-to-inclusive-leadership.

186 'What is Allyship in the Workplace', Great Place to Work, accessed 4 April 2023,

https://www.greatplacetowork.com/resources/blog/what-is-allyship-in-the-workplace.

187 'What is Psychological Safety at Work? How Leaders can Build Psychologically Safe Workplaces', Centre for Creative Leadership, accessed 14 April 2023,

https://www.ccl.org/articles/leading-effectively-articles/what-is-psychological-safety-at-work/.

188 Tirzah Enumah and Mike Arauz, 'Looking at Psychological Safety Through an Equity Lens' August, accessed 4 April 2023,

https://www.aug.co/psychological-safety-and-diversity-equity-and-inclusion-august-whitepaper

189 Sheryl Estrada, 'Twitter to pay resource group leaders, saying the work shouldn't be a 'volunteer activity', *HR Dive,* 6 October 2020, accessed 4 April 2023,

https://www.hrdive.com/news/twitter-to-pay-resource-group-leaders-saying-the-work-shouldnt-be-a-volu/586489/.

190 Donald Hicks, 'The Future of Tech and Silicon Valley Isn't Super Gadgets: It's Amplifying Black and Brown Voices', *Medium,* 1 September 2020, accessed 4 April 2023,

https://medium.com/@donaldhicksj/the-future-of-tech-and-silicon-valley-isnt-super-gadgets-it-s-amplifying-black-and-brown-voices-a3f37d39a9b3.

191 Josh Bersin, 'HR Predictions for 2023', joshbersin.com, accessed 14 April 2023,

https://joshbersin.com/josh-bersins-predictions-for-2023/ .

192 Josh Bersin, 'The New World of Talent Mobility; Flexibility Rules', joshbersin.com, April 2021, accessed 4 April 2023,

chrome-extension://efaidnbmnnnibpcajpcglclefindmkaj/https://joshbersin.com/wp-content/uploads/2021/04/2021_04_Bersin-Talent-Mobility.pdf.

193 Kimberley Leonard, 'Best HCM Software (April 2023)', *Forbes Advisor,* 6 March 2023, accessed 4 April 2023,

https://www.forbes.com/advisor/business/software/best-hcm-software/.

194 Prarthana Ghosh, 'Top 10 Applicant Tracking Systems (ATS) Software for 2022', *Spiceworks.com.* 1 March 2021, accessed 14 April 2023,

https://www.spiceworks.com/hr/recruitment-onboarding/articles/top-applicant-tracking-systems/.

195 196. Josh Bersin, 'Talent Marketplace Platforms Explode into View',

'https://joshbersin.com/2020/07/talent-marketplace-platforms-explode-into-view/' accessed May 2023.

196 Jill Duffy, 'The Best Project Management Software for 2023', *PC Mag UK,* 24 March 2023, accessed 4 April 2023,

https://uk.pcmag.com/project-management/9161/the-best-project-management-software.

197 'Skills Based Organisation, Facilitating Internal Talent Mobility', Deloitte Insights, 8 September 2022, accessed 2 May 2023,

https://www2.deloitte.com/us/en/insights/topics/talent/organizational-skill-based-hiring.html.

198 Faye Wai, '15 Best Employee Benefits Software & Platforms in 2023', Snacknation, accessed 4 April 2023,

https://snacknation.com/blog/employee-benefits-software/.

199 'Improving Employee Connection and Strengthening Workplace Culture: Pfizer's Story', Workhuman, accessed 4 April 2023,

https://whc.workhuman.com/webnwh-improving-employee-connection-and-strengthening-workplace-culture-pfizer-story-emea-replay.html.

200 'Best Analytics Platforms', G2, accessed 4 April 2023,

https://www.g2.com/categories/analytics-platforms.

201 Blathnaid O'Dea, 'Irish start-up Abodoo to connect rural remote working talent across Europe', *Silicon Republic*, 1 March 2022, accessed 4 April 2023,

https://www.siliconrepublic.com/careers/abodoo-remote-working-european-commission.

202 Josh Bersin, 'The Employee Experience Platform Has Arrived. Employee Service Delivery as a Foundation for Great Experiences', Bersin & Associates, accessed 4 April 2023, c

hrome-extension://efaidnbmnnnibpcajpcglclefindmkaj/https://joshbersin.com/wp-content/uploads/2021/01/Employee_Experience_Platform_v4-EXP-BERSIN.pdf.

203 Josh Bersin, 'The Employee Experience Platform: A New Category Arrives' Joshbersin.com, 24 May 2021 accessed 4 April 2023,

https://joshbersin.com/2019/02/the-employee-experience-platform-a-new-category-arrives/.

204 Hayfa Mohdzaini, 'Bringing on the brain bots – a missed opportunity for HR?', CIPD, 13 December 2022, accessed 4 April 2023,

https://www.cipd.co.uk/knowledge/work/technology/workplace-people-management/intelligent-automation#gref.

205 'People analytics,' CIPD, 30 September 2022, accessed 4 April 2023,

https://www.cipd.co.uk/knowledge/strategy/analytics/factsheet#gref.

206 Dimple Lalwani, 'Data Story-Telling – the human Art of Evidence based HR', AIHR, accessed 4 April 2023,

https://www.aihr.com/blog/data-story-telling-the-human-art-of-evidence-based-hr/.

207 Maureen Haaker, 'Giving a voice to the lived experience', ukdataservice.ac.uk, broadcast date April 2017, accessed 14 April 2023,

https://ukdataservice.ac.uk/learning-hub/qualitative-data/.

208 Josh Fechter, 'What is HR Analytics', HRUniversity, accessed 4 April 2023,

https://hr.university/analytics/hr-analytics/.

209 'HR Metrics for Success', Gartner, accessed 14 April 2023,

https://www.gartner.com/en/human-resources/insights/hr-metrics.

210 'People analytics: driving business performance with people data', CIPD, 13 June 2018, accessed 4 April 2023,

https://www.cipd.co.uk/knowledge/strategy/analytics/people-data-driving-performance#gref.

211 CEB 2013 HR Business Partner Survey, CEB, ©2013-2016.

212 'Are you SMCR ready? A 10 point guide for Human Resources', accessed 22 April 2023,

https://shepwedd.com/sites/default/files/190809%20-%20SMCR%20Senior%20Managers%20and%20Certification%20Regime-compressed.pdf.

213 'Are you SMCR ready? A 10 point guide for Human Resources', accessed 22 April 2023,

https://shepwedd.com/sites/default/files/190809%20-%20SMCR%20 Senior%20Managers%20and%20Certification%20Regime-compressed.pdf.

214 'People Risk Management – A Practical Approach to Managing the Human Factors That Could Harm Your Business', Institute of Operational Risk, 10 August 2015, accessed 4 April 2023,

https://www.ior-institute.org/publications/people-risk-management-a-practical-approach-to-managing-the-human-factors-that-could-harm-your-business/.

215 Ibid.

216 Risk in Focus: Hot topics for internal auditors, European Confederation of Institutes of Internal Auditing, 2023, accessed 4 April 2023,

https://www.iia.org.uk/media/1692515/risk-in-focus-2023.pdf.

217 Executive Perspectives on Top Risks for 2023 and 2032, Protiviti and NC State University's ERM Initiative, December 2022,

www.protiviti.com/gl-en/survey/executive-perspectives-top-risks-2023-and-2032.

218 Sue Cantrell, Michael Griffiths, Reem Janho and Zac Shaw, 'Elevating the focus on human risk', Deloitte, 9 January 2023, accessed 4 April 2023,

https://www2.deloitte.com/us/en/insights/focus/human-capital-trends.html? id=us:2sm:3li:4diGLOB175985:5awa:6di:MMDDYY:hct23:author&pkid=1011 052#elevating-the-focus.

219 'Managing people risk', PwC, accessed 4 April 2023,

https://www.pwc.co.uk/services/human-resource-services/managing-people-risk.html.

220 Ibid.

221 Andrew Edgecliffe-Johnson, 'Why personnel departments need to return to basics', *Irish Times* 7 December 2022, accessed 4 April 2023,

https://www.irishtimes.com/business/work/2022/12/07/why-hr-needs-to-go-back-to-basics/.

222 Richard Nieva, 'What The Mass Tech Layoffs And Job Cuts This Year Mean for 2023', *Forbes*, 30 December 2022.

223 Sinéad McSweeny, 'What do you want to be when you grow up?', TEDxStormont, accessed 4 April 2023,

https://www.youtube.com/watch?v=rGr1uOLaY-4.

224 Sandra Durth, Neel Gandhi, Asmus Komm and Florian Pollner, 'HR's new operating model', McKinsey & Company, 22 December 2022, accessed 4 April 2023,

https://www.mckinsey.com/capabilities/people-and-organizational-performance/our-insights/hrs-new-operating-model.

225 Erik van Vulpen, 'Data-Driven HR mindset: Only 2 out of 10 HR departments use data to guide their decisions', AIHR, accessed 4 April 2023,

https://www.aihr.com/blog/data-driven-hr-mindset/.

226 Eric Garton, 'HR's Vital Role in How Employees Spend Their Time, Talent, and Energy', *Harvard Business Review*, 30 January 2017, accessed 4 April 2023,

https://hbr.org/2017/01/hrs-vital-role-in-how-employees-spend-their-time-talent-and-energy.

227 Ibid.

228 *Increasing HR's Strategic Impact*, Gartner, 2022, accessed 4 April 2023,

https://www.gartner.com/en/human-resources/trends/increasing-hr-strategic-impact.

229 Ibid.

230 Josh Bersin, 'HR Predictions for 2023', The Josh Bersin Company, accessed 13 April 2023,

https://joshbersin.com/josh-bersins-predictions-for-2023.

231 Janelle Gale, Lori Goler, Adam Grant and Brynn Harrington, 'The 3 Things Employees Really Want: Career, Community, Cause' *Harvard Business Review*, 20 February 2018, accessed 4 April 2023,

https://hbr.org/2018/02/people-want-3-things-from-work-but-most-companies-are-built-around-only-one.

232 Jennifer Geary, *How to be a Chief Risk Officer, A Handbook for the Modern CRO* (Kindle Direct Publishing, 2022).

233 Trista Bridges and Donald Eubank, *Leading Sustainably: The Path to Sustainable Business and How the SDGs Changed Everything*, (London: Routeledge, 2020).

234 'What is corporate social responsibility (CSR)?', Business Development Bank of Canada, accessed 4 April 2023,

https://www.bdc.ca/en/articles-tools/entrepreneur-toolkit/templates-business-guides/glossary/corporate-social-responsibility.

235 'What's the difference between CSR and ESG', Novisto.com, 11 October 2022, accessed 14 April 2023,

https://novisto.com/whats-the-difference-between-csr-and-esg/.

236 Witold Henisz, Tim Koller, and Robin Nuttall, 'Five ways that ESG creates value', *McKinsey Quarterly*, November 2019.

237 *Our Common Future, The Brundtland Commission Report*, 1987.

238 Yvon Chouinard and Vincent Stanley, *The Responsible Company: What We've Learned from Patagonia's First 40 Years* (Ventura, CA: Patagonia Books, 2012).

239 Paul Polman and Andrew Winston, Net Positive: How Courageous Companies Thrive by Giving More than they Take (Brighton, MA: HBR Press, 2021)

240 Ibid.

241 www.esb.ie.

242 Sdgs.un.org/goals.

243 Ibid.

244 Dave Ulrich, 'ESG and Human Capability: Connecting Emerging Intangibles', LinkedIn.com, November 2022, accessed 9 May 2023.

https://www.linkedin.com/pulse/esg-human-capability-connecting-emerging-intangibles-dave-ulrich/.

245 '10 best nature quotes from Sir David Attenborough', wwf.org.au, 18 November 2021, accessed 15 April 2023,

https://www.wwf.org.au/news/blogs/10-best-nature-quotes-from-sir-david-attenborough#:~:text=%22It's%20surely%20our%20responsibility%20to,for%20all%20life%20on%20Earth.%22.

246 Dave Coplin, *Business Re-imagined: Why work isn't working and what you can do about it* (Petersfield: Harriman House Publishing, 2013).

247 David Green, '12 HR Trends for 2023: Humanising (the Future of) Work', LinkedIn.com, 8 December 2022, accessed 4 April 2023,

https://www.linkedin.com/pulse/12-hr-trends-2023-humanising-future-work-david-green-/.

248 Adam Grant, 'The four-day work week: luxury or necessity?' Re:Thinking, November 2022, accessed 4 April 2023,

https://open.spotify.com/episode/3ze4HZF5U3WgQugPdUXOqb?si=dKx-5ALQ3RGK_YD3g7BTQ6g&context=spotify%3Ashow%3A0uFXKiNiC-05GOrjE9AXnkn&nd=1.

249 Aaron De Smet, Sarah Kleinman and Kirsten Weerda, 'The helix organization', *McKinsey Quarterly,* 3 October 2019, accessed April 2023,

https://www.mckinsey.com/capabilities/people-and-organizational-performance/our-insights/the-helix-organization.

250 Kevan Hall, *Making the Matrix Work: How Matrix Managers Engage People and Cut Through Complexity* (London: Nicholas Brealey Publishing, John Murray Press, 2013).

251 Diane Gherson and Lynda Gratton, 'Managers Can't Do It All', *Harvard Business Review*, March-April 2022.

252 Dave Ulrich, 'HR from the Outside-In', The RBL Group, 3 July 2019, accessed 4 April 2023,

https://www.rbl.net/insights/videos/hr-from-the-outside-in.

253 Jean Cushen, 'How did layoffs become the answer to every business problem?', RTE, 22 February 2023.

254 Melissa De Witte, 'Why are there so many tech layoffs, and why should we be worried? Stanford scholar explains' *Stanford News,* 5 December 2022, accessed 4 April 2023,

https://news.stanford.edu/2022/12/05/explains-recent-tech-layoffs-worried/.

255 Shop.greyston.org.

256 Sir Winifried Bischoff (ed), *Corporate Culture and the Role of Boards,* Financial Reporting Council, 2016.

257 Dave Ulrich, 'Six Actions for HR to Create More Stakeholder Value', LinkedIn, 29 November 2022, accessed 4 April 2023,

https://www.linkedin.com/pulse/six-actions-hr-create-more-stakeholder-value-dave-ulrich/.

258 Stuart Woollard, 'Financial depletion?' www.hrmaturity.com. 10 August 2016, accessed 14 April 2023,

https://www.hrmaturity.com/financial-depletion/.

259 *Omindex®Workforce Survey,* omservices.org, 2023, accessed 4 April 2023,

https://www.omservices.org/?page_id=1950.

Manufactured by Amazon.ca
Bolton, ON

38472171R00247